**A VITAL**

**FRONTIER**

ANDREA MUEHLEBACH

A

VITAL

# FRONTIER

Water
Insurgencies
in
Europe

DUKE UNIVERSITY PRESS
*Durham and London*
2023

© 2023 DUKE UNIVERSITY PRESS
*All rights reserved*
Project editor: Bird Williams
Designed by A. Mattson Gallagher
Typeset in Source Serif 4 and National 2 Narrow
by Westchester Publishing Services

Library of Congress Cataloging-in-Publication Data
Names: Muehlebach, Andrea Karin, [date] author.
Title: A vital frontier : water insurgencies in Europe / Andrea Muehlebach.
Description: Durham : Duke University Press, 2023. | Includes bibliographical
references and index.
Identifiers: LCCN 2022041740 (print)
LCCN 2022041741 (ebook)
ISBN 9781478019831 (paperback)
ISBN 9781478017134 (hardcover)
ISBN 9781478024408 (ebook)
Subjects: LCSH: Water utilities-Europe. | Privatization-Moral and ethical aspects. |
Rightto water–Politicalaspects– Europe.| Water-supply–Politicalaspects– Europe.|
Environmental policy-Europe-Citizen participation. | BISAC: SOCIAL SCIENCE /
Anthropology / Cultural & Social | SOCIAL SCIENCE / Activism & Social Justice
Classification: LCC HD1697. A5 M84 2023 (print) | LCC HD 1697. A5 (ebook) |
DDC 363.6/1094–dc23/eng/20230104
LC recordavailableathttps:// lccn.loc.gov/2022041740
LC ebookrec ordavailableathttps:// lccn.loc.gov/2022041741

Cover art: Photograph of the Irish Sea by the author.

I dedicate this book to my daughters Olive and Liliana, the centers of my universe, as well as to all of those protecting the water all over the world.

# CONTENTS

I write this book in the midst of an endless pandemic, the beginning of which I spent (among many other things) wondering how the global water industry would respond to a planetary crisis where the consistent washing of hands we were asked to perform makes water seem more precious than ever before. By May 2020 I had attended a virtual Corporate Water Leaders Panel organized by Global Water Intelligence (GWI), a self-described "unchallenged leader in high-value business information for the water industry." It was moderated by Debra Coy, who was introduced by the GWI representative as the "queen of Wall Street" and the "queen of water technology." Coy is an executive in residence at XPV Water Partners, the largest water-focused growth equity fund in North America. For decades Coy has provided strategic advisory services for municipal utilities, investors, and companies from a capital markets perspective, and, worldwide, she is considered one of the most experienced consultants covering the water sector. The meeting also featured corporate executives Hara Prasad

Nanda from DuPont Water Solutions, Cath Schefer from Stantec, Rafael Perez [...], and Ana Giros from S[...] their conversation th[...]nic go to waste. The at[...]he accelerating oppor[...]c offered to the water i[...]it all sectors of the glo[...]ould be uneven and sec[...]profile seemed to have[...]e private water sector l[...]roup noted that this wa[...]had within the first m[...]ernments that they co[...]s across whole regions[...]' that could be potenti[...]formance and by inve[...] in the digitization and automation of water payments (many of which were lagging, the executives noted, as the pandemic wore on). Most importantly, the water executives also noted that the pandemic was an opportunity since it would create new budgetary constraints for public institutions needing investments for water infrastructures. These needs could be met by private investment because a huge amount of capital was sitting idle and looking for opportunities for long-term stable revenue.

These ambitious visions of increased private capital expansion into water utilities came right at a moment when several United Nations special rapporteurs published a dramatic op-ed in the *Guardian*, arguing that the pandemic vividly exposed "the catastrophic impact of privatizing vital services" like water and sanitation. The rapporteurs argued that states should "no longer cede control as they have done" and that they should cease delegating core goods and services to private companies and the market on terms that will "effectively undermine the rights and livelihoods of many people" (Farha et al. 2020; MacDonald and Spronk 2021). Seemingly oblivious to these warnings, executives on the Corporate Water Leaders Panel insisted that "as a sector, we should try to get all that capital," with Coy concluding that the focus would soon shift from the management of pandemic risk to postpandemic growth and to "getting more attention, more public awareness, more dollars."

This book could easily be a tale told about the ravages of global capital expansion into water utilities; a tale of dispossession and of more and

[Handwritten note: 1. which people does she talk about at the beginning and why? Debra Coy, Hara Prasad Nanda from DuPont Water solutions, Cath Schefer from Stantec, Rafael Perez Feito from Aqualia, Alejandro Jimenez from Acciona, and Ana Giros from Suez]

more do⟨…⟩vation, envi-
ronment⟨…⟩told as a tale
about a t⟨…⟩esent historical conju⟨…⟩markets that
are "mo⟨…⟩eed of major
regulati⟨…⟩n the spaces
where th⟨…⟩gent life—by
water ins⟨…⟩ortunities for
capital a⟨…⟩ty of water as
right, vit⟨…⟩ft imaginative
projects⟨…⟩mocracy and
just pric⟨…⟩frastructural
respons⟨…⟩on that I seek
to honor⟨…⟩their hands,
and it is

[handwritten note: Intro. to her goals, purpose for writing this book, her interest in water insurgencies]

This book emerged out of the varied routes I took beginning in 2014. My interest in European water insurgencies was first peaked by the Italians and the astonishing political and legal work they performed in the lead-up to a national referendum in 2011. But it was a first conversation with Saki Bailey in Turin about the Italian referendum and the Berlin Water Table and its striking achievements that led me to live in Berlin in 2015–2016 to conduct research in both Italy and Germany. While there, Dorothea Härlin from the Berlin Water Table took me to a meeting of the European water movement in Brussels, where David Sánchez Carpio from Food and Water Watch urged me to go to Ireland because the mass insurgency against metering was still ongoing and because "water there is not priced." Claus Kittsteiner from the Berlin Water Table had also been involved in a water referendum that was held in 2014 in Thessaloniki, Greece, which is why I visited there, too. That trip was short but involved among other things, an epic motorcycle ride and lots of good food with the unforgettable Yiorgos Archontopoulos. I also conducted a month-long visit to France during the summer of 2017, where I relied especially on the knowledge and generosity of Thierry Uso in Montpellier and a number of others in Paris. The result is a story that circulates as much as the members of these diverse water movements circulate—across varied hydrological, political, economic, and cultural terrains that are always in resonance with each other as people share epochal problems and common obstacles (Mezzadra 2015, 222). What follows are not case studies that allow for symmetrical comparison. Nor am I able to capture national, regional, or local water struggles in their

f                                                                    ot of bounded com-
r                                                                    nt political and legal
f                                                                    n.

                                                                     , sometimes in con-
                                                                     ince distances could
r                                                                    ays mutually under-
s                                                                    nts via ethnographic
t                                                                    iewing in what were
s                                                                    arch trips. All in all,
I                                                                    lowed their ongoing
c                                                                    so spent a month in
I                                                                    nterview people and
a                                                                    d, on one occasion,
a                                                                    in Campania, where
I was initially fascinated by the remunicipalized Neapolitan water utility,
Napoli Acqua Bene Comune (Naples Water as Commons; ABC), but soon
got drawn into the ongoing and no less dramatic struggles faced by people
in the region's smaller rural towns and villages. Throughout, I traveled to
these towns and villages and sat in on meetings and also engaged sources
ranging from government reports, laws, and online accounts including those
available on social media—both as communicative devices and as visual
archives of protest and lively fora of debate. Taken together, the chapters
that follow can be read individually, but their message will be enhanced
through juxtaposition as readers detect resonances across the stories I tell.
Much of this book thus aims to capture the rich heterogeneity of situated
struggle. But it also seeks to grasp the often stifling political and legal parameters against which this heterogeneity must assert itself.

Sometimes, I came late to water struggles and sought to document them
retroactively. I saw that water struggles had moved on to other political
terrains, such as when I was invited to meet Irish water activists as they
were demonstrating for the right to housing for those rendered homeless
by the housing crisis. Some struggles documented in this book continue
unabated until today, even if they are more dispersed or weakened by the
exhaustion of activists. In many cases, my interlocutors were left with a
sense that their victories were fragile achievements that could easily be
overturned. They were experienced enough to know that their political
work—even if it ended in successful remunicipalization—would have to
be constantly renewed because the forces intent on extracting financial
value from their most precious resource were constantly renewing and

rebuilding themselves as well. Many thus practiced a constant vigilance in a world where no successfully won battle for water as a commons would be the last, and where battles would have to be fought over and over again, by them and by generations to come. This was a politics that was perhaps not best captured by Marx's decidedly terrestrial metaphor—that of the old mole burrowing around in the underground only to then suddenly appear as revolution—but by the hydrological metaphor of the water cycle as a politics and poetics of constant returns and recursions. Just as water is a constantly shapeshifting substance, moving from its solid into liquid and then vaporous states, so too are the politics of water insurgencies marked by a continuous, constantly transmuting cycle of renewal that has no beginning and no end, and that will likely have to repeat itself, over and over again over time. And yet, everything I document in this book points to the conclusion that water movements are offering the world an insurgent gift—that of posing radical questions about wealth, value, and inappropriability and of working in common to continue to pose these questions.

If I were to trace the routes that my own thinking took over the years, I would start with a sparkling conversation I had with my dear friend Gavin Smith in Toronto on Edward Palmer Thompson. But there were other moments of clarity that I was gifted by friends and colleagues and that make this book the fruit of thinking in common: Firat Bozcali, who coined the term "infrastructures of financialization" for me; Sardar Saadi, who reminded me that the question of democracy was crucial and that I needed to foreground it analytically in the introduction; Naor Ben-Yehoyada on the Strathernian question on indivisibility; Tania Li on financial frontiers and the possibilities of that concept; Andrea Ballestero on pushing back at that concept; Hannah Appel on how weirdly interesting contracts are when studied ethnographically; Francesca Coin on genealogies of vitalism and the defense of life; Theodoros Rakopoulos for a question on usufruct; Enzo Alliegro on the importance of the biocidio movement and the terrifying specters of aquifer contamination; and especially Kelly Gillespie and Leigh-Ann Naidoo on insurgent questions and the insurgent practices that flow from such questions. The group that convened over a volume on financial frontiers also refined my thinking infinitely as we met across impossible time zones, distances, and life challenges during a pandemic: I salute and thank Hannah Appel, Geoffrey Aung, Julia Elyachar, Karen Ho, Jorge Nuñez, Horacio Ortiz, Gloria Pérez-Rivera, and Michael Ralph. Andrea Ballestero, again, was always luminous and illuminating; I am thankful for our friendship. Others who have accompanied me along the way and whose companionship, intellectual and otherwise, I will always treasure are Gretchen Bakke, Mike Balkwill, Joshua Barker, Francis Cody, Catherine Fennell, Jessica Greenberg, Sarah Hillewaert, Bonnie McElhinny, Amira Mittermaier, Noelle Molé Liston, Shiho Satsuka, Jesook Song, Carlota McAllister, Valentina Napolitano, Alejandro Paz, Bhavani Rhaman, Todd Sanders, Anwen Tormey, and, especially, Naisargi Dave. Then there are those brave souls who read the whole manuscript with care and generosity: Andrea Ballestero, Andreas Bieler, Firat Bozcali, Tania Li, Andrew Gilbert, and, especially, Hannah Appel (I don't know how you do it all). Please let me do the same for you when the time comes.

But most of all, this story is buoyed by the water insurgents I had the joy of meeting over the last few years. In Italy, I thank Marco Bersani, Costanza Boccardi, Carlo Borriello, Renato Briganti, Paolo Carsetti, Ida Dello Ioio, Raffaele Nunzio De Mauro, Renato Di Nicola, Tommaso Fattori, Valentina Gambarella, Enzo Guadagno, Giuseppe Grauso, Alberto Lucarelli, Ugo Mattei, Giuseppe Micciarelli, Maurizio Montalto, Stefano Risso, Enzo Ruggiero, Consiglia Salvo, Simona Savini, Francesco Sessa, Enzo Tosti, Gerardo Vitale, Padre Alex Zanotelli, and Ernesto Zona. I thank Giulia Romano from the University of Pisa for prompt and clarifying emails; Francesco Fusco, who made initial fieldwork in Naples pleasurable through his humor and generosity; Sergio Marotta, who shared his wisdom in a three-hour conversation and numerous clarifying emails; and Mario Visone, who delighted me by whisking me off to hang out with a Super Mario during what seemed like a very long and adventurous night in the Campanian countryside. I also want to express my debts to Bonnuccio Gatti and Ciro Annunziata—may they both rest in power. They look back on lives well lived. In Berlin, I thank Thomas Blanchet, Michael Efler, Johanna Erdmann, Christa Hecht, Carsten Herzberg, Ulrike Kölver, Shahrooz Mohajeri, Timothy Moss, Hermann Roloff, Gerlinde Schermer, Gerhard Seyfarth, Ulrike von Wiesenau, and Herrmann Wollner. I'm particularly thankful to Claus Kittsteiner, who welcomed me into his apartment, which was really the archive of the Berlin Water Table, stuffed from floor to ceiling with papers; Mathias Behnis, who sat with me for hours sifting through and talking about this archive; Carl Waßmuth, a man who knows numbers and holds a deep well of patience; and Dorothea Härlin and Heidi Kosche, both of whom have become dear friends. In Ireland, I thank the indefatigable Lynn Boylan, Patrick Bresnihan, Karen Collins, Ann Farrelly, David Gibney, Brian Gould, Gavin Harold, John Lonergan, Anne McShane, Noreen Murphy, Maggie Ni Caoimh, Diarmuir O'Flynn, Donal O'Sullivan, Ted Tynan, and the unforgettable Balleyphehan/South Parish Says No group. I will also not forget sitting in a Dublin McDonald's with eyes wide open when I realized that the tall and burly red-haired man I was having a great old laugh with was a water fairy. Though he and others I spoke to will remain anonymous, they were some of the most raucously witty water insurgents to talk to. I also thank Karen Doyle for an incredibly illuminating conversation and Noreen Murphy for her indomitable spirit, humor, and political wisdom. As she and many others in Ireland taught me, the struggle for public water is serious, but it can also be filled with laughter. In Paris, I thank Armelle Bernard, Henri Coing, Martine Depuy, Marc Laimee, Matthieu Marquaille, Jean-Claude Oliva, Jean-Luc Ouly, and Graciela Schneier Madanes; while in Montpellier I remain indebted to Thierry Uso, Jean Baron, and Grégory Vallée. I also thank my students, who know this manuscript and all of its various ins and outs intimately. Thank you, Tessa Bonduelle and Salvatore Giusto, for being outstanding fieldwork companions along the way. Thank you, Jacob Bessen, Xiaoling Chen, Ferda Nur Demirci, Bronwyn Frey, Gina-Marie Grawe, Justin Langille, and Sandy Hyunjoo Oh, for your intellectual friendship and your willingness to work on details in such thoughtful ways.

I have also shared many iterations of this work at different institutions, members of which were gracious enough to host me and to think in common through ideas. I think of myself as having cocreated parts of the story I tell here with these audiences—and especially students—at El Colegio de México and the Universidad Nacional Autónoma de México, the University of Chicago, Manchester University, the University of Sussex, the Freie Universität Berlin, the Graduate Institute in Geneva, St. Andrew's University, Cambridge University, the University of Bergen, McMaster University, Columbia University, Simon Fraser University, and at the Temple Hoyne Buell Center for the Study of American Architecture; as well as the Departments of Anthropology at Columbia University, the University College London, Harvard University, Princeton University, the University of Zürich, the THESys Institute at Humboldt University, the University of Oslo, the NYU School of Law, the University of San Diego, Yale University, the University of Edinburgh, the University of Basel, the University of Warwick, Ludwig Maximilian Universität, the Universität Hamburg, and CUNY Graduate Center. Thank you. I was very honored by your presence and thoughtful engagement. The incredible team at Duke University Press—with Elizabeth Ault leading the way, with Benjamin Kossak helping me get my act together, and with Mattson Gallagher, Maria Katsantones, Lisl Hampton, and especially Bird Williams crafting this project into shape—has been a life raft as I tried to finish a book with children at home and manage my departure from the University of Toronto to the University of Bremen, where I am thrilled to hold a professorship dedicated to maritime anthropology and cultures of water.

Finally, it takes time and money to indulge in the writing of books. I could not have done it without funding from the Wenner-Gren Foundation for Anthropological Research, a grant from the Deutscher Akademischer Austausch Dienst, a grant from the Dean's Faculty Research Funding at the University of Toronto at Mississauga, and a University of Toronto Faculty Research and Scholarly Activity Fund. A Jackman Humanities Institute Faculty Fellowship at the University of Toronto and a half-year sabbatical granted by the University of Toronto at Mississauga provided the magical time I needed to pound the last few bits of this book out.

Words cannot express my indebtedness to my parents, Ingeborg Gerngroß Mühlebach and Hans Mühlebach, as well as to my in-laws, Judy Gilbert and Robert Gilbert, for love and childcare. So much labor went into allowing me to conduct research for and to write this book; I especially thank my Californian mother-in-law for continuously braving absurdly cold Toronto winters. My profoundest indebtedness goes to my partner, Andrew Gilbert, whom I referred to as my rock in my last book's acknowledgements. He is still that same rock (as befits rocks), and I am deeply grateful.

# A Vital
# Frontier

A TATTERED PHOTOCOPY OF A BILL, shown to me by an elderly man living in an impoverished town just outside of Naples in Southern Italy, sometime in 2016. He had rummaged through an archive in his living room, boxes brimming with papers stacked next to a piano, looking to find proof of the insane prices that the privatized water utility company *Gestione Ottimale Risorse Idriche* (Optimal Water Resources Management or GORI SpA) had made him and others pay. Eventually, he pulled out a crumpled piece of paper and showed it to me: a photocopy of what people there called a *bolletta pazza*, a "crazy bill." I had seen crazy bills like this held up high in the air during demonstrations or burned on flaming piles of wood. People were incensed by the fact that the utility was retroactively charging customers thousands of euros for water for which they had supposedly underpaid. For this elderly gentleman, the bill was a scandal, an utter betrayal of the Italian people. After all, in 2011, Italians had won an unprecedented national referendum against the privatization of water.

An image of members of the Berlin Water Table (Berliner Wassertisch), sitting in a room wearing small white and golden paper crowns, holding a paper sign that said *"Der Souverän sind wir"* (We are the sovereign). Some were smiling triumphantly after a recent citywide popular referendum that they had won in 2011 and organized under the banner of *"Wir Berliner wollen unser Wasser zurück!"* (We Berliners want our water back!). The referendum, which also included a peoples' law (*Volksgesetz*) written by the Wassertisch itself, forced the public disclosure of a secret contract that had governed relations between the city and the French multinational Veolia and the German energy utility Rheinisch-Westfälisches Elektrizitätswerk AG (RWE) for over twelve years. The disclosure caused such a political scandal that Berlin was forced to remunicipalize the utility by 2013, promising more transparency and democracy in the referendum's wake.

*Handwritten note:* Three stories about water— (1) the "crazy bill" and the privatization of water (2) Members of the Berlin Water Table after winning a referendum that forced the public disclosure of a secret contract (3) A mother protesting against water meters in Ireland with her ill son alongside her

...otesting in Ireland. I had ...hern tip of Ireland, that ...cided to block the instal- ...l 2014. Things were bad ...receive help for her ill ...tional water utility, Irish ...were going to reap even ...e, people said, the straw ...at her protest, standing ...ate with her son sitting ...the most massive social ...housands of people bar- ...nded by police as they ...ll be free!"

...cesses unleashed by the financialization of public water utilities. All are examples of the fissures that open up when global financial frontiers extend into utilities that for large parts of the twentieth century provided water as a public good. These utilities, like others in many parts of the world, have moved from providing a vital service to citizens at subsidized rates toward relying on global creditors and the selling of services to clients on a full cost recovery basis. This process of privatization initially involved smaller-scale private shareholders or infrastructure companies. Today, it involves much more powerful global financial actors such as private equity firms and large pension funds ready to invest billions into infrastructural assets.[1] Yet this attempted conscription of public utilities into global circuits of capital accumulation—that recursive process that Marx called *ursprüngliche* (original) or primitive accumulation—is often vehemently contested. As public utilities are revalued and converted into publicly traded bankable corporations, they become zones of struggle, reconversion, and reappropriation as well.

This book explores these zones of struggle and the vital politics that have erupted in their wake. It shows how the exuberant horizon opened up by the promise of future profits is often met by the fact that the population at this frontier may itself become a risk. By focusing on these zones of struggle through the lens of the frontier, I refer not to a place but to a global process both volatile and generative—a mobile proliferation of appropriation and theft, protests and violence, as well as various claims to ownership and sovereign lawmaking, legality and illegality (Ballestero and Muehlebach et al., forthcoming); Tsing 2003, 5101–2). The financial frontier is always also an attempt at revaluation—a conversion of highly localized qualities into abstract quantities and of local into global regimes of value making. When global investors argue that they are more capable of understanding "the true value of water" and that "water tends to be undervalued around the world" (Yang 2020), they project that universal market laws will replace government and local municipalities' seemingly arbitrary and particularistic forms of valuation. Proper pricing will, so the story goes, better regulate demand and supply, trigger transformations of behavior, and create the conditions for the superior valuation and conservation of scarce resources (Dukelow 2016, 144). Proper pricing will also attract shareholders who will trade their shares speculatively; shares that have become assets thus become a form of wealth that derives its value out of claims made on future payments—a specter of endless returns.[2] Investors thus seek not simply to extract value from previously public utilities but to set the terrain of valuation. They attempt to dispossess people not only of public goods but of their capacity to determine what value and wealth are (Elyachar 2005, 8).

Water movements thus struggle against more than the financialization of water and water utilities. They struggle against the hegemony of finance as a measure of value and thus against the financialization of value as such (Christophers and Fine 2020, 22). Against the life-draining necropolitics of financialized accounting (Manjapra 2019, 35), water movements posit other modes of valuation and other modes of accounting and express them both within and outside the logic of numbers. Against the insistence of the "universal fungibility of all value on Earth through the general equivalent of the money form" (Manjapra 2019, 34), water movements insist that it is impossible to render fungible the value of water. Against the durable debt that finance seeks to install through infrastructures of long-term profit, water movements insist on a transcendent debt that humans have always already incurred toward water, and thus toward life as such.

One might be tempted to think of contemporary finance as the "greatest and most monolithic system of measurements ever created, a totalizing system that would subordinate everything—every object, every piece of land, every capacity or relationship—on the planet to a single standard of value" (Graeber 2001, xi). Indeed, there is little doubt that the financial industry has arisen as a global network of exchange that creates, compares, and trades in all sorts of things that now count as assets (Ortiz 2012). Yet narratives of monolithic totality obscure the fact that a plurality of forms of valuation persist and are in fact newly provoked by and generated out of the dominance of finance. This book tracks how Europe's water movements have articulated their own "counter-valuations" (Collins 2017, 6–7) against this single standard of value, and how these movements have refused to submit what they often call "their water" to narrowly economistic ways of seeing the world. Against dreams of financial revaluation, these movements insist that water is not undervalued at all but in fact the most valuable, most sacred form of wealth. Emphasizing the ways in which water is often treasured in highly localized ways, water movements insist that water is *theirs*—a substance with specific tastes, meanings, and histories sustained across generations. For them, the value of water is, even when priced, ultimately incalculable and immeasurable and thus incommensurable with an abstract market logic. For them, water should thus be priced in ways that would allow it to remain radically accessible, especially to those in need (Ballestero 2019, 20). Against regimes of financial valuation that always increase water price, water movements posit a diametrically opposed regime of valuation that foregrounds affordability, accessibility, and just price. They argue that water justice can only be achieved if their resource is democratically and transparently managed through a just politics of societal distribution.

The financial expansion into the public sector is thus a nonlinear process and far from inevitable. It is often met with insurgency as the people burdened with replenishing speculative dreams of infinite wealth respond with their own sets of values—of democracy, social contract, transparency, and just price. As the price of vital goods is made subject to global investment schemes backed by an increasingly authoritarian state and emergency law, a series of political fault lines spring up as well. This push to privatize in the Global North came after a wave of investments into utilities in the Global South in the 1990s led to retreat as investors realized that the infrastructures needed in poorer countries were simply too expensive to build and maintain. Coupled with antiprivatization protests and the underperformance of profits, many multinationals withdrew as dozens of cities in the Global South remunicipalized their water works, with Latin America leading the way (Bakker 2013, 254–55; see also Björkman 2015; von Schnitzler 2016).[3] Water insurgencies in Europe must thus be understood as being fed by what appear to be Europe's margins, with processes that first unfolded in global "peripheries" now (re)constituting the "center" (Chakrabarty 2000; Tsing 2003, 5101; Byrd et al. 2018; Morris 2016, 47). Put differently, the privatization of water utilities is a "double arrival" to the West of both colonial and capitalist logics—two forms of predation whose "disorders have come home to roost" (Clover 2016, 167; Cesaire 2000; Comaroff and Comaroff 2006, ix; Susser 2017, 3). Financial frontiers shift across Europe just as they shift across the globe. After all, the whole world is a frontier for capital, with terra nullius "continuously declared, as if for the first time" (Cooper and Mitropolous 2009, 367).

Yet, the financial frontier is highly indeterminate terrain. Water insurgencies struggle not only over modes of financing and accounting but over political questions about democracy, sovereignty, and legality; indeed, over the very nature of the political and the lawful as such. They throw into relief philosophical questions about private, public, and common forms of property; and about contract, price, distribution, and the law. Through these politicizations, distinctions between public and private institutions, between commodities and social goods, and between profits and fees, become fields of struggle. None of these distinctions can be taken for granted as stable entities. Indeed, many of the "public" utilities that were in the process of being "privatized" were already thoroughly corporatized (Berlin, Naples) or partially privatized (Ireland). The vitalism of this financial frontier thus consists of the fact that public and private goods, institutions, contracts, or commons are constantly destabilized and restabilized in terms of what they might actually mean. Water movements are thus not restorative social movements that seek to recuperate a lost moral economy or "public." Instead, they present us with new frontiers of the political imagination that ask what the public or common might be. The financial frontier might thus appear as a global project that seamlessly conscripts public utilities into teleological circuits of capitalist self-expansion

(Fraser 2016, 166; see also Sopranzetti 2017). In fact, it is made by the equally relentless proliferation of political imagining by water movements that argue that the sell-off of their common goods is the most immoral form of theft of all—the theft of life itself.[4]

It matters that water management is usually a local affair. In many parts of the world, water is managed as a common-pool resource through community-controlled mechanisms (Bakker 2007, 442). In Europe, particularly in Germany, Italy, and Ireland where this story is set, water was for the longest time managed municipally via local water sources and infrastructures (Dukelow 2016; Fantini 2014; Lanz 2005).[5] This means that the history of water infrastructures developed very differently from other modern infrastructural systems like railroads, telecommunications, and electricity grids, which were made subject to centralized government schemes to universalize access and to unified regulatory regimes (Collier 2011, 205–6; Bakke 2016). Contrary to the regional and national scaling up of these publicly owned infrastructures that occurred in Europe and the United States beginning in the 1930s, water works almost always stayed local, in part because of transportation costs but also because water cultures and long durée infrastructures have always been communal (McDonald 2018, 49). Even in France, which has long managed its water via more centralized river-basin institutions, water basin authorities are still largely managed according to principles of subsidiarity (Juuti, Katko, and University of Tampere 2005, 37).[6]

It is these localized vital histories and their attendant material intimacies that have created the contours and ethics of the political mobilizations documented here and that make water utilities particularly resistant to financialization. The intimate intensity with which people hold "their" water dear stands in stark contrast with the abstract pricing and trading infrastructures that global finance seeks to build (Besky 2016).[7] As anthropologists have long argued, inalienable possessions hold transcendent value and are often held in common (Kockelman 2020,14). They tend to be "essential to the continuity of the thread of life between past, present, and future" (Narotzky and Besnier 2014, 9; Weiner 1992). These possessions may under some circumstances be counted and priced, but always with questions of justice in mind and never by outsiders who treat these inalienable possessions as mere resources from which wealth can be extracted. After all, inalienable possessions are never mere economic, but also juridical, political, ethical, and affective facts that cannot easily be rendered equivalent through numbers (Kockelman 2020, 15; Ballestero 2015, 2019).

Many of my interlocutors understood the privatization of their public utilities as an enclosure of a common good that should, under all circumstances, be kept public.[8] They experienced enclosure in very concrete ways: in the form of crazy bills that could not be paid and were thus unjust; in the form of water meters that sought to press the "last drop of blood out of stones"; as nominally public utilities that suddenly seemed to be governed by faraway inscrutable forces; as contracts that people argued they never signed; or as laws and violent policing that they perceived to be profoundly illegitimate, even illegal. My interlocutors thus experienced financialization not primarily as a set of abstract economic institutions but as an intimate social formation that came with often obscure practices and illegitimate effects; a "sedimented financialization" that propelled seemingly distant processes into the everyday lives of households with accelerated speed, anxiety-inducing intensity, and polarizing class effects (Song 2014, 41; Palomera 2015; Kalb 2020; Mattioli 2020). It was against these concrete, everyday financialization effects that Europe's water insurgencies arose and through which finance emerged as a highly politicized object.

Moving across Italy, Germany, and Ireland, I explore the uneven distribution, expansion, and retraction of processes of financialization—economic logics that are also always modes of political governance accompanied by modular kinds of lawmaking and circulatory moral and contractual forms (Appel 2019; Vogl 2017). As I track the political insurgencies that emerge in response to and always in excess of this apparatus of capture, I show that the financial frontier consists of a series of volatile encounters with uncertain effects. Unsurprisingly, two of the insurgencies I document appeared in Europe's racialized "peripheries" (Italy and Ireland, part of what mainstream media widely called the "PIIGS" during the 2008 financial crisis, i.e., Portugal, Italy, Ireland, Greece, and Spain [Franquesa 2018, 123–24, Schneider 1998]). But they occurred also in what is frequently thought of as one of the hearts of the European project: Berlin. Across these terrains, I track the vitality of insurgency as people relentlessly push back and thus shape the financial frontier.[9] When Allianz Global Water, a subfund of Allianz Global Investors, urges investors to "ride the wave" and invest in water infrastructures while insisting that such investments are secure because they are "immune" to "political and sentiment-driven volatility," it misrepresents what is often a precarious terrain to which global firms like Allianz must respond.[10] While investors like Allianz are constantly rearranging their narratives and tactics as they anticipate critique (such as when water corporations suddenly speak of water as a human right), movement critiques cannot always be seamlessly integrated. Instead, fault lines open up in their wake. It is only through attention to the proliferation of these fault lines that the financial frontier can be fully grasped. And it is only through a focus on these fault lines that prospects for an emancipatory contemporary politics can be discerned (Fraser 2016, 57).

I refer to this frontier as vital because my interlocutors all equated water with life—a language that bore striking resemblance to indigenous movements that have long argued that extractive capitalism is a form of thievery that relies on the world's "open veins" for sustenance (Estes 2019; Gómez-Barris 2017, xvii; de la Cadena 2015; Farthing and Fabricant 2018; Shiva 2016; Simpson 2017, 2021). As neoliberalism renews its "extractive-dispossessive form" in an era of financialized sovereignty (Gago 2015, 11), its necropolitical core is challenged by the vitality of the politics of water as life, now a rallying cry around the world.[11] I also refer to these politics as *vital* because the history of neoliberalism cannot be understood without reference to the expansion of commercial processes into life itself. Value is today produced through life, as the biotech revolution has shifted the locus of value production to the level of the genetic, microbial, and cellular (Sunder Rajan 2006; Cooper 2008, 19; Helmreich 2008).[12] While the expansion of the financial into biological life processes has been well documented (Langley 2020b), I argue that this mode of appropriating value must be understood as including the vital infrastructures necessary to make life substances like potable water circulate and flow (see Langley 2018, 2021; Bear 2015; Harvey 2004). Vital infrastructures, in short, are a crucial part of the life that capital seeks to absorb (Murphy 2017, 149; Hardt and Negri 2000). As the flows that circulate through urban fabrics are monetized via consumer payments and as potential present and future income streams, investors make claims on the future of cities and the human and nonhuman life entangled with it. They generate wealth out of the stuff of life and the infrastructural backbones it relies on, subordinating the substance of society to the laws of the market (Langley 2018, 177; La Duke and Cowen 2020; Polanyi 2001, 75). It did not matter to my interlocutors that global investors were for the most part more concerned with *infrastructural* assets (the pipes, collection wells, pumping stations, and filtration and sewage treatment systems needed to manage and move fresh water and wastewater systems) than with water as an asset class per se, though this is now rapidly changing.[13] For my interlocutors, the financialization of water infrastructures was a struggle over *their water* being taken away, and it was their water they wanted back.

Water is a charismatic protagonist at this frontier. For insurance, banking, and asset management firms, scenarios of extreme scarcity from California to Cape Town create horizons of expectation promising durable wealth that stretches far into the future.[14] Investors bank on life's infinite dependence on water as a vehicle toward infinite wealth. For them, the frontiers opened up by the structural imbalance between water supply and demand should be addressed through massive private investment—large-scale credit and the forms of public indebtedness they entail. Investors foreground infrastructural breakdown and the moral imperative to meet these material needs. What they obscure is what is really at stake: long-term financial opportunities through debt financing (Bear 2017, 2020; Mitchell 2020).

Yet water is a profoundly "uncooperative commodity" that is not readily enclosed or owned (Bakker 2003), a "limit figure" that escapes from or at least resides at the edges of enclosure (Kockelman 2016, 5).[15] As William Blackstone put it in his eighteenth-century commentary on English common law, water is "a moving, wandering thing, and must of necessity continue to be common by the law of nature so that I can only have a temporary, transient, usufructuary property therein" (Blackstone 2016, 11). As an unruly substance that constantly circulates through rock, soil, air, and flesh, water troubles the fiction of possessive ownership and bodily sovereignty (Ballestero 2019, 415; Björkman 2015, 14–15; Cattelino 2015b; Helmreich 2011; Neimanis 2019; Strang 2005; Povinelli 2016). With qualities difficult to measure and temporalities that exceed human comprehension, there is perhaps no other substance that is as out of sync with finance capitalism's short-term rhythms, modes of disembedded ownership, and modes of valuation (Bersani 2011, 89; Muehlmann 2012; Satsuka 2019, 203). Water is vital both from the point of view of everyday household reproduction as from the point of view of capitalization, creating terrains of struggle that oscillate between appropriation and reappropriation, capture and overflow. My use of the term *vital* is not meant to ontologize life or to appeal to some immanent insurrectionary power or autonomous force.[16] But it does acknowledge the fact that there are few substances that are as universally revered as sacred, such as when a Neapolitan priest sprinkles bystanders with water from a public water fountain—as if he were distributing holy water with the world and its inhabitants as his church. The privatization of this sacred good, while shrouded in the "phantom objectivity" of exchange value, seems unnatural, even evil, to many (Taussig 1980, 4). Water symbolizes a gift that money cannot buy, "the whole of potentiality; it is *fons et origo*, the source of all possible existence" (Eliade 1958, 188; Helmreich 2011, 132). A symbolically dense sign and substance, water buoys the frontiers of water movements' political theorizing, while always also existing in excess of it.

The term *insurgency*, etymologically linked to *surge* and most likely to the late-fifteenth-century Middle French word *sourge* (fountain or stream), is defined as a rising, swelling up, or ascension from below. Today, we define *insurgency* as a condition of revolt against a government whose authority is deemed illegitimate. Anthropologists have long documented insurgencies in the Global South, where, for decades, governments have had to manage populations as they became risks to the implementation of structural adjustment regimes (Peterson 2014, 54–56; von Schnitzler 2016). They have further documented the kinds of "insurgent citizenship" that have made powerful demands in countries like Brazil and Bolivia, where profound inequalities and the urban poor's alienation from the law and democratic process have seen waves of reappropriations and "autoconstructions" of law and democracy from below (Holston 2009; Lazar 2007; see also Graeber 2004, 83–84; Hines 2021). When the Berlin Water Table insisted that they were the sovereign and wrote a disclosure law to prove it, or when the Italians built and won a referendum in 2011, they similarly insisted on their right to democratic process and to auto construct the law. When the Irish blocked the installation of water meters using their bodies as barricades, they similarly reappropriated public space and engaged in a public battle over debt, justice, and sovereignty—with sovereignty implying not exclusive jurisdiction or possession but a commitment to the inappropriability of life (Simpson 2020, 686; Subramanian 2009, 171). All did so from the vantage point of deeply grounded histories and tactics of collective political mobilization, using already available cultural and historical arsenals at their disposal.

Arising from the level of households, neighborhoods, and cities, water insurgencies pose profound challenges to the liberal democratic project as it has evolved under conditions of financialized capitalism in Europe. Here, the rise of authoritarian neoliberalism has seen executive branches marginalize the policy-making function of national parliaments in order to fast-track austerity reforms and fiscal adjustment programs. They have structurally inscribed "a permanent state of exception into its legal and institutional practices" (Cozzolino 2018, 337–38; Bieler 2021, 96),[17] and they have centralized decision-making processes to reduce spaces of dissent (Tansel 2018; Mattioli 2020). Against this conflation of emergency legislation with ordinary policy-making functions (Cozzolino 2019, 340), and against what many of my interlocutors called "the illegality of the law" (see also Holston 2009, 19), European water movements have used all tools at their disposal—self-authorized lawmaking and exuberant public demonstrations; political maneuvers as well as guerilla actions; evocations of both human rights and broader questions of "life." They have done so relentlessly through a continued renewal of political will, collective organizing, and common purpose. The temporality of insurgency that I document here is thus certainly eventful (such as when the majority of a population expresses its political will through a resoundingly successful referendum against the privatization of water). But insurgency is just as often built patiently over the long term through community work, often over years, sometimes decades.

Water movements are not exclusively constituted by citizens making demands on the nation state. Rather, they often occur in the name of the human right to water and, increasingly, in the name of water and nature as kin. Bearing family resemblance to both indigenous mobilizations for the protection of water (de la Cadena 2015; Estes 2019; Simpson 2017, 2021) as well as to submerged Christian traditions, such as when Italians referred to water as *sorella acqua* (sister water) after an eleventh-century Franciscan prayer (Muehlebach 2018b), the insurgencies documented here emerge out of a profoundly contradictory historical moment in which the rise of vital infrastructures as a financial asset class coexists with the fact that rivers and other bodies of water are increasingly granted constitutional rights as persons (Warne 2019; Chiasson 2019).[18] Many of my interlocutors were aware of this mostly indigenous-led global politics that recognizes the Earth and its substances as animate, rights-bearing subjects, just as they were very knowledgeable about processes of financialization. It was these incommensurable global developments that opened up fraught ethical questions about life in its indivisibility as well as about futurity and debt—a debt that current generations owe to water as life-giving substance and to human and nonhuman generations to come. If the principle of investment "hinges upon the belief that the future is exploitable" (Papadopoulos 2017, 139), water movements raise the question of futurity and whether limits ought to be set to the future's—indeed life's—exploitability.

This book tracks how people across Europe have come together in insurgent, sometimes even riotous groups to publicly burn water bills at the stake, block the installation of water meters with their bodies, sabotage water meters, write their own laws, hold their own referenda, force the disclosure of contracts, or refuse to sign contracts. By focusing on those bearing financialization's weight as its intimate effects unfold across every day and sometimes quite unexpected terrains (Ho 2020; Miyazaki 2012), I show that people are never subsumed under a steadily expanding totalitarian financial regime (Weiss 2018, 460; Hart and Ortiz 2014, 472; Besky 2016). Instead, they exist in a frictitious, rebellious, sometimes riotous relation to this process. By conceptualizing these fault lines as a frontier, I insist on financialization's contingency and volatility. The extractive zone is always a zone of "permanent provocation" as well (Li 2007, 11; Byrd et al. 2018; Mezzadra 2015, 222). At this frontier, the extraction of wealth from life is met with a resounding affirmation of life as the only form of wealth.

### Financializing Life

In March 2019, over seven hundred "top water leaders" and business executives met in London at a three-day Global Water Summit to help investors discuss global water markets and their movements. London was a highly symbolic location, as the summit's watermeetsmoney.com website put it, since the city is not only "historic, grand, and global," but also a "hub for creativity and finance, two of the pillars of a more successful water future."[19] The main topic of the summit was the "disruptive designs" that would help investors "accelerate opportunities in the global water sector" in light of the growing capital requirement for water infrastructures. The summit was only one of many recent spectacular international events that have showcased the ways in which a huge global capital liquidity—superfluous money produced by a superfluous class with no real social function, as Hannah Arendt poignantly put it (1976, 148)—is intersecting with a growing anticipation that water and water infrastructures are rapidly becoming some of the most lucrative commodities on the planet.[20] These events hinge on the promise of ample future returns, such as when Allianz Global Water predicts that investors will derive multiple forms of "environmental, social, and financial alpha" from their investments (with alpha indicating excess or abnormal rates of profit).[21] The global "rush" (Li 2014, 4) to invest in water is thus as much a moral as it is a fiscal story, with investors accruing both financial and ethical returns.[22]

The summit included roundtables on desalination and how this technology might serve, among other things, corporate mining needs; how the effects of future water scarcity might impact beverage industries such as Coca-Cola; and what the role of smart money might be for the North

American oilfield water services market.[23] Yet one of the summit's main stated goals was to bring together investors with utility managers in order to meet the growing financial needs of aging urban water utilities around the world. Thus, even as the global rush for "unconventional hydrocarbons" is today coupled to an equally frantic search for "unconventional water" (Gandy 2014, 12), one of the summit's central concerns was the decidedly more mundane question of how and under what conditions global investors might invest in urban water utilities. As one Swiss financial company estimated, the size of the global water market was around US$591 billion in 2015, US$500 billion of which was invested, allocated, or directly managed by municipal or public utilities (Ballestero 2019, 18). Allianz Global Investors argue that in 2019 alone, "the accumulative investment gap on water infrastructure was US$81 billion. Other calculations suggest annual needs of more than US$100 billion each year for the next 20 years" (2021). The number of people globally served by privatized water companies is thus growing, from 335 million in 2000 to 1.1 billion in 2015, with political support for water privatization building globally, particularly in China, Brazil, and the United States (McDonald, Marois, and Spronk 2021, 118–21). These specters of yet-to-be completed investments along the water supply chain mean that the frontiers of water financing are gravitating toward public or municipal water infrastructures. They make up the majority of the market share, especially in larger urban areas in middle- and high-income countries.[24]

Global Water Intelligence (GWI), a firm that sponsored the Global Water Summit, is a good example of this frontier in the making. It offers members an online monthly roundup of water-related news and carefully scours world political developments to discern the laws and policies that might "unlock" water infrastructures for future investment. Is Chile's government backing the reforms to water utility regulation? How to interpret the language of a US$1.4 billion environmental bond bill introduced in Massachusetts last week? GWI does not attempt to veil what is at stake: a global war over water about which intelligence must be collected—"unpriced information" that must reach GWI's clients before the competition does (Leins 2018, 81). The urban water utility sector is, in short, a projected horizon of wealth accumulation that intersects with the urgent needs of ecological and infrastructural modernization (Bresnihan 2016, 115).

The financialization of water infrastructures sets in motion multiple layers of predation. Public utilities in post–Maastricht Treaty Europe are today compelled to raise money through debt financing, just like their counterparts in the Global South were when the IMF and the World Bank implemented structural adjustment policies decades ago (Whiteside 2019, 1478). Municipalities thus vie for global investments by rendering themselves "bankable," that is to say, legible to financial investors. A utility's bankability (or "investment grade") is measured not only in terms of how well it is able to transform itself from a previously "invisible" and "inefficient" water network into a transparent and accountable infrastructure asset (Bresnihan 2016, 117; Heslop 2020, 364–81; see also Collins 2017),[25] or in terms of how quickly it can convert "weak operational performances" into what investors call "forward momentum" that will secure future funding for large-scale infrastructure investment.[26] Utilities must, first and foremost, demonstrate that they can and will be able to repay incurred debts.

They do so by turning themselves into joint stock companies that must demonstrate their financial efficiency and regulatory compliance through the use of corporate accounting methods and the reduction of operational costs (Bresnihan 2016). External loans are repaid through the municipal capacity to secure a captive income stream from households who pay predictable water tariffs over predictable time periods (Bayliss 2016, 386). Apart from outsourcing labor or selling public assets, privatized utilities are thus also reliable debtors insofar as they can guarantee stable income streams. The capital at stake is huge. A PricewaterhouseCoopers report for Ireland, for example, estimated that the debt capacity of the national water utility, Irish Water, could rise fantastically from 606 million euros in 2015 to 2.9 billion euros by 2030 (Bresnihan 2016, 120)—a debt capacity that translates into long-term contractually guaranteed returns for investors. Investors accrue an additional layer of value through the bond and derivatives trading built on top of municipal repayment of high-interest debts (Bear 2017, 5). After all, utility shareholdings have become assets that are speculatively traded, with ownership changing rapidly according to volatile financial market indicators. Public services have thus been transformed into tradable assets, with households around the world producing the income that allows for the steady "trickle up" of wealth through their consumption of essential goods (Bayliss 2014, 295). As Global Water Intelligence put it in a 2019 global water tariff survey, the average water, wastewater, and storm water tariffs increased by 3.3 percent on average over the previous year, a trend that shows no sign of abating.[27]

Contractually guaranteed long-term profits end up increasing, not decreasing, municipal debt (Whiteside 2018, 3; Lobina 2014, 3). This is not to say that municipalities were not always financial actors or that they were not also previously indebted.[28] Rather, there has been a move from what Laura Bear has called "political debts" to "monetary debts" (Bear 2017, 3). Public infrastructures for much of the twentieth century were financed through tariffs, taxes, Keynesian deficit spending, and sovereign debt (Langley 2018, 175)—debts that were characterized by government collaboration with forms of capital such as pension funds and that entailed a fiscal policy in service of political and social reproduction (Bear 2020, 2017, 3). It is only when this debt became financialized, that is, when control over fiscal policy moved from states to banking and financial rentier classes, that debt had to be paid back with often high interest. This logic of nonnegotiable monetized debt has now saturated political governance and accounting from India to the European Union (Bear 2017, 4).

This public capture by finance has changed the forms and temporalities of political governance, with the tributary structures erected around debt repayment now constituting the very logic of public institutions. This orientation toward creditors—the "God of Debt," as one of my German interlocutors put it—means that remnants of whatever long-term political reasoning is still left have been hollowed out (Bear 2015, 51). State institutions are experimenting with biopolitical rationalities that explicitly foster and support processes of financialization. They create extensive legal and regulatory provisions for capital while pledging their own tax base to investors (Langley 2018, 172–82; Smith 2020, 329).

My interlocutors across Europe were incensed by the fact that the debts their utilities were accruing would accumulate in the long run and cascade across generations, generating future debts to be-paid by their children and grandchildren. They struggled against this intergenerational bondage to debt—a "perpetual motion scheme" where distant creditors generate money out of money by living indefinitely off interest and burdening future generations with present financial and political arrangements (Foster 2018, 298; see also Arendt 1976, 144).[29] Against this politics of municipal debt (or what scholars have called the urban "debt-machine" or "bond-market urbanism" (Peck and Whiteside 2016), European water movements articulated not only an oppositional politics of monetary debt and financial accounting, but their own, contrarian poetics of vital debt—an incalculable debt that humans and nonhumans owe to water on a daily basis. They thus articulated a very different quality and temporality of value (Narotzky and Besnier 2014, 4)—one generated out of life's indebtedness to water as it is renewed with every drop, every day, and as it holds together humans and nonhumans, bodies across space, and generations across time. Italian politician Tommaso Fattori made this point beautifully when he recounted Ovid's *Metamorphosis*, a classic of Latin literature written more than two thousand years ago. In it, the goddess Latona addresses a group of peasants who refused to allow her to drink from a pool, asking, "Why do you refuse me water? The common use of water is the sacred right of all mankind. Nature allows no one to claim as property the sunshine, the air, or the water. When I drew near, it was a public good I came to share. . . . A draught of water would be nectar to me; it would revive me, and I would find myself indebted to you for life itself" (Fattori 2001).

The financialization of life is a political process, too. Some of my interlocutors noted that their main adversary in this David-and-Goliath battle were, in fact, politicians. As Claus Kittsteiner, one of the founding members of the Berlin Water Table put it to me, "Our frontline (*unsere Frontebene*) was never the capitalist corporation, which does what we expect it to do. Our frontline was always the politicians who signed these scandalous contracts." Their most incisive critiques were thus reserved for those public institutions that had sold off what some of my interlocutors in Germany called their *Tafelsilber* (or silverware, which in English is perhaps more appropriately translated as crown jewels)—their water (Moss 2020, 284–89). Indeed, municipal water works are often desperate for investments since public subsidies were radically reduced since the 2008 financial crisis, right at a moment when infrastructure bonds and debt financing became more popular. This means that this frontier of dispossession operates also on the level of desire—of public utilities yearning to develop debt capacity and to become worthy of global investment (Morris 2016, 33; see also Björkman 2015). State actors are thus as invested in attracting global capital as they are in staging a fantasy of credit worthiness—that they are or will in the future become efficient debtors. Yet desire does not fully capture the psychic life of public indebtedness either. Consent and the commitment to good behavior matter, too, insofar as *haute finance* can only entrench its grip on politics because loans and the renewal of loans hinge on credit, which in turn hinges on "good behavior" reflected in the budget (Polanyi 2001, 14). As Marco Bersani from Italy's National Forum for Public Water put it, "Politicians and their parties have consented to the expropriation of their political function."

Parallel to this apparatus of guaranteeing and leveraging debt runs a process of political centralization, an economy of scale matched up with the administrative scaling up of water management systems (Romano, Guerrini, and Campedelli 2015, 46). In Marx's words, the concentration of property results in political centralization because centralized govern-mental structures can better accommodate large-scale investments and shared capital corporations (Marx and Engels 1967, 65). This means that states need to actively create the properly scaled political conditions for financialization. In Italy and Ireland, for example, states passed legislation to create single, consolidated (in Ireland national, in Italy regional) water companies (Bresnihan 2016, 9), as was the case in England and Wales in 1989. The regional centralization via regional water authorities was set in accordance with watershed areas; but this ecologically sound rearrange-ment nevertheless also facilitated privatization (Bakker 2001, 145). Politi-cal and administrative centralization, in short, is necessary to economic monopolization (see also Boyer 2019, 16). It is a process that runs parallel to the fact that water provisioning is a natural monopoly and not a competitive market. Because there exists only one infrastructure for the aqueduct and only one possible supplier of the resource through the network, the body running the service will have monopoly and thus access to a captive income stream—a form of monopoly rent or what some of my interlocutors called a "hostage market." Such patterns of monopolization were already evident in nineteenth-century private water provisioning, where private companies did not compete but "followed a model familiar to crime bosses: they real-ized far better profits by dividing the territory into separate monopolies where they each set their own rates as they saw fit" (Salzman 2013, 67). A century earlier, states had already intervened into highly monopolized mercantilist economic life when monopolies became dangerous because they impacted the "necessaries of life" (Polanyi 2001, 69). One of my German interlocutors, social-democratic politician Gerlinde Schermer, similarly commented on this dual process of economic monopolization and politi-cal centralization, arguing that the financialization of public utilities often reverses decades of federalism and municipalism in favor of centralized political and administrative structures. They allow for global investors to negotiate "only with one, not with several kings. That way, you only need to talk to a single decision maker to get at what is in fact *our* property!"

Infrastructural assets allow for this existing global liquidity to embed itself in durable material and social infrastructures at a moment of intense global economic volatility—a long-term guaranteed stability of returns that emerges out of the fact that water is what specialists call a "nonoptional" and "fixed-demand" service. Humans are not free to decide whether or not to use water. Their demand does not vary much in relation to contin-gencies (in moments of crisis, a family might only marginally reduce its demand for water or even increase it). Thus, even though investments in expensive water infrastructures may take years to return their value, they promise "low-risk, high-yield, inflation-proof investments" over time (Campra et al. 2014, 5; Della Croce and Yermo 2013; Harvey 2004, 63; Mitchell 2020). Value in this financialized economy is thus extracted from life and the households that produce and reproduce it, the infrastructures that sustain it, and the rent that can thereby be accrued. It lies not primarily in their infrastructural capacity to move commodities across space, but in their capacity to facilitate durable *financial* flows across time (Mitchell 2020). This durable rent structure also arises out of durable legal and political infrastructures. After all, investments in water infrastructures are made through contractual agreements that last almost the length of a generation, usually twenty-five to thirty years or more, thus guaranteeing the durability of corporations that can outlast many an elected government.[30] While the guaranteed returns on investment (12–15 percent per year) are humble in contrast to the 25 percent returns that can, say, be made through short-term corporate restructuring, the security they offer in times of market turbulence is priceless to investors like pension funds.[31] Studies of water utility privatization in the United Kingdom have shown, for example, that companies have made profits well in excess of predictions, paying dividends to their shareholders well above the average paid to stock market investors (Bakker 2001, 157).[32]

At the heart of this financial frontier lies the household—the site from which wealth is extracted, bill by bill, month by month. The spiraling debt economies that go hand in hand with the financialization into public utilities ensnares not only public budgets but people's everyday lives as well. Households are central to this vital frontier as indebtedness has become necessary for the acquisition of life's necessities. Utilities have come to rely on the steady income of household payments in order to manage debt. The current round of accumulation, in short, relies at least in part on the movement of wealth "upward" through household payments on vital goods—on water but also rent, energy, phones, and subscription fees.[33] Households have thus become anchors to which the volatile post-2008 global financial system is attached; they function as "shock absorbers" in a market lurching from one crisis to the next (Cooper and Mitropoulos 2009, 364). Yet households are volatile anchors and can become sites of refusal, too. Once stretched too thin, they are the terrain upon which fault lines appear.

## Recursions

When Adam Smith wrote *The Wealth of Nations*, the prospect of commodi-fying water was still unthinkable. Arguing that the usefulness of a good could be inversely related to its value, he gave the famous example of a diamond that was useless and yet expensive while "there is nothing more useful than water. But [water] will purchase scarce anything; and scarce anything can be had in exchange for it" (Smith [1776] 1937, 33). Smith was operating within the basic parameters of Western law, which, born out of Justinian jurisprudence, differentiated between public goods, private goods, *res nullius* (goods that belong to no one and that therefore can be appropriated by everyone), and *res communes* (goods that belong to every-one such that no one can use them exclusively for themselves, including freshwater and seawater [Fattori 2013, 382; Shiva 2016, 20]). Beginning in the nineteenth century however, that which was unthinkable to Smith and unknown within the Western legal canon became thinkable, even com-monsensical: the turning of *res communes* into assets through which future value is earned in the present (Mitchell 2020; Barlow 2005).

Of course, water itself has been priced, bought, and sold in different ways for millennia. Ancient Rome already distinguished between water, free for the taking by commoners out of public basins, versus water that was provided by the city to the upper classes via pipes running from the main system to their private houses or baths. The former were warned never to sell their free water ("A marble wellhead from the ninth century in Rome's San Marco church carries an inscription cursing anyone who dares to sell the well's water"), while the latter had to pay a water tax that was reinvested into infrastructure maintenance (Salzman 2013, 54–57). The medieval market for holy waters was similarly vibrant, as was the European trade in healing mineral waters that emerged in the eighteenth century and that still exists today (Salzman 2013, 23). Another exquisite story, told in the immediate aftermath of World War II, describes Naples' water sellers selling *acqua ferrata* (water containing iron) in rounded cups shaped like women's breasts and charging "three or four times the equivalent amount of wine" (Lewis 1978, 85–86).

Yet this provisioning of water for a price, whether in ancient Rome, medieval France and Germany, or modern Naples, always appeared as an exception against the backdrop of the fact that water, with its life-giving capacities and inimitable material qualities, is widely, indeed cross-culturally, thought of as a natural commons that ought to exist outside of the spheres of market exchange.[34] Thus, even though humans have for millennia built infrastructures to capture water or even at times sell it, they never before made it subject to the kinds of financial speculation and rent seeking that first occurred in the mid-nineteenth century and that is reoccurring again today. The quantifications of water's qualities (such as when a cup of water equals three to four cups of wine, or when ancient Rome's wealthy were taxed for the water flowing through city infrastructures) cannot be equated with current regimes of capitalization that hinge on the belief in the limitless exploitability of future returns (Muniesa et al. 2017).

The current financialization of water utilities thus differs profoundly from the buying and selling of water as it has occurred, on and off and in limited ways, across millennia. Instead, it represents the (re)emergence of interest-bearing capital in ways that facilitate accumulation (Christophers and Fine 2020, 20), thus replaying nineteenth-century speculative endeavors through which common goods were converted into financial gains, the Earth's gifts into sites of accumulation (Luxemburg 1913, 230–31). As I show for the case of Berlin, city officials signed almost identical contracts with similar political, social, and infrastructural effects in the mid-nineteenth and the late-twentieth centuries. This means that the current era of financial expansion offers insight into the enduring power of financialized infrastructures as they appear and reappear across space and time. But it also allows us to see that these incursions build on, recombine with, and complexly fold back upon earlier histories of finance while throwing open similar fissures and fault lines once again.

Scholars have explored the recurrent logics of what David Harvey, in his rereading of Rosa Luxemburg, has called a "new imperialism." Here, value is accumulated through dispossession and expropriation—a process that today dwarfs the exploitation of waged labor as a principal source of value production and capital expansion (Harvey 2004; Federici 2004; Fraser 2016). Capitalism did not evolve teleologically from a prehistory of originary (*ursprüngliche*) or "primitive" accumulation—the theft of labor, land, water, and other natural resources that Luxemburg called the Earth's free gifts and "natural treasures" (*Naturschätze*) (1913, 230–31)—toward the production of surplus value in the factory, the mine, or the agricultural estate (Harvey 2004, 73). Rather, capitalism must constantly reiterate its own violent origins, especially in periods of crisis (Morris 2016, 38; Arendt 1976, 148). Originary or salvage accumulation—the conversion of noncapitalist into capitalist forms of value (Tsing 2015)—is thus recursive rather than teleological, structural rather than temporal (Morris 2016, 62; Federici

2004, 12–13). It exists permanently as "capitalism's disavowed confiscatory underside" (Fraser 2016, 168). While both mechanisms of accumulation—by dispossession and through labor exploitation—are constitutive parts of the same capitalist whole (Luxemburg 1913, 203), the latter has today been demoted as the principal source of surplus value (Cooper 2008, 24).

This recursivity of dispossession means that frontiers must constantly be remade, as natural commons like land, air, and water, or cultural forms like music, public goods, and universities are pillaged (Harvey 2004, 75). Indeed, the insurgencies documented here bear striking resemblance to insurgencies documented across history, such as those made famous by Edward Palmer Thompson in his work on peasant crowds during the early modern English era of enclosure—people rendered "turbulent" not by an "irrational" desire to riot (or not pay for their water, as critics of water movements often falsely accuse them of), but by a moral and political consciousness that responds to the plunder of the commons.[35] Then as now, wealth was ruthlessly extracted from the "prime necessities of life" (Thompson 1993, 270, Muehlebach 2018a). Then as now, these insurgencies are profoundly gendered, as women were most directly impacted as the everyday reproduction of household life became the cusp of frontiers of finance (Roberts 2008, 236; Federici 2004).[36] Through the mobilizations of women, the deprivations suffered by private households were politicized and rendered public for all to see—through the public burning of bills, for example.

The term *frontier* comes with much historical ballast not only from the US American West but also from Latin America (Tsing 2003, 5100). Yet I here turn to Rosa Luxemburg's analysis of the building of the Suez Canal in late nineteenth-century Egypt because it is a paradigmatic example of a financial frontier fueled by British and French imperialism. I find her analysis particularly helpful as it bears resemblance to the forms of dispossession explored in this book. Describing how London's nineteenth-century stock market was engulfed with a fever for exotic bonds, she shows how emerging states such as Argentina, Mexico, Uruguay, Turkey, Greece, and Egypt took out loans worth hundreds of millions of pounds sterling from England, most of which were immediately spent buying English commodities including coal, steel, and the machinery needed to build railroads, mines and, crucially, water infrastructures (see also Khalili 2021). Lurching from one cycle of bankruptcy to another, these countries again turned to England for even more high-interest loans. English investors—soon followed by the Germans, French, and Belgians—were more than happy to oblige (Luxemburg 1913, 283–84). As both Luxemburg and Arendt insist, this "export of money" relied foundationally on the material power of the state, which utilized its political institutions exclusively as vehicles for the protection of private property (Arendt 1976, 149).

In Egypt, the collusion between French and British investors with Egyptian political elites in the second half of the nineteenth century saw the country's debt grow like an avalanche—the weight of which was carried by impoverished Egyptian peasant households (Luxemburg 1913, 286). Here, dams, irrigation systems, wells, and canals were built to provide water for plantation crops cultivated for European consumption: indigo, sugar, cotton. Yet it was the Suez Canal that was the most fatal infrastructural project for Egypt. The Egyptian state offered tens of thousands of corvée laborers to the French Compagnie de Suez and bought company shares worth 70 million mark, 40 percent of the Companie de Suez's total assets. The ensuing debt was "mercilessly beaten" out of the peasantry that had already been not only dispossessed of their land and labor but forced to pay land taxes, head taxes, and cattle taxes as well as a tax on every single date tree and every single mud hut they owned. Once plantation irrigation systems were built, peasants were charged for the water they needed for their fields. The more debt grew, the more peasants were coerced into paying taxes. Everyone, writes Luxemburg (1913), was drawn into the immense labor of repayment—humans, animals, even the earth itself was expropriated (289).[37] By 1875, Egypt was so indebted that it sold its Suez shares to the British government, only to be met with another round of crippling interest payments (291). By 1879, Egypt's finances came under permanent European control. By 1882, Egypt was occupied by the British. The Egyptian king's land was confiscated just as he had forcibly confiscated that land from peasant households. Large parts of it went to the Compagnie de Suez (292).[38]

I tell this story because Suez looks back on being one of the longest running corporations in the world. Until a short while ago, it operated in the global water sector under the name of Suez Environnement and was, together with another French multinational Veolia Environnement, one of two dominant transnational players in the water privatization market today (the companies have since merged).[39] Some of the water utilities that my interlocutors waged years of struggle against are partially managed by subsidiaries of Suez. Suez today accumulates wealth through fiscal mechanisms and political maneuvers very similar to those utilized in the past, with similar effects on those situated at the center of this financial frontier—often already impoverished households.

I also tell this story because the building of the Suez Canal in nineteenth-century Egypt is one historical example of the ways in which fairy-tale profits could be captured through investments in water infrastructures (Luxemburg 1913, 290). Many other water infrastructures were built by British and French investors at the time as they moved effortlessly between the colonies and their home countries—an empire of finance driven by the quest to draw modern cities' growing demand for water into global financial circuits (Kar and Schuster 2021). In 1850, the British East India Company drew up plans to provide water to Bombay (Anand 2017, 34). Indeed, it was in India where some of the earliest forms of speculative capitalism and its colonial forms of corporate and contract law first arose (Bear, Birla, and Puri 2015, 389). In 1852, a group of British aristocrats founded the Berlin Water Works Company, a London-based joint stock company. In 1878, the Anglo-French General Credit and Discount Company founded the Naples Water Works Company.[40] Water infrastructures, in short, were already once part of a global regime of accumulation seeking to absorb life's dependency on water into its speculative orbit.

I tell this story, finally, because it invites a reflection on the recursive modes of financialization, their tactics, long durée cycles, and often volatile and open-ended effects. I here draw on social theorists who have conceptualized recurrence in the capitalist economy as a tripartite sequence that broadly began with the financial expansion led by merchant or finance capital in the nineteenth century and then was replaced by manufacturing and industrialism in the early twentieth century. When the limits of this system were reached by the 1970s, capitalism moved again into an age of financial expansion—an era currently characterized by evermore desperate attempts at accumulation. This tripartite structure moved from circulation to production back to circulation, from asset to commodity back to asset, and from rent to profits back to rents. This cyclicality, so the argument goes, has generated a concomitant cycle of political action that has moved from riots (over the price of vital necessities) to labor strikes (over the price of labor power) back to riots.[41]

While this historical framing certainly elucidates historical patterns in highly abstracted ways, I am as an ethnographer most committed to historically grounded, contextually specific, often also nonlinear and surprising social struggles. I am thus more interested in attending to the granularities and specific genealogies of political protest, such as when the Irish mobilized anticolonial registers in their water meter protests or when my German interlocutors reminisced about the historical importance of having held a key trial in a particular court room with a chilling Nazi history. This book thus attends to capitalism's "genuinely weird temporality" (Sewell 2008, 533)—the fact that it is characterized by a "strange stillness" (as its mechanisms and forms recur across time and space) *and* intense volatility and nonteleological contingency at the same time (519).

Likewise, I attend to the weird temporalities of political protest—the fact that they periodically recur and bear resemblances to each other while also being characterized by great contingency. Many of the protests I document here bear striking similarity to protests that others, including Rosa Luxemburg (1913), documented for the late nineteenth century when communally held "natural economies"—those noncommodified worlds that capitalism so foundationally depends on—put up bulwarks against capitalism's unbridled expansion. For "natural economies," there was "no other attitude than opposition and fight to the finish" (371). Similar bulwarks were put up in European cities in the late nineteenth century, where early financial investments into water infrastructures were accompanied by political upheaval because they created problems of unequal access, distribution, infrastructural inefficiencies, and corruption—all coupled to often unpayable municipal debt. With hostility growing against the "functionless" investor and rentier (Hardt 2010, 348), many late-nineteenth-century cities decided to municipalize their water infrastructures, with water utilities falling (or being pulled into) public hands. As liberal statesman Joseph Chamberlain declared in 1884, "It is difficult, if not impossible, to combine the citizens' rights and interests and the private enterprise's interests, because the private enterprise aims at its natural and justified objective, the biggest possible profit" (Juuti, Katko, and University of Tampere 2005, 41).[42] Today, remunicipalizations abound again as cities from Paris to Berlin and Naples take back their water utilities and place them under local control (McDonald and Swyngedouw 2019), yet we cannot assume that the meaning of "the public" or of "property" or of "the commons" have remained static over time.

In part, these initial, early-twentieth-century municipalizations occurred because municipalities had gained the right to borrow money at low interest rates, versus the high-interest loans cities had previously taken out from private creditors—a local fiscal sovereignty that allowed them to take on debt for long-term infrastructural investments (Hall and Lobina 2012, 4). Municipalities underwrote these loans with their municipal capacity to tax and thus their capacity to guarantee future fiscal revenue (Smith 2020, 329). They began to invest in the development of their own infrastructural systems in the name of modernity, public health, and poverty alleviation—an investment that resulted in more effective control (of pricing, for example), better infrastructural coverage, and higher employment for locals. It could also be quite lucrative for cities (Juuti, Katko, and University of Tampere 2005, 42).[43] Most contemporary water infrastructures were thus built by municipally owned public enterprises during the twentieth century, with central governments playing a crucial role once municipalization had been achieved. This included major extensions of networks into rural areas following World War II—a hydro-social contract managed through the taxation of urban populations, low-interest loans, and massive cross-subsidizations (Hall and Lobina 2010, 4). Here, the term *profit* was often not used in reference to water provisioning. Rather, *surplus* was considered more appropriate for an industry supplying a vital service (Bakker 2001, 144; Ballestero 2019, 52). All of this changed as the noncommodified spheres of public water utilities got drawn into financialized modes of valuation.

### Milieus of Enclosure

The public-private partnership is a key device at the financial frontier. It uses the guise of a fair contract between partners to deeply integrate public utilities into highly unequal circuits of accumulation (Pistor 2019; Appel 2019). Water movements have long criticized this particular kind of entanglement of the public with the private sector. The public-private partnership is contractual, not concessional, which means that "the state becomes an "equal" *commercial* party to a legal agreement" (Appel 2019, 141). As water movements across the world have shown, this arrange-ment almost unfailingly works to the detriment of the public because it is a contradictory marriage between two incommensurable entities: one dedicated to the maximization of profits, the other (at least nominally) to public service. Presented as a partnership, the public-private partnership is a classic frontier ruse where contracts mask expropriation.

To my interlocutors, the crisis facing water utilities was a *political* crisis that emerged out of this mutual imbrication, a state that had not simply been captured but that had actively colluded in this process of disposses-sion (Kalb 2020, 26). The result was the entrenchment of an economized style of government whose "forms of command" were distributed across public institutions, private corporations, banks, and financial institutions; it was a "milieu of enclosure" that entangles public and private actors and institutions in formal and informal reciprocities (Vogl 2017, vi–vii). All bore uncanny resemblance to the ways in which public institutions under pressure from structural adjustment in the Global South soon ceased to exert actual powers. Commercial law began to organize public resources; and "the public" came to arrange itself along private lines (Tsing 2003, 5102; Peterson 2014, 90; EuroNomade 2018).[44]

There is no single European model for this highly malleable and constantly evolving form (Whiteside 2018, 3)—an arrangement between the public and private sectors that allows for the funding, construction, renovation, management, or maintenance of public infrastructures or services. The Organization for Economic Co-operation and Development (OECD) defines public-private partnerships as an alignment of the public with the private, an agreement between the government and "one or more private partners according to which the private partners deliver the service in such a manner that the service delivery objectives of the government are aligned with the profit objectives of the private partners and where the effectiveness of the alignment depends on a sufficient transfer of risk to the private partner" (OECD 2008). Public-private partnerships have been implemented for many public services worldwide, including bridges, highways, hospitals, and schools, thus inserting the logic of private property and profit seeking "into the heart of public infrastructure" (Whiteside 2018, 4). They are in fact not, my interlocutors argued, particularly risky. On the contrary, as Carl Waßmuth, a German engineer and member of the Berlin-based Gemeingut in BürgerInnenhand (Common Goods in Citizens' Hands) put it to me, public-private partnerships are "beautiful formal structures" that allow for what are often risk-free investments—a financing, not funding of infrastructure, and thus a way for governments to "rent money." Even in case of failure, the vital service must still be guaranteed by the state, which remains the last instance guarantor when all else fails.[45]

The battle over elementary water infrastructures, Waßmuth explained, was occurring because the "big stuff" like telecommunications, energy sectors, postal services, railways, and waste management had in many countries already been fully privatized during the 1990s. Investors soon realized that the maintenance of these huge infrastructures was prohibitively expensive. Public-private partnerships provided an elegant solution to this conundrum. Rather than pay for infrastructural investments themselves, investors today offer high-interest loans to cash-starved municipalities who are looking for quick monetary fixes in times of financial crisis.[46] The municipality, in turn, offers a long-term concession to a consortium that obtains the right to extract revenue directly from end users (Campra et al.

2014, 33–39). Contractually guaranteed returns oblige public institutions to fulfill this obligation by whatever means necessary. In practice, local governments, whose debts are now often millions higher than if they had kept their services under public operation, scramble to repay debts—sometimes by relinquishing their own profits, at other times by taking out new loans to pay off old ones. The public-private partnership thus conjures a fantasy of contractual equality where there is none.[47]

The marriage of incommensurables between the public and private also does violence to the holism of water. After all, the "unbundling" of the utility into several spheres of operation—with municipalities, for example, being responsible for the protection of water while broader competencies are handed over to a "more efficient" private consortium—means that water, a hydrological totality, is managed across various institutions with different institutional cultures, forms of knowledge, and economic and ethical commitments (Mohajeri 2006, 180–85). European municipal governments came to the contractual table under duress of a post–Maastricht Treaty politics that sacralized (and in the Italian case, constitutionalized [Cozzolino 2019]) the fetish of balanced budgets, inaugurating what Walter Benjamin called a cult of blame and debt (*verschuldeter Kultus*) (Vogl 2017, 160). Having introduced fixed public debt ceilings—the "Black Zero" (*Schwarze Null*) as the Germans call it—Maastricht created a landscape of intense fiscal discipline where many municipalities create what my German interlocutors called *Schattenhaushalte* (shadow households)—complex nested corporate structures that do not appear on the official books even though they become the instruments through which high-interest loans are procured by the public. They operate under the auspices of private law and pursue their own policies and water pricing (the calculation of which now ceases to be disclosed publicly [see Ballestero 2015]). Public-private partnerships thus often increase opacity and render the governance of vital resources not more, but less transparent.[48] In many cases, European municipalities have incurred billions of euros of debts that are not only higher than if they had borrowed directly but also hidden from view (Massarutto 2020, 8).[49] This debt lives in the shadow of the officially "balanced" municipal budget—a negative space that haunts what appears as good budgetary behavior.

Public-private partnerships further unsettle the terms of how ownership within the still nominally public utility is organized and conceived. Even if politicians insist that the utility is still publicly owned (which they always do since the municipality still owns a majority of the shares in the utility-turned-joint-stock-company), water movements everywhere were worried about the de facto deactivation of the distinction between public and private spheres. Not only had the purported public or private nature of a utility "lost traction as an index of distinct legal and economic logics" (Ballestero 2019, 47), the question of ownership had also become deeply obscure, as is always the case in frontier situations (Tsing 2003, 5104).

To be sure, asset ownership within public-private partnerships typically rests with the public authority, and all rights to those assets revert to that authority when the partnership ends (Campra et al. 2014, 39). But ownership means little if the utility orients much of its activity toward creditors rather than toward the public.[50] Indeed, just as the corporations publicly traded on Wall Street during the 1990s began to understand shareholders as the "true owners" of companies (Ho 2009, 3), so too do public-private partnerships inaugurate a form of utility ownership that ultimately rests with distant creditors. The surplus generated out of the utility, previously owned by the public and redistributed back into the utility, is made to trickle far upward, an apotheosis of what Veblen (1923) called "absentee ownership."

Against this indeterminate milieu of enclosure, water movements argued for a reinvigorated discussion about what "the public" is or ought to be. Many even argued against the recuperation of a public and instead for a much more democratized sense of the commons. In this discussion, water utilities were owned and accountable to those who had built them— "the people," over decades, through their own labor, taxes, and fees.[51] My interlocutors thus refused the public-private partnership as a model for ownership and public association (Birla 2009, 25) as well as the theory of the public it entailed. As joint stock companies, the selling of shares ("going public") allows for the public to be imagined as nothing more than an agglomeration of investor individuals. And while joint stock companies are a collectively held form of wealth (Martin 2002, 137), the publicly traded public utility consists of nothing more than a public of individual traders, a "non-totalizable multiplicity" (Elyachar 2012) where "private interests are treated as identical to the interests of the public" and where public life appears as nothing more than the totality of private interests (Arendt 1976, 145). The single purpose of this public, in short, is to be "mined as a collection of financial assets for elite and private gain" (Ho 2018, 149; Birla 2009, 3–4), leading to a profound reconfiguration of what the "public interest" is (Whiteside 2018, 3; Langley 2020a, 133). Water movements attempted to reimagine this perversion of the public by insisting that water ought to be treated as a particular kind of property, a property that is not really property at all, but a *Gemeingut* (common good) in Germany or a *bene comune* (commons or commonwealth) in Italy.

## Terrains

In this last section, I track some of these parameters across the European context that tie otherwise often disparate European terrains together. These ties were achieved not only through the vibrant circulation of people, images, and texts through movement networks or through the fact that many activists were producing similar analyses of their predicaments despite living in different countries and speaking different languages; ties were also achieved because they emerged from the fact that movements dealt with similar corporate tactics as they recurred across time and space. Monopolized capitalism comes with a relentless monotony of corporate forms—contracts that recur across time and space, tactics of obfuscation that remain numbingly consistent, and discursive techniques that insist that water is a human right even as they work to undermine it.

At the same time, the European water movement also created ties of its own, for example, through shared origin stories that they rehearsed and repeated about their movements' genesis. Many of the Irish people I met looked to the United States, specifically the desperate water struggles in Detroit and Flint, as the dystopian figure against which they measured their own possible future. But my Italian and German interlocutors pointed to Cochabamba, Bolivia, as the foundational moment for their water movements, a moment when certain modes of struggle and conceptual registers first came to their attention. There, Aguas del Tunari, an international consortium of US, British, and Italian multinationals, had signed a forty-year concession with the Bolivian government in 1999 that had guaranteed investors a 15 percent annual rate of returns, the result of which were a series of water tariff hikes people could not pay for. The people of Cochabamba responded by founding the Coordinadora de defensa del agua y la vida (Committee for the Defence of Water and Life), a mass coalition of unions, peasant organizations, ecologist movements, and students that captured the political imagination of millions around the world with its protests for "life" and against neoliberalism's necropolitical culture of death. By April of that same year, the Coordinadora had kicked the consortium out of the country (Olivera and Lewis 2004; Bakker 2010; Hines 2021).[52] The Cochabamba victory rendered visible the fact that "the battle over common goods was the new frontier in the struggle against neoliberal globalization," a realization that came at a moment when alter-globalization movements were already focusing on the illegitimacy of growing international financial institutions (Bersani 2011, 21–23; De Angelis 2017, 306–10). But a turning point came during the 2001 World Social Forum in Porto Alegre, when one representative from the Coordinadora turned to activists from the Global North and said, "Dear comrades, we are happy about your solidarity, but I want to say one thing to you: Of the ten water multinationals on the planet, nine are European and they are also trying to grab your water. When will you understand that the best way to help us would be to fight these corporations in your home countries?" (Bersani 2011, 24). An identical story featuring Kenyan activist Wangui Mbatia was told to me by the Berlin Water Table's Johanna Erdmann. In both cases, it was to provocations from the Global South that European water movements responded, not least because the effects of the financial crisis had engulfed Europe, too. At the same time, my interlocutors displayed a keen sense of the fact that struggles had to be fought in plural and situated ways, on particular terrains and through locally grounded tools and mechanisms.[53] Argentina, which had managed to kick out Suez, was different from Paris, which had refused to renew its contract with Veolia and Suez in 2008 after twenty-five years of privatization. The Berlin Water Table, named after Venezuela's *mesas de aguas* after founding member Dorothea Härlin encountered them while traveling in South America, knew that its worlding—its attempt at building worlds otherwise—must always consist of projects growing out of distinct watery histories and political terrains.

There is a European history to be told here, too. Most of the people I met told the history of water enclosure from the vantage point of the 1992 Dublin Statement on Water and Sustainable Development, which was the first global document to insist that "water has an economic value in all its competing uses and should be recognized as an economic good (Principle No. 4)."[54] While Principle No. 4 recognizes "the basic right of all human beings to have access to clean water and sanitation at an affordable price," it also notes that the misuse of water was the result of the "failure to recognize the economic value of water." The Dublin Statement thus inaugurated a paradigm shift—that it was only through a new regime of financial valuation that water could be used efficiently and equitably. Soon, the World Bank argued that it was state subsidies that *caused* the global water crisis, with private markets providing the solution (Ballestero 2019, 57; Collins 2017, 5–6).[55]

The year 2000 saw the adoption of the European Union's Water Framework Directive. While a substantial and ambitious piece of environmental legislation (the Directive calls for an integrated river basin approach that reflects the ecological dimensions of the water cycle), and while stating that water is not a commercial product, the Framework also uses economistic and technocratic registers that are hard for communities to navigate (Moore 2019, 17).[56] Article 9 of the Water Framework Directive is of particular concern for water activists as it calls for full-cost recovery and requires member states to use economistic analyses in managing their water resources.[57] Much of this early legislation was met with critical pushback—a fault line immediately opened up. This is why member states today have some subsidiarity power to determine how social, environmental, and economic aspects are included and priced (Lanz and Scheuer 2001). Because of this political pushback, a number of controversial passages of the Water Framework Directive were written in ways that allow for different interpretations and implementations (Kaika 2003). This is also why water services have remained outside the European Union's single market and are somewhat protected from the pressures facing other public services in the region (Moore 2019, 14).

The European Commission, in contrast, continues to demand that member states appropriately value water as assets, including rivers, lakes, groundwater, and coastal waters. For the Commission, both nature and infrastructures ought to be (re)valued in terms of the economic and ecological services they perform (Bresnihan 2016, 121). This means that EU water management has moved from simply maintaining existing infrastructures to reassessing them in response to future risks. Understood as part of Europe's "natural capital," water resources are conceptualized as providing economic and ecological functions, all of which need to be accounted for (European Environment Agency, 2015). Public utilities and their infrastructures, indeed nature as such, have thus been drawn into an "asset management culture" (Bresnihan 2016, 121). "Raw" nature, previously conceptualized as a market externality, is now "rendered commensurate through a common apparatus of measuring techniques and technologies" (Bresnihan 2016, 122; Brockington 2011; Cattelino 2015a; Robertson 2006; Sullivan 2013). In these technocratic dreamscapes, assets are conceptualized as soon-to-be performing rents that are measured in terms of financial *and* ecological value and evaluated, compared, and potentially traded (Bresnihan 2016, 122). All sorts of unlike entities—water, pipes, managerial systems, and nature—are reworked to appear as quantified, standardized, and priced, rendering their value commensurate and thus comparable and movable across time and space (Kockelman 2016, 16). Against these technocratic regimes of valuation and pricing, in 2013, the European Water Movement launched an unprecedented European Citizen's Initiative called Right2Water. It gathered almost two million signatures in an effort to call for the United Nations (UN) to legislate the human right to water and sanitation at the European level.[58] In direct response to this provocation, the European Parliament recognized water as a public good that should be priced appropriately. It also called for good working conditions in the industry and for the banning of water cutoffs in response to nonpayment (Laaninen 2018, 3).

None of these political mobilizations were carried out by single "activist" figures alone. On the contrary, some people I spoke to bristled at being described as such. Some preferred to call themselves "democracy experts," since they saw themselves engaging in the work of pushing for people's direct participation in the management of common goods. Others eschewed that terminology altogether, emphasizing the work that communities perform to organize themselves relationally and reciprocally through everyday concerns (see also Cody 2016, 179).[59] I thus understand these water insurgencies in Fred Moten's terms, as mobilizations that are "constantly renewed in small groups, on front porches or around kitchen tables, in clubs and lunch rooms" long before the figure of the activist comes into full view (Sirvent 2018). Moten's insistence on the social source of insurgencies is important here because it speaks to the ways in which households are sites of extraction but also sites of mobilization.[60] Cutting across party politics and other social distinctions, the violence of financial abstraction is met with deeply grounded and often highly gendered collective responses that grew out of the "ordinariness" of the troubles people were facing.

Women were often prominent in water mobilizations, mostly because of their role in the social and material reproduction of the household. As one interlocutor in Berlin put it to me, "[w]ater is a women's thing (*Frauensache*). They cook, do the laundry, clean, bathe the children, water the plants. Water is central to our everyday experience and work" (see also Weston 2017, 18; Barnes 2013, 2014, 33–34; Limbert 2001; Naguib 2009). In Ireland, I was told that it was women, not men, who were responsible for doing the household bills "99 percent of the time." It's never the man, "even if they're both not working. She knows her bottom line . . . about the electricity, the mortgage. If there's another bill, she knows it's going to stretch them more." Women in Ireland were thus repeatedly referred to as the backbone of the water movement. Time and again, I heard people say, "When you have the women out with you, then you can rebel. It was the same in 1916 (when the Irish rose against British colonial rule)." One Sinn Féin member, a party that resurged during the Irish water protests, said, "I remember being an activist for Sinn Féin a decade ago, and while we were canvassing we had a saying: 'If you get the woman you get the house.'" In Italy, too, the men still active in the local water committees that lingered on after the national referendum in 2011, reminisced about the days when the women and youth were on the streets as well, "Because that is when we understood that we had a movement." All shared a collective outrage that a substance as life giving as water would be privatized. "What next," I was repeatedly asked, "the privatization of air?"

Moving from these more general parameters, the chapters in this book unfold across the following terrain: Chapter 1 tracks the financial frontier as a contested zone of lawmaking, where the law of the many is pitted against the law of the few. Situated in the Southern Italian region of Campania and crisscrossing a landscape that includes protesting majors and a collective love affair with old public water fountains, I connect these small political and infrastructural battles with the national water movement's "making" of a referendum—a practical, highly innovative frontier of political imagining that people insisted was an alternative to the "authoritarian democracy" that had engulfed them from above. Carl Schmitt once argued that land appropriation is the primeval act of all possible law since fences divide but also bring order (Zimmer 2015, 138). Yet there is evidence that it was rules establishing access to water in arid regions that might have predated property law for land (Salzman 2013, 46).[61] The Italian water movement used water to do precisely that—to experiment with law, democracy, and property through their struggle for water. The frontier, in short, consisted of novel ways of "the many" collectively enunciating and self-authorizing both law and new forms of property—a commons organized around use rather than possession. Chapter 2 focuses on the financial frontier as a zone of state violence and policing as its infrastructures of financialization— the water meters—became an object of intense contestation. Situated in austerity-ridden Ireland, I track how the meters—an important step in the anticipation of contracting with global investors—was met with the largest social movement seen in the country since independence. As Rosa Luxemburg (1913) put it long ago, the conversion of indivisible common property into private property (*ungeteiltes Eigentum* or *Gemeineigentum* into

*Privateigentum*) is never uncontested at the frontier; the thicket of local social relations is always the strongest bulwark against the violence of capitalist expansion and valuation (245). In the process, the struggle over water meters was always also a struggle over legal and political boundary making: What was legal, what illegal, what criminal, what political? The criminalization of social protest under conditions of authoritarian neoliberalism proved to be the alter ego to the power of the popular barricade—both protesting device as well as vehicle for the building of sociality, community, and a moral and fiscal vision of societal distribution (Simpson 2021). Chapter 3 is set in Berlin and focuses on an intrepid group calling itself the Berlin Water Table as it worked itself through several court cases and toward a citywide popular referendum that eventually forced the disclosure of a private contract and the secret embedded therein: that the city had guaranteed global investors a return on investments in direct contravention of a ruling by Berlin's Constitutional Court. I thus treat the financial frontier as a zone of illegibility but also as a zone where profound clarity can be reached: that capitalism must rely on expropriation and theft, not on equilibrated contractual exchanges, in order to accumulate wealth. The Berlin case shows that capital accumulation always relies on mystified mechanisms of value accumulation, but that there are also moments where these mystifications are rendered legible and visible for all to see. What resulted was a scandalous popular referendum that forced Berlin to disclose the water contract and to remunicipalize its water utility. Chapter 4 returns to Campania and focuses on the financial frontier as a zone of contested valuation and of struggles over what constitutes just price. Here, I explore what people called *crazy bills*—bills so high that they could not be paid. This last chapter thus explores two very different regimes of valuation—one deeply committed to the treasuring of local waters, the other to the pricing of water in ways that would allow for its value to move "upward" into global trading circuits. If "command over price is not so easy to distinguish from sovereignty" (Clover 2016, 53), then the struggles I track here are struggles over the local, sovereign right to determine value through price and to determine what a moral economy of just price might look like as well. I conclude by offering a glimpse into Paris's remunicipalized water utility Eau de Paris, asking how it offers us insight into imaginative frontiers that are political, moral, legal, and fiscal. These frontiers are constantly renewed in water struggles all over Europe as they demand a future as ethical possibility and material promise (Gillespie and Naidoo 2019, 237) and the possibility of a world and the commons as inappropriable and inviolable.

# 1

## You Cannot Sell to Us
## What We
## Already Possess!

ON NOVEMBER 28, 2015, five-thousand people from the southern Italian region of Campania staged a protest in the city center of Naples. Demonstrators included environmentalists, trade unionists, and workers from Naples' public water utility who were criticizing a recently passed law that centralized water management in Campania under a single entity called the Ente Idrico Campano (EIC). The EIC would take control of all springs; all strategic planning; and all regional, national, and European funds—all in the service of a more "efficient" management of water. It would also determine water price and manage concessions, and people feared that these maneuvers would set the stage for water privatization (Marotta 2015). The demonstration was one of several that occurred in the last few years. Previous demonstrations had been organized against the already privatized water works in one of the Campanian districts, the Sarnese-Vesuviano district, where a public-private part-nership called Gestione Ottimale Risorse Idriche (Optimal

1.1        Naples, November 28, 2015. The banner, framed by some of the
           municipal flags displayed that day, says, "Whoever manages water
           manages life. Give water back to our territories!" (Image courtesy
           of Rete Civica ATO 3.)

Water Resources Management or GORI SpA) was already serving seventy-five municipalities. Water prices there had soared, and water shutoffs (prohibited in France but legal in Italy) had begun to proliferate. What was striking about the demonstration was not only that Naples' iconoclastic mayor at the time, Luigi de Magistris, walked shoulder to shoulder with protestors, but that more than thirty mayors representing the small towns and villages in the Sarnese Vesuviano district did so as well. Many were part of a network of mayors (the Rete dei Sindaci) that had been formed in 2013 to protest privatization and to underscore their commitment to the public and participatory management of water.[1]

One by one, these Campanian mayors walked, donning their mayoral *tricolore* sashes in green, white, and red and carrying banners emblazoned with municipal coats of arms. Potent symbols of popular sovereignty and self-determination, the banners are beautifully embroidered with golden crowns that mimic ancient city walls and serve as reminders not only of local sovereignty but of the municipality's duty to protect and care for its citizens. The crown-as-wall also signaled the link between the architectural and the jural. As Hobbes put it, "Laws [are] the walls of government, and nations" (Comaroff and Comaroff 2006: 22–24).[2] The public must be secured and a structure built wherein subsequent actions can take place—the space being the public and the structure being the law (Arendt 1998, 194–95). The appearance of publicly protesting mayors, holding their municipal coats of arms high into the air, was thus a protest against more than the looming dispossession of local communities' right to publicly own and manage water. It was a protest against the dispossession of their capacity to effective legal and political action as such.

The demonstration of so many small-town mayors must be understood in relation to the fact that Naples, the city around which the Sarnese-Vesuviano area is nestled, was at the time the only major Italian city that had remunicipalized its almost-privatized water utility after an unprecedented 2011 popular national referendum that had explicitly forbidden the privatization of Italy's water utilities. De Magistris, a politically nonaligned antimafia magistrate who became mayor of Naples that year, had, in 2012, transformed Napoli's water utility from a joint stock company called the Azienda Risorse Idriche Napoli (Water Resources Company Naples, or ARIN) back into a "special public company" (*azienda speciale*) called Napoli ABC (Napoli Acqua Bene Comune or Naples Water as Commons), thus averting the specter of privatization.[3] Much of his political platform consisted of the promise that Napoli was "not for sale," and that the water flowing from the city's taps and public water fountains would always be *l'acqua del sindaco* (the mayor's water), a phrase that, in Italy, has become synonymous with publicly provided water. To make this point, Napoli adorned many of its public water fountains with plaques reading *acqua del sindaco*, and with signs in both English and Italian, assuring the public that the water was "good to drink" (*buona da bere*).[4] The presence of so many small-town majors in the demonstration signaled their desire to be able to determine the fate of their water utilities too, just like de Magistris in Naples had. After all, the looming centralization of water utilities under the EIC meant a loss of the small sovereignties still available to them, such as the capacity to influence water pricing, make small infrastructural changes, hire a municipal worker or two, or issue ordinances against water shutoffs.

This chapter explores the financial frontier as a political process of de-democratization and centralization—an authoritarian democracy orbiting around the accelerated temporality of neoliberal political and legal decision making. Against this authoritarianism, people sought to "recover pieces of a sovereignty" that they felt had formerly belonged to them but that had been taken away (Fattori 2013, 381; see also von Schnitzler 2016, 83; Graeber 2004, 7). They did this by using the law as a means to perform and prefigure a participatory democracy, with lawmaking becoming a distinct form of political work.[5] I thus track the financial frontier as a zone of contested lawmaking: by the state as it created pathways for finance through emergency decrees, and by the people who sought to repossess democracy and sovereignty through the slow, deliberate, and collective making of popular laws. Against a government for whom the market had begun to assume the function of the law (Vogl 2017, 34–35), the Italian water movement sought to "make" a referendum that would have the people assume the role of sovereign lawmakers. The law of the few was countered by the law of the many, as the Italian water movement insisted that water can only be governed as a commons if it simultaneously also included the recuperation of meaningful popular democratic participation as well.

The fact that the water movement attempted to reclaim peoples' rights to effective democratic action through lawmaking suggests that frontiers are far from being zones of lawlessness (Pastenak and Danfos 2018). Rather, these are zones of law creation wrought out of protracted battles between very differently positioned lawmakers—in this case, "the people" and their mayors on the one hand versus technocratic political elites who rule by emergency decree on the other.[6] By asserting themselves as lawmakers and "constituent powers" in their own right, Italians engaged in the making of the law in counterhegemonic ways, questioning not only normative liberal spaces of law creation (i.e., the legislatures and courts) but the processes of lawmaking and the meaning of legality and illegality as such (Bailey and Mattei 2013).

I thus track the financial frontier as a political and legal process as people feel not only economically dispossessed but dispossessed of their capacity to determine their political futures and to rely on the rule of law. I expand on a narrowly economistic concept of dispossession to argue that dispossession—of water as a kind of commons, for example—is always accompanied by the evacuation of legal process and democracy as well (see also Susser and Doane 2014, 4; Gill and Cutler 2014). Enclosure, in short, is marked by the use of the law as a mechanism for plunder (Pistor 2019). Prominent Italian lawyer Ugo Mattei and Laura Nader have called this the "illegality of the law" (Mattei and Nader 2008, 4), echoing many of my interlocutors who similarly used the term *illegality* as a diagnostic to comment on the state of disrepair their democracy had fallen into. The financial frontier is thus a zone where the distinction between legality and illegality is fraught and unstable (Nichols 2017, 16–17), an illegality of the law that bends older legal forms and creates new laws designed to legitimize new property relations (Thompson 1975, 260–61). An elderly man made this clear during a townhall meeting in 2015 with Luigi de Magistris, the then incumbent major of Naples, by arguing that people were "fighting against the illegality from above! We are being governed by a band of delinquents!" Here, the speaker meant not only that the law and lawmaking itself had become evacuated of democratic substance and moral legitimacy, but that the sell-off of public assets—including electricity, gas, railroads, telecommunications, highways—all "synonymous with citizenship itself" (Marotta 2014, 40)—had occurred in highly discretionary ways, usually authoritatively by decree and without due democratic process (Bieler 2021, 96).

Protesting mayors are thus a symptom of authoritarian neoliberalism as they provocatively pose the question of who represents the demos and how politics can still be crafted under conditions where the parameters of political action have radically contracted. They posit a sovereign public diametrically opposed to the privatized public instituted from above, thus pitting one more "proximate" part of the state against those parts that many Italians consider to be "distant" and beholden to financial capital. The Italian water movement thus offers insight not only into the profound de-democratization of the public sphere that comes with the financialization of public services, but also into how popular lawmakers can work from within the remaining, sharply circumscribed parameters of political action as well as, sometimes, outside of them.

In what follows, I track the legal and political fault lines opened up at the financial frontier, moving from what I call the law of the few, where the political executive illegitimately captured law and the right to make it, to the law of the many that simultaneously proliferated from below. I understand the proliferation of irreverent popular lawmaking not simply as an attempt to repossess the law as an expression of democracy but as an attempt to recapture the very material, practical, and lived sociality of the public, indeed of the demos as such (Brown 2015). People were, in Arendt's sense, rebuilding the walls of a thoroughly redemocratized public through the autoconstruction of the substance and process of the law.[7] Thus, unlike social theorists who have focused on the recent proliferation of emergency rule on the part of the state (Agamben 2005; Di Costanzo and Ferraro 2013, 19; Vogl 2017), I argue that popular lawmaking is the alter ego to emergency rule—two forms of lawmaking that inversely mirror and coconstitute each other.[8] It is only through attention to these two forms of lawmaking that the financial frontier can be more fully grasped.

### The Law of the Few

If tales of cities can be told through their histories of water (Gandy 2014), tales of the financial frontier can be told through water, too. The history of Naples' waterworks is illustrative of the recurrence of finance in the lifetime of European water utilities as well as the frontier fault lines that they also always provoked. Like the story of Berlin's water utility that I recount in chapter 3, the Naples Water Works Company (NWW) emerged in 1878 out of a contract the city signed with two Anglo-French engineer-investors associated with the General Credit and Discount Company (De Majo and Vitale 2004, 43–44).[9] Primary shareholder was the French Compagnie Générale des Eaux's subsidiary, the Compagnie Générale des Eaux pour les Étrangers, which also built aqueducts in Venice, La Spezia, and Bergamo (De Majo and Vitale 2004, 25).[10] The city received a large credit from the Compagnie Générale to refurbish an ancient Roman aqueduct by 1885. As one of the first public-private collaborations in Europe (Campra et al. 2014, 28–29), it was clear to investors at the time that the rise of centralized water provisioning would become quite lucrative as the need for modern infrastructures increased with growing cities. Soon, investors faced first hurdles. The Naples Water Works Company lagged far behind its promised expansion of necessary services. The city was increasingly unwilling to repay its extraordinary debt, especially because it faced increased popular complaints about the private management and distribution of water (De Majo and Vitale 2004, 47; Juuti, Katko, and University of Tampere, 2005, 41). Soon, at least two-thousand households were in arrears with pay (De Majo and Vitale 2004, 60). Investors took the city to court in 1886. Litigation lasted several years, with the courts siding with the Compagnie Générale. By 1895, the city of Naples had paid the Compagnie Générale tens of millions of lire—a sum that allowed for the Naples Water Works Company to pay out ample dividends to its British and French investors (De Majo and Vitale 2004, 46–47).

But by 1922, Fascist nationalism reared its head, and with it came a commitment to large public works. The Naples Water Works Company was "Italianized" when the Italian banker and businessman Emanuele Fizzarotti became a major shareholder. He renamed Naples' heavily indebted water works Società Acquedotto di Napoli and immediately raised the water price by 15 percent (De Majo and Vitale 2004, 60). Rumors abounded that Fizzarotti was just a front for French and British capital (De Majo and Vitale 2004, 65). By 1926, he was sidelined. The Società Acquedotto di Napoli came under control of a maxiprefecture (*maxiprefettura*) created by the Fascist regime. An emergency management—a High Commissariat for the City and Province of Naples (l'Alto Commissariato per la città e la provincia di Napoli)—was installed, with the majority of the utility's shares passing into the hands of national banks (De Majo and Vitale 2004, 65). A number of works left unfinished by Fizzarotti were completed. Many other infrastructural improvements, including massive canalization and the extension of pipelines into Naples' industrial and peripheral neighborhoods, were also overseen by the Fascists in the 1930s (De Majo and Vitale 2004, 69–71). By 1945, Naples fully remunicipalized its water utility, creating a municipal corporation (*azienda municipalizzata*) under full local control (De Majo and Vitale 2004, 75). This move from private toward public management was one that occurred in all larger European cities by the beginning of the twentieth century as well.

Yet by the 1990s, dreams of privatization began to rear their heads again. A panoply of successive laws geared toward the management of Italy's highly fragmented local water provisioning systems were passed over several years (Massarutto and Ermano 2013; Guerrini and Romano 2014). On the one hand, these laws represented a turning point in Italy's water management in that they sought to regulate the country's fragmented and often starkly mismanaged water services system (Massarutto and Ermano 2013). A first comprehensive national law, passed in 1994 (Legge Galli 36/1994), called for the integrated management of water services and recognized both surface waters and groundwater as "public property" (*proprietà pubblica*) and "environmental patrimony" that should be left in its entirety to future generations (*patrimonio ambientale da consegnare integro alle generazioni future*); the recognition that human consumption had priority over industrial and agricultural use; and that water services must be integrally managed (Bersani 2011, 2–3). It also legislated that all water, including groundwater, came under the control of the state, meaning that all water use needed to be registered, licensed, and metered. The law was important because groundwater use was relatively unregulated in Italy's rural areas where water use was largely based on a model of self-supply. There were many small rural towns and even individual households that abstracted water from wells and other small sources until the 1990s with very little license, oversight, and pay (Massarutto 2015, 208).[11] On the other hand, the Galli law and the others that followed represented a turning point in that they also attempted to create the conditions for more "efficient" private management and, ultimately, debt financing. The doors were now slowly opening for private investors.

The Galli law tasked Italy's regions with identifying "optimal areas" (Ambito Territoriale Ottimale; ATO) where water and wastewater were to be managed integrally by intermunicipal authorities (Autorità d'Ambito Territoriale Ottimale; AATO) (Romano, Guerrini, and Campedelli 2015, 46). These entities were governed by assemblies of mayors who continued to maintain statutory responsibility for municipal service provisioning. Mayors were made responsible for the planning and licensing of water concessions, the management of European funds, and the appointment of members of the board of directors and the president. While bundled into these larger management units to achieve economies of scale and increased professionalism (Massarutto and Ermano 2013, 23), water was ultimately still governed from below, through the decision-making powers of mayors.

These laws must be understood from within a European context where a number of water utilities had already been privatized, notably in Britain in 1989 (Bakker 2004). These early European privatizations paved the way for the consolidation of large French, British, and Spanish water companies, which soon diversified their activities across the globe (Bakker 2013, 254). By the mid-2000s they sought to make incursions back into the rest of the European water market itself, including Italy, which had for a decade or so already been under pressure by the European Union to reform its water sector (Carrozza and Fantini 2013, 102). Many public utilities began to shift ownership structures by transforming their municipal corporations into public limited companies (*società di capitali*)—joint stock companies that offered their shares up for sale. Naples' water utility became a joint stock company (*società per azioni*) in 1996. Although the city was initially the unique shareholder, it was widely assumed that Naples would soon enter into a public-private partnership or be fully privatized (Landriani et al. 2019, 44; Massarutto 2011, 252). By 2000, law 267/2000 insisted on more "diverse" (i.e., more privatized) forms of management. A 2001 law (448/2001) then tried to irreversibly privatize water, with Article 35 noting that all water utilities must be transformed into joint stock companies (*società per azioni*, or SpA). Law 269 in 2003 again tried to legislate the corporatization of public water utilities (Bersani 2011, 35–36). By 2006, a ministerial decree mandated a

7 percent "adequate remuneration of invested capital" (*adeguatezza della remunerazione del capitale investito*) to investors.[12] A milieu of enclosure was steadily being erected through the law, creating pathways for an incursion of finance into the public realm.

By 2009, the Italian parliament passed the so-called "Ronchi decree" without discussion or public consultation. This decree mandated the privatization of all public services, including water, by turning all water utilities into joint stock companies with at least 40 percent private capital (Bersani 2011, 36). From that point on, all water and wastewater had to be managed as fully private or public-private partnerships. No water utility was to be entirely publicly owned after December 2011 (Guerrini and Romano 2014, 10; Mattei 2012, 369). At that point, Italy ranked second worldwide after Great Britain in terms of the value generated through the privatization of state assets—about 140 billion euros (Mattei 2013, 368; Marotta 2014). As Ugo Mattei, professor of law and first director of Napoli ABC, put it to me in an interview, "the government has basically started behaving like a private individual—and like a private individual badly in debt. It sold off public property as if it were private property; as if it were selling a bicycle." Private property, in short, is inviolable in liberal constitutions, while there exists no analogous inviolability of public property at all.[13] As a result, Italy was within two decades able to rapidly sell off goods that had been marked as "public property" within the Italian Civil Code.[14]

This financial incursion into public property occurred in ways that many Italians found to be profoundly undemocratic. Law decrees, such as the one named after Minister Ronchi in 2009, are provisional measures that emerge out of situations of necessity and that only later achieve the force of law. They are always passed with unusual rapidity and with little if any parliamentary input, a kind of baroque political style operating like a "permanent coup d'état" that bypasses parliamentary involvement, avoids popular referenda, and eschews democratic convention (Vogl 2017, x). As Marx put it, the enclosure of the commons and its transformation into private property always relied on a parliamentary coup d'état, that is to say, on the laws of the few. Operating within and performatively asserting a state of exception, these laws grew out of a "no-man's-land" between law and political fact—the extra-juridical zone out of which sovereign law is generated (Agamben 2005, 24–25).

The history of Italian lawmaking shows this very clearly. The modern Italian state emerged at a moment in the late nineteenth century when the state was constantly proclaimed to be under a "state of siege," with royal decrees regularly passed in order to maintain public order. The Fascists would later convert into law several thousand outstanding law decrees that had been issued in the preceding years under conditions of "economic emergency."[15] While later considered to be a Fascist abuse of emergency decrees, this practice of executive legislation had in fact long been the rule of law in Italy. Emergency law decrees had long been transformed from exceptional into ordinary sources of lawmaking (Agamben 2005, 14–17). Indeed, the history of the Italian republic is characterized by the increased use of states of emergency to govern what are normally ordinary issues of contemporary society (D'Alisa and Armiero 2013, 31). Initially, extraordinary commissioners were appointed after natural disasters like floods and earthquakes that happened in the 1970s (Pipyrou 2016). Soon however, they were also appointed for the management of traffic and mobility control, global events like G8 summits, international sports meetings, or religious conventions. Since the end of the 1990s, the accelerated practice of emergency management has allowed the national government to spend vast amounts of public funds by entrusting contracts for public works to private companies, often without respecting the rules for procurement or European and national laws. The number of ordinances (law decrees that serve as public injunctions) proliferated, making it difficult to determine which norms were being implemented in specific cases (Di Costanzo and Ferraro 2013). The Italian case thus illustrates one of the foundational conceits of modern liberal democracies—that it is supposedly parliament, that is, the legislature made up of elected officials, that makes laws, with the executive branch carrying them out and the judicial branch interpreting them. In reality, many of my interlocutors noted that the parliament was no longer the sovereign legislative body holding the exclusive power to bind citizens by means of the law. On the contrary, it had been reduced to ratifying the decrees issued by the executive—the legislative having been absorbed into executive power.[16]

The acceleration of rule by decree is historically variable and accelerates and de-accelerates at specific historical moments. Many scholars have pin-pointed the year of the 2008 financial crash as the moment that saw the rise of a highly moralized austerity discourse as well as of declarations of economic emergencies (D'Alisa and Armiero 2013; Cozzolino 2019). In the United States in 2008, for example, the Fed used an emergency paragraph 13(3) of the US Federal Reserve Act for the first time ever, thus allowing it to "exceed its legal remit and support" (Vogl 2017, 5; Blyth 2013). This was a global phenomenon that was evident also in the controversial interventions of the European Stability Mechanism (ESM) and the European Central Bank (ECB).

The post-2008 financial crisis thus led to an acceleration of rule by decree in the name of cutting national debt and balancing budgets, particularly in countries like Italy, which carries one of the highest debt burdens as a proportion of its economic output in the EU. The velocity with which such law decrees came to pass shows how the overstimulated climate of debt-fueled financial markets can translate into a manic delirium of lawmaking directed toward the plunder of the public sphere. The Italian government has since passed a slew of emergency law decrees with almost no parliamentary input, all paving the way for the sell-off of public assets, including public water utilities. By 2011, the government passed a barrage of reforms that liberalized the pension system, labor market, and public administration. It also changed the constitution to include the principle of balanced budgets. As Cozzolino (2019) calculates, 63 percent of total lawmaking activity between 1976 and 2015 consisted of emergency legislation (337).

Yet if Italy is a juridico-political laboratory (Agamben 2005, 14–17), some of its regions are more so than others. In the southern Italian region of Campania—currently the poorest region in Italy and a highly racialized "periphery" that Italian northerners have long thought of as being populated by "biologically inferior beings" (Gramsci [1926] 2005; Schneider 1998), the imposition of states of emergency has long existed as the method to undergird private interests and disempower democratic participation (D'Alisa and Armiero 2013, 30).[17] Indeed, declarations of states of emergency and the creation of ad-hoc executive agencies such as emergency commissioners (*commissari*) have an almost routinized history in this region and have long served to reinforce regimes of political patronage and "the transfer of funds from the public to the private sector" (Armiero and D'Alisa 2013, 9–14). Writing about the tragic waste scandals in the region, Di Costanzo and Ferraro show that many Campanians have become "totally habituated to emergency rule" after national governments on both the right and the left of the political spectrum perpetuated this state of emergency. They did so, for example, by delegating waste management to an agency with exceptional powers, the Commissariat for Waste Emergency in Campania (Di Costanzo and Ferraro 2013, 19). Extraordinary government and the concentration of powers in one agency (as opposed to local, decentralized authorities such as mayors) have thus become normalized and have closed off spaces for political dissent in the name of quickly and efficiently dealing with "crises" (Di Costanzo and Ferraro 2013, 19). The battle around Italy's water must thus be understood from within a highly volatile legal climate that is both a continuation and an inversion of Fascist-era law. The habit of passing laws by decree has been reactivated, but this time not to build grand public projects as was the case in 1920 and 1930s. Instead, this law is used for the opposite purpose of privatizing state infrastructures, with capital expansion relying not on the retraction but, conversely, on the adoption of centralized state power.[18] Even the 1994 Galli Law's declaration that water was a "public good" did nothing to change this transfer of the wealth of the many into the hands of the few.

The mayors marching side by side with Luigi de Magistris must be understood from within this context. After all, mayors, especially in smaller towns, have always been complex mediators between the powers above and pressures from below. Brought to their knees by the steady impoverishment of their towns and unable to provide for their constituencies—an incapacity exacerbated in the destitute communities of Southern Italy where infrastructures and services exist in growing states of utter disrepair—it was easy for GORI to "buy the mayors, and this not even in a veiled manner," as one member from a local water committee bitterly explained. Indeed, none of the mayors in the ATO 3 had asked any of the townspeople in 2003 whether they wanted to contract their water utility out to GORI. And for years, people said, mayors did nothing—letting price hikes happen and frequently not even attending the ATO's meetings. It was not until pressure began to build from below that their mayors began to listen. Soon, they began to question (or were forced by their constituencies to question) GORI's water prices and the shutoffs it oversaw—a pressure that became so explosive that the entire water district was eventually placed under emergency rule in 2013. By 2016, the water district's emergency manager nominated members to the board of directors of GORI even though his mandate had expired and was declared illegitimate by a local court. The Campanian case thus stood as a supreme example of a more general trend toward postdemocratic forms of government that come with privatization and the rise of finance—layers and layers of expropriation and illegitimate lawmaking that ordinary people sought to reverse.

With water, it seemed like the rolling financial tide of de-democratized privatization could be stopped. There was something about water, its symbolic weight and intimate link to life on Earth, that made it a potent vehicle for political mobilizations. Many Italians thought of water as a commons and as an inalienable local abundance—an "immovable wealth" that should never be rendered movable through commodification and capitalization (Rakopoulos and Rio 2018, 4).[19] In 2011, Italian citizens soundly rejected the privatization of water through a national referendum initiated by one of the largest social coalitions ever seen in the country.[20] Bringing together alter-globalization activists, Leftist unions, the Catholic church, activist lawyers, and a proliferation of local water committees, the movement dedicated itself to a "new water culture" that arose in defense of life and against life's commodification. Pointing to the problems of exorbitant pricing, unequal access, and increased water pollution, the movement argued that these were growing crises not just in the Global South but in the Global North as well. In a historically unprecedented move, twenty-seven million Italians rejected the compulsory privatization of water and guaranteed profits to private investors.

Through the referendum, the Italian water movement insisted that water was to be treated as a *bene comune* (a commons) that ought to be governed democratically and outside of the logic of profit. Water offered the opportunity for people from across the political spectrum to do something quite unusual, allowing a nation to create a common lexicon of anticapitalist refusal and revolt. Water allowed people to generate a scale of values diametrically opposed to those offered by the market, its empty promises of commodification, its doctrines of private property, efficiency, and full-cost recovery, and its authoritarian wielding of the law. With the referendum, Italians affirmed a vision where pure fiscal calculus was to be replaced by an expansive vision of the commons. There was something about the clarity of the message that made this movement flourish. As Tommaso Fattori, a key figure in the Italian water movement and prominent Tuscan politician put it to me, "You cannot sell to us what we already possess."

Deeply indebted to autonomist Marxist theorizing while also buoyed by the Catholic imaginative universe, the water movement juxtaposed water as life with neoliberalism's "culture of death" and water's sacrality with its desacralization through market exchange.[21] The movement thus saw the convergence of a plurality of genealogies of vitalist thought that

1.2        *San Rubinetto* (Saint Tapwater). Mineral waters in Italy are often named after saints and for centuries were thought to have miraculous healing qualities. One of the most famous, for example, is San Pellegrino, which is named after Saint Pellegrino Latiosi, the patron saint for people suffering from cancer or other illnesses. Today, San Pellegrino is owned by Nestlé. In this image, the Italian water movement sought to capture some of those meanings by transferring the miraculousness of mineral water to its humble brethren, the water flowing from Italian taps. The halo circling the tap signals the water movements' humorous attempt to capture some of that sense of sacrality. (Image courtesy of Forum Italiano dei Movimenti per l'Acqua.)

intersected and enhanced each other, including a generation of activists influenced by Antonio Negri's reading of Spinoza, as well as the Catholic commitment to the defense of life.[22] These convergences resulted in the water movement often representing its battle as "a conflict between the stock market and life" (Bersani 2011, 88). Indispensable, then, were not only Italy's vibrant social centers and groups coming out of the country's deeply rooted Communist traditions, but also the "frontier priests" (*preti di frontiera*; Bersani 2011, 54) who preached from the pulpit about "sister water" (*sorella acqua*), a form of address borrowed from St. Francis of Assisi's 1224 Canticle of the Sun, which refers to water as a "sister" who is "useful, and humble, and precious, and pure."

Such language of kinship added additional symbolic potency to water as inalienable relation through which individuals are rendered profoundly nonsovereign, tied not only to water as kin, but to each other in this shared intimacy. People used the refrain "we are water," reminding each other that their collective bodies were intimately composed of the specific watersheds they drank their waters from and that the human body is not so different from the blue planet itself. Like the earth, which is made up of about 71 percent water, newborns consist of about 75 percent water, a percentage that decreases only as we age. Our blood is not only mostly water but contains a concentration of salt and ions that is remarkably similar to that of the oceans—about 3.4 percent (Angier 2008). Such numbers, more than merely mechanically rendering the human condition, serve as potent signs of poetic communication about the alliances of human and nonhuman matter (Ballestero 2015). People were buoyed by this message, from the "old lady who said she would remember us every evening in her prayers," to the convicts serving life sentences who, while not allowed to vote, nevertheless promised to disseminate the movement's information on the prison radio." Nuns who usually lived in strict seclusion (*clausura*) would come forth to request meetings with movement representatives (Bersani 2011, 49), while the mayors of towns all over Italy were photographed drinking "the mayor's water" from public water fountains.[23] This popular victory was built out of many years of political work that was remarkable in its degree of organization and capillary penetration of the national terrain. The referendum, in short, served not only as a vehicle against predatory market incursions or for the recuperation of a sense of democracy, popular sovereignty, and collective sociality. It also brought the common into full and recognizable view. Theft, as Nichols writes, recursively generates property (Nichols 2017, 8). But it can also recursively bring the common to life.

A first step in this collective generation of the commons was a social forum on water, held in 2003 in Florence, the capital of Tuscany, in part because Tuscany was the first to implement the Galli law and to transform its public water utilities into public-private partnerships. Tuscany was by then already aflame with citizens' protests, notably in Arezzo where people had begun to organize against "crazy bills" (or *bollette pazze*, discussed in chapter 4). It was here where the idea of a regional popular initiative law (*legge regionale d'iniziative popolare*) was born. In the meantime, water struggles proliferated in the country. People discussed the regional law in five national assemblies in Cecina, Florence, Rome, Pescara, and Naples, but then decided that they needed a national law (*legge nazionale d'iniziativa popolare*; Fattori, personal communication). Soon, "waves of activists washed over the national territory" with thousands of initiatives, signature collections, and mobilizations (Bersani 2011, 39). Many of the people I spoke to years later still remembered these activities with joy. The hundreds of assemblies (*assemblee* or *agorà*, the Greek term people also used) that were held in the lead-up to the passing of the law were built around open discussion and consensus building. As Tommaso Fattori (2013) explained, "We never voted; not a single time." Tens of thousands of people experimented with participatory democracy through assemblies—a political form that Fattori calls one of the movement's key achievements (380–81) and that have clear precedents in indigenous Latin American assembly-based democratic theory and action (Lazar 2007, 241). En masse and in common, they envisioned what the common might mean and how it could be used to build new modalities of public and participatory governance.

Importantly, this national conversation drew on the energies of already existing local mobilizations as well. Many assemblies were deeply grounded in longer traditions and tactics of already existing political movements, as was the case in Campania where weekly assemblies were already held as early as 1991 to protest real-estate speculation in Naples and, later, the unimaginable toxic pollution that had gripped parts of the Campanian countryside (Armiero and D'Alisa 2013; De Biase 2015). Soon, a core of activists began to work closely with the Comboni missionary priest Padre Zanotelli, a charismatic figure in the Italian water movement whom I visited twice in his home—a narrow belltower that hugs the side of the Church Santa Maria alla Sanità in Napoli's Sanità neighborhood. Having returned to Italy from Kenya, Zanotelli discovered that his own country needed his help just as much as his "brothers and sisters in the Global South" did. He was incensed by the actions of successive Italian governments. "*Maledetti voi!*" (May you be damned!) he frequently lamented, at times while standing next to one of Naples' public water fountains and sprinkling bystanders with water. "Water is sacred, it is life! Man is water walking and thinking. Water is a supreme good, and it is becoming increasingly scarce. Water is not a commodity, and its privatization is a sin!"

The national conversation thus drew strength from preexisting battles, often over environmental extraction and toxic contamination. Their mechanisms of engagement were deeply rooted, decentralized, and participatory (Capone 2013). Through the translation, dissemination, and circulation of these territorially grounded democratic practices, the movement familiarized ordinary Italians with the process of *making* law and *making* a referendum, thus creating one of most inclusive mobilizations in the country's recent memory. Like Latin American social movements before them, people referred to themselves as part of constituent assemblies (*assemblee costituenti*), a politics that oriented itself toward the remaking or rethinking of some of the basic principles of the national constitution and that reimagined this foundational document as a lively site for the reimagination of collective life (Ballestero 2019, 115). This was not surprising, since many Italians felt that the constitution, the "mother of all laws, the mothership of all laws" (*casa madre dei diritti*) was either not being applied or in urgent need of reform. This is why people took it upon themselves to write new laws. As one of my interlocutors put it to me, "this is why we have become creators of constitutionality" (*creatori di costitutionalità*). Tens of thousands of Italians engaged in what Bersani has called a long process of "political alphabetization."[24] The law, reappropriated by citizens, was the vehicle through which the logic of enclosure would be overcome and through which atomized social relations could be recomposed collectively as a "social wealth" (Roggero 2010, 359). By 2006, a national law was approved by the National Assembly of Water Movements, with its Articles 1 and 2 explicitly defining water as a non-commodifiable "national patrimony" and "commons" that the state has the duty to guarantee to current and future generations. By 2007, it was presented to the Italian Chamber of Deputies, but it has until this day not been passed.[25]

Soon, the Italian Forum for Water Movements (Forum Italiano dei Movimenti per l'Acqua) was formed. By 2008, the Forum launched a campaign on local lawmaking with the goal of changing local and regional statutes through popular resolutions (*delibere d'iniziativa popolare*). Many smaller municipalities, but also some larger cities, began to approve the modification of their statutes to affirm that water is a "common good and a universal human right," and that "water services ought to be excluded from commercialization" (Bersani 2011, 41). They thus attempted to build their legal walls around a public to be protected, small sovereignties responding to what was widely perceived to be illegitimate lawmaking from "above."

Preparations for the 2011 national referendum went ahead with the depositing of two referendum questions to the Court of Cassation in Rome. The first aimed at repealing the hated Ronchi decree and asked, "Do you want to annul Article 23bis [i.e., the article in the Ronchi Decree that made the privatization of all local social services mandatory] from the Law Decree Nr. 112 of June 25, 2008?" The second aimed at repealing the regulations

1.3    The ubiquitous image used during the referendum stating "Water cannot be sold. Remove water from markets. Remove profits from water." Noteworthy is the image of the public water fountain, its water being pumped and priced as if it were oil. The dilapidated nature of the public water fountain must not be read as signaling a need for renovation. On the contrary, it evokes an affection for the older, public water system and the social values it stood for. (Image courtesy of Forum Italiano dei Movimenti per l'Acqua.)

governing the determination of water prices, specifically the guaranteed rate of return to investors. It asked, "Do you want to annul Comma 1 of Article 154 of the Law Decree Nr. 152 from April 3, 2006, specifically the formulation 'adequate remuneration of invested capital'" (*dell'adeguatezza della remunerazione del capitale investito*)?[26]

These technical questions were asked from within a movement resolutely dedicated to the imagination of a novel form of property. But what did Italians mean when they conceptualized water as a *commons*? The meaning of the term was and continues to be indeterminate—a polysemy that is part of the concept's power and capacity to mobilize across different social terrains and groups (Carrozza and Fantini 2013, 100; 2016). But, at its heart, it always signals "the principle that the relation between the social group and [the commons] shall be both collective and noncommodified—off-limits to the logic of market exchange and market valuations" (Harvey 2013, 73), and that these commons are protected in the interest of future generations (Mattei 2013, 369). The commons thus inaugurated a radical re-envisioning of property, a property distinct from public and private ownership and in need of special constitutional protection (Mattei 2013, 369). It meant refusing both the idea that the distribution of goods ought to be channeled through the market and that collective decision making ought to be channeled exclusively through the state (Browne and Susen 2014, 218). The debate around the commons has thus long emphasized the collective and noncommodified management of property first and foremost through remunicipalization. This meant not only revalorizing labor in the public sector as more than just a cost to be rationalized; it also meant rethinking ownership as such, with citizens demanding the right to directly and democratically participate in the governance of a vital good (Lucarelli 2013; see also Razsa and Kurnik 2012; Razsa 2015). At stake, then, was not the elimination of public services but "their radical deprivatization and democratization" (Fattori 2013, 385). Small- and medium-sized communes—like the protesting mayors introduced at the beginning of this chapter—were especially receptive to this demand, since it was evident that they would barely be represented in the boardrooms of large, centralized multiutilities (Bersani 2011, 72).

With this demand for democratization came an attempt to remake political subjectivity as well: Italians explicitly conceptualized the commons as both tangible and intangible, both natural and social. The commons were those goods that "no one can claim to have produced individually: goods that the collectivity receives as a gift of nature (no one produces water or the global water cycle, air, or forests) or receives as an inheritance from previous generations." But the commons were also thought of as the condensation of collective thought and action—knowledges, languages, institutions (Fattori 2011). Drawing on the Italian commons movement, Michael Hardt and Antonio Negri (2009) similarly wrote that the commonwealth consists not only "of the material world—the air, the water, the fruits of the soil, and all nature's bounty" (viii) but of shared knowledges, languages, codes, information, and affects—everything that forms the basis for social relationships (8).

I myself often witnessed this common social labor while conducting research in 2015–2016—long after the referendum in 2011. Groups of activists continued to meet in social centers to discuss a range of political issues, including how their own institutions and spaces could be transformed into and maintained as a commons. Many of their assemblies were long winded and full of repetition. But that was, it seems to me, the point. It was as if the lexicon out of which the commons was to be imagined and inhabited had to be mouthed by as many mouths as possible, circulated through as many minds as possible and reworked, mimicked, replaced, and incessantly produced by bodies assembled together repeatedly in material space, over time. These were moments where people made democracy a lived experience, where bodies dwelled together, repeatedly and in common (Razsa and Kurnik 2012, 249; see also Lazar 2007, 242–43; Butler 2015) and where the "fundamental relation between corporeality and resistance" (Hardt and Negri 2009, 30) was tested, lived, and pragmatically enacted. "We made a referendum" (*Abbiamo fatto un referendum*), as many people repeatedly put it to me, almost like a refrain. These vividly remembered moments where a "slow democracy" that was lived, a revolution that organized time in ways that powerfully contrasted the "authoritarian democracy" of accelerated temporality and rule by decree from above (Greenberg 2014, 10). As Fattori put it to me, "For this kind of political work we needed a path that was not too hurried" (*ci vuole un percorso che non abbia troppa fretta*) because "everyone needed to be made to feel that they can make a contribution without feeling left out . . . and without feeling that this is only a thing for specialists. We dedicated ourselves to a process that took many, many months, and we had many, many meetings that were open to all." In contrast to the economic giving form to the juridical in these neoliberal times (Brown 2015, 151), the juridical took the shape of the social through a prefigurative and slow politics of becoming (Greenberg 2014, 2; Razsa and Kurnik 2012, 251–52). The law, in short, became an expression of an embodied and collective practical activity through which insurgent citizens came to know themselves and each other as self-determining actors. Strikingly resonant with the popular rewriting of the Brazilian constitution in 1988, Italian citizens became their own legislators as they imagined both law and democracy as something that ought to be collectively made and owned.[27] Law and democracy, like water, were the property of the people. *Si scrive acqua, si legge democrazia* (We write water and read democracy), was one central slogan of the movements. It was as if water, law, and democracy had become part of the same organism, intimately wedded to each other into one substance.

On June 12 and 13, 2011, 95 percent of Italians voted against the privatization of their vital public services, including water. They thus clearly voted for water utilities to either stay or return to being communal public-law institutions. They also almost unanimously voted against the "adequate remuneration of invested capital" in water services provisioning. It had been twenty years since a referendum had reached quorum in Italy. An unprecedented achievement, many people I met said, almost like a miracle.

## Toward a Redefinition of Property

The attempted financialization of all of Italy's public water utilities opened up another legal and political fault line as well—one that had Italians engage in a national conversation about liberal property regimes and their limits. The conversation was initiated during the short-lived reign of a center-left government between 2006 and 2008 and in the midst of the eruption of water struggles all over the country, when Prime Minister Romano Prodi issued a decree that tasked a special commission with reforming the provision on public property contained within the Italian Civil Code. The group consisted of illustrious lawyers who discussed the fact that liberal legal frameworks could not protect public assets from privatization. The goal was to establish principles that might limit the privatization of these assets. This Commission on Public Goods (Commissione sui Beni Pubblici, famously known as the Rodotà Commission because it was presided over by prominent Civil Law Professor Stefano Rodotà) published a 2010 report with a searing critique of the very foundations of liberal constitutional law. This was noteworthy since this was, politically, a group of largely centrist lawyers who could nevertheless explicitly agree that liberal constitutional law privileges private over public property by protecting the former over the latter.

The Commission found that while the concept of eminent domain (*demanio*) allows for the expropriation of private property by the state (*espropriazione per pubblica utilità*), that form of expropriation is always judicable because private property owners can claim just compensation. The opposite scenario—the selling of public property to private actors—is governed by no such framework and accomplished via political, often highly discretionary decisions on the part of the state. Indeed, no already existing legal concept, such as eminent domain (*demanio*), patrimony (*patrimonio*), or public property (*proprietà pubblica*), was capable of protecting the rights of citizens to common goods, as the Legge Galli, which used both the terms *patrimonio* and *proprietà pubblica*, showed. Additional concepts such as "cultural property" and the "landscape," embedded within Article 9 of the Italian

Constitution and increasingly interpreted as meaning "the environment," have also not adequately protected common goods like water (Bailey and Mattei 2013, 983).

As one of the members of the Commission on Public Goods, Ugo Mattei, put it to me in an interview we conducted in February 2017 in front of his eager students at the International University College in Turin, this is exactly what had happened in Italy during the 1990s: "Privatization was made up of discretional choices taken by the government with things that were taken to be its property. But the property of the government is not really the property of the government! It's the property of the people—the government is just the representative of the people!"[28] How, then, could this property be protected? Ancient Justinian legal concepts such as *res nullius* (things that belong to no one), *res communes* (things that belong to everyone), and *res extra-commercium* (things that lie outside of the realms of commerce) were too ambiguous for contemporary use. In the end, the Commission proposed that there was a need for a general reform of the property regime and that a new legal category and form of property different from both private and public property—that of "the commons" (*beni comuni*)—had to be invented. As the Commission defined it, the commons are essential to collective life and social solidarity as well as to the satisfaction of fundamental rights of the person. In all cases, the commons must be protected in the "interest of future generations" and given special constitutional protection (Commissione Rodotà 2010, 6).[29] The Commission thus saw itself engaging in what Mattei called an exercise in "creativity and fantasy," the playing with the law in an era of "illegality."[30] Not unlike the techno-legal playfulness and craftiness displayed by hackers engaged in legal tinkering (Coleman 2009), Mattei treated the law as an "open text" rather than a rigid form, a set of principles that could be resignified and appropriated rather than be forever set in stone (Merry 1996, 68; Subramanian 2009). Grinning cheekily, Mattei ended our conversation by stressing how much he was in love with the law, but also how much he was "trying to break it as much as possible."

These horizons of noncanonical lawmaking offer insight into the politics of lawmaking at the financial frontier. This broader move toward experimental legal practices—the writing of popular laws, the making of referenda, and the workings of the Commission—must be understood as the alter ego to the emergency law being produced at intensified rates in austerity-ridden Europe. This form of emergency rule appears "illegal" to people even as it is perfectly "juridical and constitutional" (Agamben 2005, 28). Ugo Mattei and many others I spent time with used a similar language: "We consider the law illegal when without legitimacy it [rams] through impotent legislatures without adequate disclosure, debate, or hearings" and when it is used to "facilitate unconscionable bargains at the expense of the people." In such instances, the law is a vehicle of "plunder, not of legality" (Mattei and Nader 2008, 4; see also Capone 2013; Pistor 2019). The writing of popular laws was thus an attempt to assert a true form of legality—a legitimate legality representing the law of the many beyond and outside of the illegitimate state.

### Counterrevolution

A counterrevolution reared its head immediately after the referendum, when rightist Prime Minister Berlusconi immediately issued a decree to reintroduce the compulsory tendering norms repealed by the referendum. ACEA SpA, the largest of four major Italian water corporations (and one of "the four sisters of water"—*le quattro sorelle dell'acqua*—that are "masters of Italian taps" as a newspaper article sarcastically referred to them [Giovannini 2017]),[31] immediately acquired the expert opinion of Giulio Napolitano, son of then sitting president of the republic and a well-known law and economics expert. Napolitano argued that no legal obligations followed from the referendum results and that business was to continue as usual.

Water activists were incensed ("This was a *golpe*, a coup!" as Mattei put it to me), a language echoed by others I met in Italy and Germany who referred to the political class as "kings" making decisions without democratic input. Yet my point here is not simply to add another page to the many already written on authoritarian neoliberalism—that form of oligarchic "autocratic governance" that has long been pioneered and now perfected by the architects of neoliberalism (Swyngedouw 2018, 170; Bieler 2021, 96). Rather, I foreground the ways in which the financial frontier is a zone where political authoritarianism is in fact responding to the fault lines it inevitably generates, including direct democratic lawmaking from below. A group of lawyers including Mattei immediately launched a constitutional challenge to Berlusconi's pushback, to which the Italian Constitutional Court responded a year later. It ruled that "the will of the people expressed in the form of direct democracy by the referendum could not be overturned by means of representative democracy (i.e., by the Parliament) at least for a reasonable period of time" (Mattei 2013, 372).

Critics argue that this doctrine of "succession of law in time," expressed in the phrase "at least for a reasonable period of time," should not apply to popular referenda, since direct democracy is one of the strongest political tools available to citizens and should therefore enjoy "a surplus of constitutional force compared to ordinary legislation" (Bailey and Mattei 2013, 987). Indeed, the water movement would argue that the legitimacy of popular referenda exceeds that of laws made by elected lawmakers since the latter only *indirectly* represent the will of the people, if at all. In principle, then, successful referenda should become law. But in a context where "democracy is screwed because of the huge amount of private money that has influenced the political process," Mattei said, "there is a very thin line between law and politics."

Soon, a new government coalition headed by Matteo Renzi passed a series of laws that, while not obliging local municipalities to privatize, instead created a set of fiscal and administrative conditions that achieve water privatization through different means. The 2015 Stability Law (Legge di Stabilità), was specifically designed to undercut local attempts at remunicipalization by obliging municipalities to prioritize private management companies in the allocation of public funds and by incentivizing the selling of whatever municipal shares in water services still existed. Continuing a trend begun by the EU Stability Pact of balanced budgets and egged on by the EU and ECBs heavy pressure to fully liberalize local public services through large-scale privatizations (Bieler 2021, 68), the law obliged municipalities who wanted to keep their water public to set aside a sum of money that equaled that of planned investments every three years—an absurd demand in an age of austerity. It also explicitly forbade that municipalities use profits made from the sale of shares to reacquire private shares with the goal of remunicipalization (Forum Italiano dei Movimenti per l'Acqua, 2014b).

By mid-2017, the Madia law reintroduced the same language that the referendum in 2011 had struck from the books: the legal provision that guaranteed investors an adequate remuneration of invested capital. This language was confirmed in parliament amidst a massive groundswell of protest. That same year, the main office of the Forum Italiano dei Movimenti per l'Acqua was evicted in Rome—ironically by a mayor from the Five Star Movement (the Movimento 5 Stelle), the only party that had made the remunicipalization of water a major aspect of its political platform (the first of the five stars after which the party is named stands for water). By 2019, the Five Star Movement managed to introduce a reimbursement for all "consumer victims" (*consumatore vittima*) who had received crazy bills. It allowed these victims to seek reimbursement and to have their service providers pay them a fine. Still, this did not stop people from lamenting that even the first star of the Five Star Movement was now in "free fall."[32] At the time of this writing, a new Draft Law for Competition (Disegno di Legge per la Concorrenza) is being discussed in the Italian Senate, with the goal of subjecting all public services, including water, to more market competition. This law, writes the Italian Forum for Water Movements, risks "placing a final tombstone on the results of the 2011 referendum and cancelling out the popular will." The fault lines, in short, remain, and Italian public opinion continues to be shot through with a sense of foundational betrayal.

### Small Sovereignties

One day in February of 2015, I was driving toward Roccapiemonte (or 'A Rocca, as it is called in Campanian dialect), a small town famous among water activists in Campania because it was the only town that had (at least until the time of this writing) managed to keep its tiny municipal water utility public. All other surrounding seventy-five municipalities in the Sarnese Vesuviano district had, in 2003, agreed to contract with GORI, creating a public-private partnership (*società di capitale pubblico-privato*) that will last at least until 2023 (so, approximately twenty-nine years). The water district (called ATO 3, one of the five ATOs in the Campanian region and the only one that had at that time contracted with GORI) owned 51 percent and GORI 49 percent of the total shares. As one water activist put it to me with much bitterness, it was the privates who got to determine GORI's chief executive officer as well as its board of directors—despite their minority shares. "The politics of GORI is thus made by a minority that corrupt the majority (public) shareholders and organ of control—and that organ of control is the mayors of the entire ATO." Only about half of the mayors of the water district had signed up to be part of the Rete dei Sindaci, the network of mayors dedicated to public water. Some joined the network voluntarily out of respect for the referendum's results and because they loathed GORI's high water prices and clientelistic politics. Others had to be forced into it, as was the case in the town of San Giorgio di Cremano, where activists presented a motion to the municipal government "proposing" that the mayor join the network (the municipal council voted in favor, forcing the mayor to join).

But not 'A Rocca, as Antonio, an elderly water activist put it to me as we stood on the top of a hill overlooking the valley where Roccapiemonte lay. It soon became clear that this valley, cut through by a highway leading to Salerno, was, for him, a highly politicized cartography of public versus private water, good versus evil. He pointed out to the right side of the highway and said "here, we have public water, and water is free" (*acqua e libera*). He elaborated, "When water is public, it belongs to citizens! That means that there is democracy and liberty. On the other side of the highway, it is private. There, it's a dictatorship. There, water belongs to the water thieves, the *ladri dell'acqua!*"

I had read many stories over the years that the Roccapiemontesi had physically stopped GORI representatives from entering their village, sometimes by blocking access to the mayor's office, sometimes with kicks and punches into GORI representatives' stomachs, which sent them to the hospital. I had heard many admiring tales from other activists who recounted how the people of Rocca had "literally pulled the contract away from underneath the mayor's pen!" Eventually, the mayor sent GORI away, citing a problem of public order. GORI soon sued Roccapiemonte, a town of barely nine-thousand inhabitants, for several millions of euros for losses incurred because of the town's refusal to contract with it; however, at the time, the courts (the Tribunale Amministrativo della Campania, or TAR) did not rule in GORI's favor.[33] "Our town was never scared of them," members of the local water committee told me. "We are continuing our battle."

I reached Roccapiemonte and soon found myself in the public library, bare except for a humble row of books with yellowing spines. I was the only woman among a group of about eight men, all of us sitting at a single table on white plastic chairs. When I asked them about the history of their water committee, all started speaking simultaneously. A very long, very loud discussion ensued, which I was not at all a part of. At one point in the midst of the din, a man sitting next to me kindly slid a drawing he had just made along the table into my direction in an effort to clarify what it all was really about.

The current situation (*attuale*), the man explained, was that GORI officially stood for "Optimal Management of Hydric Resources" (*Gestione Ottimale Risorse Idriche*). His "personal consideration" (*considerazione personale*) was that GORI should actually be called "Optimal Management of the Collection

ATTUALE

GORI = ( GESTIONE
OTTIMALE
RISORSE
IDRIGHE

CONSIDERAZIONE PERSONALE?

GORI ( GESTIONE
OTTIMALE
RISCOSSIONE
INTROITI

SOLUZIONE
OTTIMALE

FONTANINA

PEDALE

P.C.

1.4     The meaning of GORI reconsidered. Image drawn by P.C. (Photo: Andrea Muehlebach.)

of Profits" (*Gestione Ottimale Riscossioni Introiti*). But the "optimal solution" (*soluzione ottimale*) in his eyes was the old-fashioned water fountain (note the pedal!), lovingly referred to in the diminutive as "*fontanina*." He signed his drawing with his initials, "P.C.," reminding me with a wink that PC also used to be the acronym for Italy's Communist Party. For him, the old water fountain was democracy's infrastructure par excellence (von Schnitzler 2016), an infrastructure that was "life-giving in its design, finance, and effects" (LaDuke and Cowen 2020, 245). In one of the poorest regions in Italy, the symbolic weight of the old fountain as an emblem of subsidized municipal provisioning cannot be overstated.

I end this chapter with this image of the humble, life-giving water fountain because I want to reflect on the small, sometimes highly territorialized battles that today linger on as vibrant remainders of the 2011 referendum—battles that exemplify the degree to which the struggle over democracy and sovereignty continues. Public water fountains are one of the central symbols in this struggle. Their materiality and symbolic presence—their levels of disrepair or renovation, the quality of the water, the question of whether people drink from them or not—have long constituted a potent sign of the tensions governing the financial frontier. Indexing more than merely publicly owned water, the old *fontanina* was a love object that stood for a kind of social contract where politics was oriented toward citizens rather than toward shareholders. "You know a good family head," as one of my interlocutors put it. "My father, before buying shoes for himself, would buy shoes for my brother and me. Today, our *servitori* (public servants) do nothing but pay their [the banks,' investors,' financiers'] gambling debts, and they do that by selling off our public assets" (see also Subramanian 2009, 2).

Roccapiemonte was able to divorce itself from the grasp of GORI because it owned three wells and managed its own municipal infrastructure (with one employee, I was told).[34] The *fontanina* thus stood for municipal self-provisioning and self-determination—a small enactment of sovereignty by a community that directly took from the ground what the ground offered and that used its municipal infrastructure to do so (see also Strang 2005, 114). Roccapiemonte's successive mayors have thus been central symbolic characters in the vibrant civic network of mayors. As "defenders of the community," they stood as a shining example of legitimate governance and were respected and admired for the principles they embodied. In contrast, the mayors who were beholden to privatized water utilities like GORI ceased to behave like mayors at all. All over Italy, Bersani (2011) writes, mayors "began to reinterpret their role in an authoritarian way," compulsively behaving like "sheriffs" and issuing ordinances in the privatized utility's name (71).

By 2018, the statutes of the centralized Campanian water institution called Ente Idrico Campano (EIC), which people had demonstrated against on that November day in 2015, were approved. The regional centralization of a previously decentralized political structure has since been accomplished. The people I met argued that this act of political authoritarianism would spell the death knell for mayors who wanted to democratically participate in the management of their waters. The region is "acting like a little king," as one person tellingly put it. As the late Ciro Annunziata from Nocera Inferiore's water committee said, throwing his hands in the air in desperation: "Let us territorialize the management of water again. Let us restore the assemblies of mayors and reflect on water as commons!" Ciro was exasperated because his local water district, ATO 3, had been under receivership for years despite the fact that a local court ruled against the continuation of this emergency management regime in 2019. He was also frustrated by the fact that the regionally centralized Campanian water body would take away small-town mayor's competencies, thus "expropriating" them of their capacity to govern their water systems from below.

Such centralization processes, people complained, would take away local knowledge about local infrastructures as well. After all, as many people in the Campanian towns noted, they had personally known the municipal workers employed by the water utility and could point out leakages and other problems directly. These workers knew the water infrastructure intimately, invisible to everyone except them. Regionalization and privatization would see many of these local utility workers dismissed, leaving gaps in the infrastructural expertise needed to *know* and often intuit local water systems and their vulnerabilities. Adding to that, critics warned that regional centralization and future privatization would render the remunicipalized Neapolitan water utility Napoli ABC (Napoli Acqua Bene Comune or Water as Commons) vulnerable: "They are attacking it," one interlocutor fumed, "because the mere existence of Napoli ABC shows all of Italy the concrete evidence that the public and democratic governance of water as commons is possible."

Against these authoritarian politics, the mayors of the Rete dei Sindaci agreed to use the law for the good of the community, for example, by issuing legal ordinances against the water shutoffs that at the time continued unabated in the district.[35] Some members of the water committee in Nocera Inferiore, for example, recounted how people in Casalnuovo had involved not just the local health authorities and the local police but eventually the mayor to make a case for the serious health and safety effects of water shutoffs. With the help of an indefatigable young lawyer, Giuseppe Grauso, the mayor eventually issued an ordinance against water shutoffs—a tool that was being used increasingly by mayors in Campania and beyond at the time of my research in 2015 and 2016. Mayoral ordinances are small but crucial legal tools in an era when the law has become an instrument of dispossession. These ordinances were last-resort tools that mayors were using to erect the legal infrastructure needed to maintain and strengthen the public realm (Arendt 1998, 194–95). Yet this capacity to issue ordinances was annulled by Campania's Regional Administrative Court in 2015, as was the case in other Italian regions, too—a devastating blow to the little maneuvering space left to mayors in their attempt to protect their citizenry (Colamonaco 2015; *Agro 24* 2015).

It did not matter to critics that GORI had responded to these upheavals by offering thirty-thousand liters of free water every year to all users, or that it had, on top of that, introduced a water bonus (*bonus idrico*) allowing for deductions to be made off of bills for those in need. For critics, these were just short-term Band-Aids that obscured the healthy profits GORI was making. Indeed, the powerful Rome-based multiutility ACEA's Chief Executive Officer Giuseppe Gola presented its 2020–2024 plan in October 2020, signaling to markets that it was continuing its pattern of steady growth. In the meantime, GORI, 37 percent of whose shares are owned by ACEA through its subsidiary Sarnese Vesuviano SRL, is still shutting off water. Campanian movements, at least until the time of the writing, cite examples of families receiving crazy bills of over two-thousand euros, not being able to pay, and subsequently having their water shut off. That same month, demonstrations took place in front of ACEA's main seat in Rome, where protestors held up a sign reading "Water is Life! Give it back to us!" This is why the sidelining of mayors was such a tragedy. It not only dispossessed mayors of small sovereignties such as the capacity to issue local ordinances; it also dispossessed local communities of one of the few powers still available to them: that of holding their mayors accountable and of pressuring them to protect them from the "water thieves."

Roccapiemonte has, until the time of this writing, refused to cede its water utility to GORI and continues to provide water to its citizens at incredibly low prices, using its own three wells to do so. While a fourth well was being built, Roccapiemonte relied on buying water from GORI to fulfill the town's water needs, but GORI retaliated by cutting its water supply to the town. For a few months in 2020 and in the midst of the COVID-19 pandemic, Roccapiemonte was forced to suspend the town's water supply for several nights a week. Its current mayor, Carmine Pagano, went so far as to launch a fundraising campaign to help with the maintenance of the municipal aqueduct and water mains (*SalernoNotizie* 2020). In an interview with local media, Pagano committed himself to what he called a "democracy of appropriation," where citizens would reappropriate their capacity and right to participate democratically in matters meaningful to them. It was only through a reappropriation of this capacity that a "democracy of trust" could be reestablished (*Agro 24* 2020).

These ongoing battles show the relentless tensions and small provocations that continue to shape this financial frontier. Indeed, many leading water activists would never admit to defeat. Both Tommaso Fattori and Ugo Mattei noted that the Italian water movement had achieved something phenomenal in that a large number of smaller local utilities still remain publicly owned (about 50 percent of Italian water utilities remain in public hands, the rest are either entirely or partially privatized [Guerrini and Romano 2014, 15]). Today, most water utilities do not distribute any returns to shareholders and instead reinvest profits in self-financing (Romano and Guerrini 2019, 1). This was, as Mattei put it, "a big damage to capital. That's not nothing." But more than that, both also insisted that Italy's political and legal universe has changed forever. The concept of *beni comuni* has been introduced into many communal and regional statutes and used in legal scholarship and many courts of law, including the Italian Supreme Court. I met members of water committees in Campanian towns who had managed to present their local council with amendments to their communal statutes, insisting that they acknowledge water as a commons. "The referendum was a clear articulation of our popular sovereignty," these people said. "It is *we* who should be able to determine our destiny!"

In 2014, one of the protagonists in the push for a popular water law, Tommaso Fattori, continued the work he spearheaded by passing a popular regional law regarding a public and participatory model of water management in Lazio. In 2018, he again launched the same initiative in Tuscany, hoping to pass the same law there. Alberto Lucarelli, another prominent lawyer who was also a member of the Commission for Public Property, a professor of constitutional law at Federico II in Naples, and the first Assessor to the Commons (Assessore ai Beni Comuni) in Naples when mayor de Magistris took office in 2011, continues to argue for the introduction of several new legal concepts within the Italian Constitution precisely to safeguard the protection of common goods: the concept of the "commons" (*beni comuni*) to protect natural resources; of "social goods" (*beni sociali*) to protect education, work, and health; and of "sovereign goods" (*beni sovrani*) to protect strategic infrastructures and essential public services. Only this would "properly respond to neoliberalism and finance capitalism" (Lucarelli 2018).

Yet others are embittered by the outcome of years of struggle. On September 17, 2020, Neapolitan missionary Father Zanotelli wrote a public lament in a widely publicized piece called "A Five Star Betrayal" ("Tradimento a 5 Stelle"). Ten years after the referendum, he wrote, not a single one of the seven successive Italian governments on either the right or the left of the political spectrum had managed to implement the referendum. This included the Five Star Movement, part of whose political platform had been dedicated to the public management of water and that was unable to push the popular law on the management of water as commons through parliament even after three successive years in government. Obstructions on all levels of government still abound—proof that it was ultimately beholden to corporate pressures. Indeed, the last few years have seen a national discussion where politicians have conjured the frightening costs of remunicipalization—fifteen to twenty billion euros. The water movement attempted to combat this specter of unaffordability with its own, significantly lower countercalculations, arguing that Napoli ABC proves that remunicipalization is eminently possible. Such a move toward remunicipalization, pleads Zanotelli, would be a "sign of life" in a world orbiting around a neoliberal necropolitics where "so many of us feel threatened by death" (Zanotelli 2020).

Many people I met thus felt that they have been dispossessed of a thing (public water) and capacity (that of efficacious democratic action). But they have not been dispossessed of the sensorium and embodied memory of democratic assembly, achieved after many years of making laws from below in response to what they see as illegitimate government from above. Having "made a referendum," activists spoke of having labored together democratically for more than a decade, as a social body in all its "corporeal materiality" and "resistant subjectivity" (Butler 2015; see also Hardt and Negri 2009, 26). Having made democracy their own, the Italians I met remembered and reminisced not just about the life-giving vitality of water, but about how their struggle for water gave life to a practical democratic process as a kind of inalienable commonwealth. Even as they face the state's refusal to recognize their demands, they remember and continue to struggle for a lived democracy that cannot be transacted and therefore cannot be captured or taken away. This is an inalienable wealth whose value derives purely out of its everyday, practical use (Foster 2018, 292)—a use and practice as vital as the air we breathe.

2

**No More Blood
from These Stones!**

IN APRIL 2016, I was sitting in Suzanne O'Flynn's kitchen in Ashbrook
Heights, a working-class estate in Togher in the southern Irish city of
Cork, listening to her story over coffee and chocolate cake. Neighbors
wove in and out of her house's open front door, adding bits and pieces to
her story as she spoke. I had been told that Suzanne was one of the first
people in Ireland who had decided that she would block the installation
of a water meter early one morning in April 2014.[1] Things had been bad
enough already—she repeatedly failed to receive help for her ill son in
austerity-era Cork, where services had been savagely cut. Now, in one of
the most ambitious water metering programs of any water utility worldwide (Bresnihan 2016, 121), the newly established national water company, Irish Water, was going to install over one million meters in
sidewalks all over the country. Irish Water was moving from
charging fixed rates through a water tax system to a system
where charges for water were proportional to the amount

of water consumed.[2] Households were to receive their first water bills in January 2015 (Dukelow 2016, 153).[3]

The meters came at the tail end of an intense post-2008 austerity regime that had seen 10 billion euros worth of budget cuts in the country, including radical cuts to social welfare and a reduction of the minimum wage. The metering of water was thus—as almost every person I spoke to in Ireland said to me when I first visited in April 2016—"the straw that broke the camel's back." Little did Suzanne know that images of her standing in the middle of the road at the entrance of her working-class housing estate would soon circulate on social media and in the national press, and that she would help galvanize hundreds of similar water meter protests all over the country. Almost a year later, the *Irish Times* would report that 22,700 video recordings of anti water-meter protests and blockages, marches, and demonstrations had been uploaded onto YouTube.[4] Over a hundred groups all over Ireland set up Facebook pages urging people to protest against metering, with memorable titles such as "You Can Stick Your Water Meters up Your Arse." All of Ireland was in turmoil. Local upheavals in what is known as the "rebel city" of Cork soon merged into a union-led national antiausterity mass mobilization, the scale of which the nation had not seen in decades.[5] This was a moment when the nation let it be known that "You are not getting any more blood from these stones."

While those first protests at Ashbrook Heights occurred peacefully through the intransigence of a few people blocking a road, tensions soon rose as Irish Water continued to install meters. By the time I arrived in 2016, social media was ablaze with videos of scuffles between protestors and police, with beatings and arrests documented and shared online. While it is hard to assess the magnitude of physical altercations that actually took place between police and protestors, the online circulation of these altercations took on an outsized place in the media landscape surrounding the water-meter protests. They rendered profoundly visible the degree to which the state was going to place the full force of its weight behind Irish Water. Many of these posts received tens of thousands of views. An iconic image on social media shows four Irish Water workers installing a meter on a street surrounded by a tight circle of more than a dozen Gardai (members of the Irish police, Garda Síochána [Gaelic for Guardians of the Peace]). Soon after, reports surfaced that Irish Water had also hired private security firms such as Guardex, which according to its website provides "specialist operational security support to clients in support of their corporate and operational goals."[6] Some people insisted

2.1        Water meter installation in Dublin, 2014. (Image courtesy of Dublin Says No.)

that guards had arrived wearing black masks and sunglasses, refusing to be identified. As one interlocutor put it to me, "They were trying to say that meters were 'strategic infrastructure' and that interference would be an act of terrorism." The situation escalated to such a degree that center-right politicians such as Noel Coonan went so far as to say that the country was "facing what is potentially an ISIS situation." By 2015, 188 protestors had been arrested and taken to court.

This chapter tracks the financial frontier as a zone of violence and as a terrain where "violent clarity" can be reached (Tsing 2003, 5101). I build on Marx and Luxemburg's points that accumulation by dispossession is always accompanied by force.[7] Luxemburg makes clear that violence is the *method* of capitalism: "Force is the only solution open to capital: the accumulation of capital, seen as a historical process, employs force as a permanent weapon, not only at its genesis, but further on down to the present day" (Luxemburg 1951, 371). Luxemburg differentiates between different kinds of capitalist violence—the violence of capitalist command (*Kommandogewalt*) that relies on war and that in the colonies was able to rapidly mobilize hundreds of thousands of people into a combination of slavery and bonded labor; and a violence that articulates itself through institutions like taxation and debt systems that create new forms of collective fiscal bondage across generations (240). Violence, in short, articulates itself differentially—economically through long-term forms of structural debt, but also through the brute force of the police—a distinction that Irish protestors made as well. Protestors often lamented the violence of austerity, just as they thought of the police as corporate enforcers of a state captured by finance. The Irish water insurgency thus revealed the open secret behind the appearance of formal liberal democracy (Swyngedouw 2018, 27)—that a politics of violence is "vitally necessary" for capitalism's survival and that this violence takes on many forms (Luxemburg 1913, 287). In the process, the Irish water insurgency insisted that theirs were political protests, not criminal actions, "noble law breaking," not "mob rule." As Cobh community organizer Karen Doyle said, "We will break those bad laws, and we will fill your courts with noble law breakers and supporters of our collective resistance."[8] Everywhere the consensus seemed to reign that "when injustice becomes law, rebellion becomes duty." This chapter is thus not only about violent clarity but about the profoundly generative challenge posed by the people and their barricades (Simpson 2021).

The riotous disruptions of these infrastructures of financialization—the "hardware for water commodification," as union organizer Brendan Ogle (2016) put it—were a direct response to the elaborate regimes of securitization that often accompany contemporary infrastructural projects (2). A number of scholars have noted governments' increased merging of their security apparatus with the protection and securitization of critical infrastructures, with states hedging against system vulnerabilities and investing in infrastructure protection against "terrorists" or "subversives" (Collier and Lakoff 2015). The state thus backs accumulation by dispossession and secures the circuitry of capital through its monopolies over violence and its (re)definition of what is legal and what is not (Pasternak and Dafnos 2018; Harvey 2004, 74). National economies will only remain vital if they are able to project "infrastructural resilience" and the state's capacity to secure it against volatile politics and other risks (Pasternak and Dafnos 2018, 751). Riots and blockages are thus provocative chokepoints within infrastructures that states have set up to facilitate financialization (Halpern 2019, 10), with stoppages not only strictly policed, but closely watched by firms like Global Water Intelligence (GWI). It was Irish water activist Noreen Murphy who first alerted me to the fact that GWI had at least on one occasion invited a counterinsurgency specialist as keynote speaker to its yearly conference.[9] The battles fought over these "toll booths on our human right to water" (Ogle 2016, 2) were as much on the streets over blocked meters as they were over the question of what violence was in the first place.

The Irish water insurgency drew its initial impetus from highly localized street-level barricades in working-class neighborhoods as people tried to stop the entry of Irish Water into their estates. Bodies became barriers—the barriers that Rosa Luxemburg (1913) notes are often erected against enclosure (241). They bore resemblance to the "tumults and riotous assemblies" that arose in the eighteenth century against the enclosure of vital goods—riots that King George I first described in 1714 as a "violent disturbance of the peace by an assembly or body of persons, an outbreak of active lawlessness or disorder among the populace" (Thompson 1971, 83; Clover 2016, 8–9).[10] Then as now, the fury of protestors was propelled by the fact that they were unable to manage basic subsistence (Clover 2016, 10), with rioters targeting the violence of the market—embodied by the figure of the police.[11] Then as now, it was women who were "most sensitive to price significances" and who "most frequently precipitated the spontaneous actions" (Thompson 1993, 234). It was also again on the level of the household—among the women who do the laundry, wash the dishes, bathe the children, and, in Irish households, almost always do the bills—where the question of vital goods and their relation to a household's capacity to social reproduction became politicized for broad swaths of the population.

Some authors would interpret the Irish water insurgency as a return of struggles previously fought against financial expansion originally led by merchant capital in the seventeenth and eighteenth centuries (Clover 2016). While recognizing these resemblances, I also move beyond these abstract cyclical histories across centuries to trace another set of returns. It was striking, for example, how the Irish water insurgency replayed the prepaid water and electricity meter protests that occurred in South Africa and India just over a decade earlier (von Schnitzler 2013, 674; Björkman 2015, 49–51). In Johannesburg, for example, the government had corporatized water companies under the pressures of the World Bank's structural-adjustment measures and transformed them into publicly owned for-profit companies run by personnel contracted from Suez. There, the installation of prepaid meters was heavily resisted through sabotage and protests, with police eventually enforcing their installation and use (von Schnitzler 2013,

2016). These scenarios in the Global South anticipated those unfolding in the Global North today. The recursive violence of previous frontiers of accumulation are hurtling back into European terrains (Césaire 2000, 35–36).

It was striking, too, how the Irish water struggle clearly drew on the long aftereffects of the Irish decolonial struggle against the British, as evidenced in protestors' frequent use of the terms "enslavement" when describing their bondage to the European Union. For many, this was a revolutionary struggle over resource sovereignty and self-rule and thus steeped in the language of Republican anticolonial protest.[12] As Maeve Curtis from Dundalk powerfully put it during an enormous, union-led Right2Water demonstration that took place on March 21, 2015, "We've heard a lot about violence and the violence of protest, but I want to talk today about another violence, the violence of austerity. There are two ways to enslave a nation, one is with the sword, and the other is with debt. And make no mistake, that's what this Government has done, and the previous Government has done. They have enslaved a nation" (Ogle 2016, 149).[13] Critics in turn often denigrated water protestors as irrational "mobs" and "savages," with protestors' message of a more just social contract initially going unheeded (Phemister 2019, 36–42).

Peoples' frequently evoked specters of enslavement bore the historical weight of a capitalism that has since its inception relied on the production of racial difference—a racial difference that reverberates into the presence through the language critics used to condescend to protestors. Indeed, the Irish, together with the Slavs, have always been part of an "inventory" of Western racial hierarchy, "lower racialized orders" and "savages" located at the bottom of this hierarchy and that made up the cheapest exploitable labor (Robinson [1983] 2000, 2). These patterns of racialization grew out of feudalism and intensified with the enclosure movement, as "wild" landless Irish peasants were herded into the newly industrializing cities—a process that occurred at the same time that African labor was violently drawn into the world system through the slave trade. The birth of the "Negro," in short, found precedence in the "racial fabrications" surrounding the Irish and the Slavs (Robinson [1983] 2000, 4; see also Federici 2004, 17).[14] It is thus perhaps no coincidence that Irish protestors found their disproportionate shouldering of the European bank bailout to be profoundly unjust, the product of a Europe bent on "enslaving" them just like the British had before.

It was also no coincidence that a number of the Irish water activists I met looked more to their Black brethren in Detroit than to other water struggles that were simultaneously occurring on the European continent. The affinities between the plight of the American underclass with the working classes in Ireland were on display in December of 2014, when Right2Water invited the Detroit Water Brigade to Ireland in what became a series of widely disseminated events on social media. The brigade had arrived in Dublin to speak to Irish protestors about the ongoing water struggles in their own city. Detroit's water utility (which, while not privatized, has nevertheless been thoroughly corporatized under an emergency manager appointed by Governor Rick Snyder, notorious for the Flint water scandal) has for many years been rocked by water shutoffs, with 141,000 households having had their water shut off since 2014 (Fennell 2016).[15] In the cruelest of twists, children have in some cases been taken away from parents by social services since their families were living without water and thus "in unsanitary conditions" (Vande Panne 2018). One of the brigade's members, DeMeeko Williams, put it as follows: "Do not let them take this water," he said. "Or else you will end up just like us. A lot of the things that have happened in Detroit will come to Ireland. . . . When we were out in Crumlin and we saw the water meters being installed, [we said] 'Why are you letting them put them in? Shut them down!'" "You have 1.7 million people in Ireland with less than one hundred euros at the end of the month," said David Gibney from Right2Water, using figures from the Irish League of Credit Unions. "And they're told, 'It's only three euros a week.' [That's] a lot to somebody who has no money, when their rent has just gone up 10.5 percent. You can only shake a can of Coke a certain amount before it explodes" (Fitzpatrick 2015).

The Irish water struggle was very much a working-class led mobilization, with early protests emerging in working-class housing estates and soon after being taken up by unions (Bieler 2021). Yet some of the earliest protests, I show, also emerged out of an infrastructural peculiarity of working-class neighborhoods insofar as many Irish working-class estates consist of a particular architecture and an attendant sociality. I show how the built environment, itself a result of working-class mobilizations in the late nineteenth and early twentieth centuries, created the material grounds for these mass insurgencies to occur. As the water insurgency unfolded, the population insisted that fiscal arrangements are always also moral arrangements and expressions of a body politic that is either fragmented and polarized through regressive taxation or united through redistributive politics and progressive taxation. In an era where citizens in some countries like the United States have since the 1970s paid more interest to finance than they have paid taxes to the state (Robbins 2020, 56), the radical nature of this protest with its insistence on tax justice cannot be underestimated.

Ireland is only one of two European countries (Scotland being the other) that until a short while ago metered its water on the district level, not on the level of the individual household. Water was thus measured via district meters, with costs covered through general taxation (the motor tax and VAT).[16] This system was introduced in 1977, when water began to be paid through a "domestic rates grant" allocated by the central government to local authorities. This collectivized payment structure hinged on a culture of cross-subsidization, subsidies that were tolerated because water was considered an essential public-health service and because it was considered equitable for costs to be distributed according to capacity to pay. Meters, in contrast, make households pay for the actual cost they "impose" on water and sewerage systems and have been interpreted as a move away from "social equity" to "economic equity" (Bakker 2001, 147), from social need to individual demand (Collier 2011, 25).

The unusual situation of unmetered water in Ireland is the result of a long and controversial history that has seen the consistent politicization of domestic water charges, with communities repeatedly up in arms about numerous government attempts to introduce them (Dukelow 2016, 151). The arguments made by communities were wide-ranging over the years, as people criticized major water price hikes in the 1970s or an attempted introduction of domestic charges amidst a more general tax hike in the 1980s. Often, the critiques were saturated with a lyricism and poetics. After all, Ireland is a country "drowning in water" as I heard many people say, its abundance translating into a deep popular conviction that water should "run free." Like the Italians I cite in the previous chapter ("*Acqua e libera!* Water is free!"), the argument about the "freedom" of water is commonly misunderstood (or actively misrepresented) as a naïve insistence on nonpayment (see also Ballestero 2019, 16) and, as one interlocutor put it to me, "that we wanted everything for nothing and that we don't understand economics."

In fact, the term *freedom* implied that water as a common good ought to be universally paid for through general taxation and thus through a system of cross-subsidization. General taxation and cross-subsidization were understood to be the fiscal and political expression of water as a collectively held form of property—an indivisible social good that should never be turned into a divisible resource, counted and paid for via individual bills. The seemingly intuitive argument that water charges should reflect the amount used by individual households (where everyone pays the same for amounts of water used—the principle of "economic equity") was vehemently criticized by a majority of Irish protestors who argued that this purportedly equalizing measure would be felt differentially across a social fabric already deeply divided along class lines. Many households already stretched thin at the end of the month would struggle to pay yet another bill if they had to pay exactly the same as their richer neighbors.

Irish protestors attempted to clarify this meaning of freedom. As one interlocutor said to me, "our waters are running free, and we want them to continue to run free. We won't pay for our waters because we're already paying for them through our taxes." The fiscal collective rather than the individual bill was thus the most ethical way to pay for water. As one long-time Socialist activist and Cork city councilor put it when recounting the domestic water charges protests in 1984, "We have always paid for water [including sewage] and waste through our taxes; and I've always paid . . . I pay my taxes every week, like the vast majority pay their taxes . . . though the super rich don't pay taxes as we all know . . . and we got angry when they wanted to introduce fixed water charges. 'No way we've already paid!' It was like a double taxation at the supermarket! It was like going to the supermarket and paying for your goods at the check-out and then being stopped again at the door to pay again" (see also Ogle 2016; Murphy 2019). Metering thus not only represented a "double payment"—an additional tax that would burden already burdened households—but would violate the principle of distribution through taxation in an indivisible system of (at least attempted) social equalization. It was also unethical because it would not hinge on distributive equity, that is to say on the principle that class disparities between municipalities (often the result of a differential municipal ability to raise local revenue) should best be addressed through centralized (re)allocation. Minimum funding levels for, say, water utilities, are in a distributive ethic maintained through nationally established priorities that make sure that local governments have access to sufficient resources (Humphreys, van der Kerk, and Fonsecca 2018, 105).

There were other layers of meaning that attached themselves to the use of the term *freedom* and that drew on the Irish anticolonial struggle against British enclosure, when the British violently restricted Irish access not only to land but to waters, specifically fishing rights. To many, the current European Union mandated austerity regime was similarly violent and predatory. Water, after all, was a commons and thus indivisible and not amenable to metered division, counting, and measurement. One interlocutor mobilized a distinctly Native American Indigenous perspective when he said to me that "water is a commons. Water is like the land. We don't own the land, the land owns us." This was more than a mere act of ventriloquism, since some of the older anti–water charges activists I met reflected vividly about their long involvement in struggles for resource rights in and around Cork. Standing in his car repair shop while chatting with myself and Dorothea Härlin from the Berlin Water Table, Cork city councilor Ted Tynan reminisced about how in the 1970s he and a group of eleven other men had occupied Lismore Castle, then owned by the Duke of Devonshire, because they wanted to "exercise our right to fish our own rivers, which were not free."[17] At times they drew on water's sacrality (scholars have estimated that there were as many as three-thousand holy wells in Ireland, with waters not only endowed with vital substances that hold miraculous powers (Ray 2011; Carroll 1999) but with wells also functioning as sacred locations where Irish Catholic parishioners held secluded mass during the era of British colonial oppression (O'Brien 2008, 327). Protest chants such as the (Palestinian-derived) "From the river to the sea: Irish water will be free!" thus profoundly resonated historically and culturally and in ways utterly misunderstood by critics, who misread it with the assumption that "the Irish don't want to pay."[18] What it was, instead, was a call for freedom from the fetters of crypto-colonial (Herzfeld 2002) debt economies initiated by Europe's brutal austerity regime, not a right to nonpayment.

Water charges were so contested over decades that Ireland sought exemption from the water charges element of the EU's Water Framework Directive (WFD) in 2000, together with a number of other southern European member states (Kaika 2003). The fact that the EU WFD includes a Section 9.4 known as the "Irish Exemption" (it allows for member states to exempt themselves from billing households for water) is a poignant reminder of how controversial the commodification of water has been for decades in Ireland. Renewed attempts to charge households for water through household metering in 2002 and in 2006 were again and again met with protests and eventually dropped (Dukelow 2016, 151).[19]

This lack of metering, almost unique within the contemporary European context, meant that the principle of full-cost recovery could not be implemented. The post-2008 demands of the European Union could not be met, nor would Irish Water ever appear legible to future global investors. The infrastructure—the technical devices needed to transform unmetered water into a predictable and legible infrastructural asset circulating in secondary financial markets (Bresnihan 2016, 120; Christopherson, Martin, and Pollard 2013; Leyshon and Thrift 2007)—was simply absent.

The situation rapidly changed when the so-called Celtic Tiger's real-estate bubble burst with the financial crisis in 2007. The Irish government issued a huge bailout for the entire banking system's liabilities by 2008. By perverse alchemy, a banking crisis was transformed from a banking into a sovereign debt crisis and suddenly became the Irish public's problem, a socialization of risks and costs (Blyth 2013, 66). The Irish government spent some 70 billion euros to shore up its banking system, allowing banks to walk away scot-free. The country, in turn, suffered the largest decline in GNP of any industrialized country between the years 2007 and 2010 (66). By December 2010, Ireland received 85 billion euros in bailout funds from the "troika"—the European Commission, the European Central Bank, and the IMF. Like the other members of what many newspapers called the PIIGS or GIPSI (two highly derogatory acronyms tinged with long-standing intra-European racisms and used to refer to the five Eurozone countries that had "partied too hard" and indulged in "excessive lifestyles" during the boom: Portugal, Italy, Ireland, Greece, and Spain), Ireland implemented 10 billion euros worth of austerity cuts. Public sector salaries were reduced by 20 percent while taxes and user fees increased. To make matters worse, low corporate taxes had tech giants like Google, Apple, Facebook, and Microsoft set up headquarters in Ireland, paying only 12.5 percent corporate taxes in contrast to the 35 percent they would have paid in the United States.[20] Apple in particular has been embroiled in a long simmering scandal in Ireland after the European Commission ruled that the Irish state had given the tech giant undue tax benefits—a total of 13 billion euros. When it ordered the Irish government to recover this tax, Ireland refused since the country wanted to send a message to the international investment community that Ireland is a safe place to invest. These dynamics existed side by side with Ireland's debt to GDP—108.2 percent in 2013 versus 32 percent in 2007 (Blyth 2013, 236–7). In the end, the Irish paid the highest per capita cost of bailing out European financial institutions, proportionally speaking (Hearne 2015)—a form of violence that would "enslave" the nation through debt.

The impact of austerity produced a deprivation rate that rose from 11 percent of the population in 2007 to 25 percent in 2011 and then, in 2014, to a staggering 31 percent—almost 1.4 million people. A staggering 13.2 percent of the population suffered food poverty, while male suicides increased by

57 percent (O'Shanahan 2015).[21] Homelessness and unemployment rates soared. Emigration rates were the highest among European states. Former Minister for Finance Brian Lenihan noted that many European countries were "amazed" at Irish budgetary adjustments since there would be riots if they were introduced elsewhere. Ireland (unlike Greece) was held up as an example of a successful bailout model that maintained social order during both austerity measures and financial sector bailouts (Hearne 2015, 4).

That acquiescence would not last long. In early March 2011, a small group of people in the tiny North Cork village of Ballyhea decided to march in protest along their main road. It was lunchtime, right after church, and they walked slowly, blocking rows and rows of traffic behind them. As Diarmuid O'Flynn, a mustached and bespectacled engineer-turned-journalist who in 2016 was working for European parliamentarian Luke Ming Flanagan in Brussels, told me, "We walked up to the end of the village on the main road where the speed limit sign is. And then we turned around and just walked back. And that was it." O'Flynn had initiated the group after repeatedly writing and emailing politicians about the injustice of the bailout. But that day in March, he "made an A4 sheet and pinned it to a little bit of plywood, and that was the first step. We then did it again the next week, with a banner that read 'Ballyhea Says No to Bond-Holder Bail-Out.'" Soon, the group began to film its marches and circulate the images and videos through their Facebook page, "Ballyhea Bondholder Bailout Protest." Journalists from all over came to report on what came to be known as "Ballyhea Says No." Other villages and neighborhoods began to form their own "Says No" groups. All marched Sundays after mass, some marchers wearing yellow reflective vests, others silently holding antiausterity banners, all bringing traffic to an almost standstill behind them. When I walked with Dublin Says No on a Sunday in April of 2016, I was struck by the identical tactic used—the slow march, the blocking of traffic in the middle of busy Dublin for almost an hour without a policeman in sight. When I asked how the marchers were getting away with causing traffic chaos in downtown Dublin every Sunday, one of the marchers said, "I'll tell you why. Because if they touched it, I swear, there would be 100,000 of us here next Sunday, marching again. And they know it." Ballyhea Says No continued to march for six more years. "They've been marching every Sunday for years!" as one of my interlocutors admiringly put it, "They're fucking mad!"

As the Says No movement grew, with innumerable groups emerging all over Ireland, changes to the financing and management of Irish Water services were already underway. The Troika program had come with a specific set of conditions regarding water provisioning in Ireland. An initial Memorandum of Economic and Financial Policies had included provisions for water charges that would help secure fiscal targets. A National Recovery Plan of 2011–2014 similarly contained plans to introduce domestic water charges based on water use, in order to fund local authority water services (Dukelow 2016, 152). This meant that, over a twelve-year period, the management of water and waste-water services would be transferred from thirty-four local authorities to a new, centralized, and self-financing state water company. The goal was to take Irish Water off the general balance sheet (since that would show up as "public debt"), but this could only occur once Irish Water passed the EuroStat "market corporation test." As Bresnihan explains, this test checks whether independent state companies or utilities can operate within European competition regulations, a process that involves the company demonstrating that it can wean itself off government subsidies, efficiently marshal a captive income stream, and thereby effectively orient itself toward global financial markets (Bresnihan 2016, 120). The desperate attempt on the part of the state to manage unruly populations and to subdue working-class mobilizations must be understood from within a context of intense state desire for global investor approval and validation, a craving to demonstrate the capacity to become a good debtor.

By April 2012, the government announced that water charges would be introduced in 2014 with water meters installed that year; it was a huge infrastructural project that would see about 27,000 installations a month on average over three years. The Minister of the Environment at that time, Phil Hogan, infamously warned that those who refused to pay would see the reduction of their water pressure to a mere "trickle" (see also Anand 2011, 546). By 2013, the government passed a Water Services Bill, rushing it through the Dáil (the Irish parliament) in just four hours in mid-December amid protest from the opposition. The bill established Irish Water as the new state water company responsible for the operation, maintenance, and improvement of all water services infrastructure, customer billing, and charging.[22] All these decisions were made despite protestations on the part of local authorities, including Dublin City Council, which worried that the side-lining of local authorities would adversely affect local democracy and accountability and negatively impact the quality of the service itself (Bresnihan 2016, 120). The government paid an initial 250 million euros for the transformation of local Water Services Authorities into Irish Water, including a weekly 81,000 euros on legal fees, 500 million euros for meter installation, and around 450 million euros for everyday management.

Many of these transformations coincided with a national scandal over the so-called Anglo Tapes, where a phone conversation between two Anglo Irish Bank executives talking about their request for rescue funds out of state coffers after the 2008 banking collapse was secretly recorded. Asked how they had come up with the initial figure of 7 billion euros, one banker said that he had "picked it out of my arse," with the pair heard laughing about how the debt could never be paid back. At the same time and in the midst of public anger over cynical bankers, Irish Water's CEO, John Tierney, showed up on TV holding a glass of water and a new water meter in his hand, noting that fifty million euros would be spent on consultancies and contractors to help set up the company. The money spent to establish Irish Water was taken from the government's National Reserve Pension Fund (now Irish Strategic Investment Fund) and the Irish motor tax that would have otherwise gone to the thirty-four local authorities (Fitzpatrick 2015; Bresnihan 2016, 118; Ryan 2015). Eighty-five million euros were spent on external consultancy services. Leaked reports described Irish Water's new corporate culture as one that included massive bonuses for staff, laughing yoga classes, and a fully equipped gym (Murphy 2019). Referring to the Irish economy during the boom years, "we were told that we partied," as David Gibney, a union organizer from Mandate, a private sector union of low-paid bar and retail workers and a key figure in Ireland's Right2Water movement put it. "A lot of people believed that. But as time has gone on people said, "Hold on a second—that wasn't me partying. [A small number of] people partied, and we have to pick up the bill" (Fitzpatrick 2015). To many people at the time, Irish Water was simply the latest manifestation of a bailout that was nothing more than a sell-off of vital public goods to laughing bankers.

At the same time, there is no question that Irish water utilities are in dire straits. An antiquated nineteenth-century infrastructure—60,000 kilometers of mostly underground piping—is leaking at a dizzying rate of 40 percent. An estimated 23,000 people are currently (or have for years been) on boil water notices due to the risk of microbiological contamination as well as, more recently, lead that has dissolved into the water supply from aging water pipes (Bresnihan 2016, 117; Doris et al. 2013). Hundreds have fallen ill with cryptosporidium poisoning. Ireland has also failed to meet the requirements of the EU Urban Waste Water Treatment Directive, leading to the European Commission initiating an Infringement Case. Ireland, like Italy, is facing a "colossal task" that requires major financial and technical resources (Bresnihan 2016, 3)—a task that austerity-era Irish government decided would be achieved through the move from local water utilities into a more efficient, centralized corporation.[23]

Importantly, however, the move to metering was not a move from fully public to privatized water provisioning. In fact, private sector involvement in local Irish water utilities had already grown exponentially via public-private partnerships since the late 1990s. A full 63 percent of all public-private partnerships already in operation in Ireland are contracted in the water sector; Ireland, along with Greece, sported the second highest level of public-private partnerships in wastewater services in Europe as of 2008 (Dukelow 2016, 157; Bieler 2021, 134–35).[24] What this means is that the bad condition of Irish water utilities cannot be reduced to so-called inefficiencies of the public sector. Rather, it must be analyzed from within the context of already almost thirty years of partial privatization, with 115 public-private partnerships managing 232 utilities across Ireland (Bieler 2021, 134). The turn to a centralized company thus meant the rescaling and intensification of an already ongoing process of privatization. The water meter was in this context the crucial device through which already partially privatized utilities could demonstrate their availability and amenability to global financial markets.

Ecological arguments were mobilized, too. Irish Water and the Green Party consistently argued that meters would help the Irish save water better.[25] But the question of metering as an environmentally more ethical practice was highly controversial among many of my interlocutors, who cited an Irish Water report that noted that people in the United Kingdom (where water was metered almost thirty years ago) use 68,505 liters of water per person per annum. In unmetered Ireland, people use 54,750 liters per person per annum, about 20 percent less (Ogle 2016, 24–25). Metering, in short, can but need not lead to better water governance.[26] It is a technical fix to complex social, political, and environmental challenges that can but do not necessarily lead to better water stewardship. In this case, water meters were clearly a prelude toward accelerating an already ongoing process of privatization and infrastructure financialization.[27]

The Irish water insurgencies thus politicized both infrastructural and environmental emergencies, arguing that these dual disasters were the result of political decisions that had led to chronic underinvestment in vital infrastructures. By 2013, groups like Ballyhea Says No and Ballyphehane/South Parish Says No were actively campaigning around the issue. Many other community groups, the Unite and Mandate trade unions, antiausterity campaigners, and members of parliament also began to organize by that time, insisting that "Our Water Is Not for Sale" (Murphy 2019). Creating a national network of Right2Water groups that spanned the territory, unions like Mandate organized townhalls that introduced a certain financial fluency among ordinary citizens, with complex debt and bailout economies patiently explained in a peer-to-peer process (Ogle 2016). One interlocutor commented on the "fantastic educational programs" that these unions organized, allowing her to "join the dots from my stopcock [the valve that regulates the flow of water through pipes or faucets] right across the world." This education "literally helped to create the water movement" by rendering political not only infrastructural and ecological decline, but the structural violence of debt-fueled national accounting.

### No More Blood from These Stones

When Irish Water began to install the meters in sidewalks, it argued that this would allow the company to read meters via a drive-by method. Irish Water also assured its customers that it would not need to enter their properties to take readings and that it could instead be done more efficiently. Yet these dreams of efficiency quickly turned into Irish Water's nightmare. Little did it anticipate that people like Suzanne were waiting for them already. Suzanne had been warned by members of an antiausterity neighborhood group called Ballyphehane/South Parish Says No that Irish Water would be coming and telling her that metering would lead to yet another bill that she would have to pay. When Irish Water arrived that morning in April of 2014, Suzanne immediately called the group, asking for reinforcement. Soon, "the lads" from Ballyphehane came to stand beside her, as did Noreen Murphy, a prominent Cork water activist whom I've never once seen without her self-designed black t-shirt, boldly emblazoned with neon pink letters reading WATER IS A HUMAN RIGHT. "There were three to four Irish Water trucks at the time," Suzanne told me, "but I wouldn't get off the road."

The first standoff lasted all day. Ashbrook Heights is built in a loop-like structure with only one entrance for cars. Blocking the entrance was easy, which is why Irish Water tried to sneak in at 5:00 a.m. the next day but only managed to dig up five holes in the sidewalk in the back of the estate, installing five meters. Chuckling, Suzanne told me that Irish Water workers soon also tried to jump over the walkway and get the machinery in from the back, hauling it in manually. "Yeah," said Suzanne, "there were those shenanigans. But really, we were lucky because we only have one entrance. Once they were in we kept them in, and stopped the work, obstructed and drew it out for the day . . . creating havoc, basically." As city councilor Ted Tynan put it, "In the working-class areas, the poverty is greater, the people are more determined, and women are tougher, y'know. They'll smoke their cigarette, and no one's fucking going in there, y'know!" Ashbrook Heights negotiated for three days for the five meters to be removed. "By that time," Suzann said, "we had TV3 and reporters and everything ready to go and put it on video. We wanted to say [to the people of Ireland], 'It can be done if you stand your ground.'" Soon, "Palmbury came up to stand with us and then Sharon Dean took it around Ellenville. It was a domino effect. People just came and stood their ground. The day they took out our meters was the day we made history, I suppose."

A video showing five new Ashbrook Heights meters being removed and replaced with the old ones, with Suzanne's booming voice in the background as she oversaw the workers backtracking on their work, received over 28,000 views.[28] Residents, especially in other working-class neighborhoods, soon followed suit in their effort to express the fact that they wanted to reinstall older, district-level ways of measuring and paying for water. Groups became increasingly coordinated with people standing alert in the early morning and using social media and text messaging to warn each other of Irish Water trucks' arrival (Muehlebach 2017). In Cobh, the "Great Island" located just off Ireland's southern coast, which can only be reached via Belvelly Bridge, people stood guard on the mainland side of the bridge very early in the morning, texting each other as the Irish Water trucks approached and letting their neighbors know which direction they were heading. By the time the trucks arrived at their destinations, people were often already waiting for them in groups, blocking the trucks' entry into their estates.

In part, it was the infrastructure of working-class neighborhoods, designed and built as an "insurance against socialist revolution" in early twentieth-century England and Ireland, that created the material conditions for mass insurgency (see also Chu 2014). Irish housing estates are often built in the British postwar "garden suburbs" style, with houses built along cul-de-sacs with few entrances and a single road lined with sidewalks. Parts of the housing area is reserved for open spaces ("greens"), which almost always take the form of a single block of nonlandscaped land (McManus 2011, 260–61). These features of the working-class estate—the cul-de-sacs with single entrances that allowed for the easy erection of barriers, the open greens that created space for public assembly, and the sidewalks that allowed for meter installation—created the material conditions for women, men, and children to assemble and strategize in the vicinity of their homes after work and then go on to collectively block meter installation in front of their houses.

Often, it was thus precisely the publicity of sidewalks (in Italy for example, meters are usually installed within or along the sides of private residences) that allowed for members of working-class households to appear in public in highly mediatized and widely shared scenes of meter blockages. The cul-de-sac structure of many housing estates similarly allowed for the staging and rapid multiplication of scenes of struggle that pitted uniformed police with batons and helmets against ordinary people. It was thus certainly poverty and the rapid intensification of inequality that propelled people into protest. But it was also the material legacy of publicly provided working-class housing and its shape and sociality that allowed for people to gather together in their refusal of metering. The "architecture of the riot" (Clover 2016, 138) in short, was grounded in the architecture of the working-class estate, which allowed for people to come together to performatively claim the weight of the sovereign—the people—with their own bodies (Butler 2015).[29] If meters signaled the divisibility of a previously indivisible resource, then the public nature of the metering in sidewalks and the organizing that took place on the greens allowed for an indivisible public to appear through assembly, and for this public to make a clear set of political and ethical demands. Put differently, the barriers and blockages had a highly symbolic resonance as they conjured a recursive relationship between public infrastructure, the collective body of protest that gathered on them to assert its indivisible sociality and publicity, and the political demands that were made—progressive taxation, where all members of society, including corporations, pay their fair share. This was a share that all ought to contribute to according to ability, rather than individual meters and bills where everyone pays the same depending on metered use. At a moment when both the livability of private life and the politics of the public sphere have been radically questioned under the weight of financialization, the Irish water insurgency posed "insurgent questions" about the public, its indivisibility, and tax (Gillespie, 2022; Gillespie and Naidoo 2019, 229). It thus performatively staged the demand for a polity that protects the nation from a logic of extraction and instead collectively gathers its monetary resources and redistributes them back in—into the aging water infrastructure in need of repair, into the labor that makes water flow, and into the water that needs to run free.

By the time the Irish Water trucks arrived, people were often already waiting for them in groups or sat, lay, stood—often for hours—on sidewalks and streets. Most of the people mobilizing were those who were at home during the day: the elderly, the unemployed, and, most importantly, the women. As one interlocutor who spoke to me on condition of anonymity because he was still active as a "water fairy" at the time said, "Make *sure* you include this. The women are the backbone of this campaign. Absolutely without a shadow of doubt. They are the ones who took to the streets, they are the ones who told their husbands to get out there! When history is written on this, it was clear that women were driving it." Cobh community organizer Karen Doyle confirmed this by saying to me in a follow-up conversation in 2020, "[The water movement] allowed our voice to be heard and not be afraid and to be bold. To be really bold and obstreperous and get out there and speak when we felt rage. . . . It gave me the confidence to later stand up about abortion rights and marriage equality, and I was able to kind of frame discussion around that [in ways] that I may not have been able to do before being involved with water."

During the blockades, elderly ladies brought out folding chairs and sipped cups of tea as they sat outside. Young men crouched in the holes the company had already dug, or sometimes clung to diggers. Men and women blocked the trucks' entry into the estates, or crowded around them and imprisoned the workers, sometimes for hours because protestors simply would not budge. People locked arms. Women, men, and children sang. Blockages sometimes lasted days, which meant that neighborhoods had to get organized into shifts and hold nightly meetings on the central greens about everything from what to wear to who would collect the children from school and make food. As one young woman said, "People had each other's backs. Many of the working-class estates all over the country were in complete lockdown. We simply wouldn't let Irish Water in. Communities, so alienated from each other and broken by poverty, evictions, unemployment, came together. It was magic" (see also Brophy 2015). The barricade here was much more than a blockading device. It became, as Leanne Betasamosake Simpson (2021) put it, a vehicle for the building of sociality, community, life.

By the first deadline of October 21, 2014, only a third of the 1.5 million would-be customer households had registered their details with Irish Water, forcing it to seek permission from the regulator to extend the registration deadline to November 29 (Murphy 2019). By that time, Right2Water had also taken off, a union-led attempt to gather local protests together into a more coherent national umbrella movement that resulted in several huge national demonstrations, the first of which took place on Sunday, October 11,

2014, and that drew tens of thousands of protestors, numbers that went well beyond organizers' expectations. It was in these initial community actions and at later, even larger mass demonstrations, where a coherent national conversation not simply against austerity but also over the question of violence began to emerge. The financial frontier, in short, unfolded not just as a scene of violence, but as a conversation about what violence is in the first place. Protestors were explicit about what they argued was the violence of austerity, thus juxtaposing their own political protest with the systemic, "ambient" forms of economic violence that saturated the social fabric (Clover 2016, 13).

The political message was as simple as it was profound: like other antiausterity critiques where protestors lamented the declining taxability within welfare states, Irish protesters insisted on the reintroduction of progressive tax or water tariffs, where everyone, including corporations, pays their fair share. This argument around tax justice was particularly poignant in Ireland—a country with a particularly low tax model (Dukelow 2016, 150). For protestors, a direct connection existed between the socialization of banking debt and the planned regressive meter charges, meaning that the debts created by private banks would be carried equally by both rich and poor. Regressive water charges, while commonsensical on the surface ("we all use water equally and should therefore pay equally for its use"), appeared absurd in light of the fact that all Irish were asked to equally shoulder bills within a context of a spiraling wealth gap. Water charges would be felt differentially if spread equally across the body politic. As was the case in the South African struggle against prepaid water meters, and as similarly stated by several US mayors in light of the Detroit catastrophe, uniform pricing structures create enormous burdens for lower-income households (von Schnitzler 2016; Lappé 2014). It was thus not just that "a millionaire would pay the same for water as someone on social welfare," as one interlocutor put it to me, but that the bottom income decile of Irish households would soon be at risk of water poverty, which is defined as occurring when households spend more than 3–5 percent of their disposable income on water (Dukelow 2016, 154; Bradshaw and Huby 2013).[30] The point was to do away with water charges and Irish Water altogether and to reintroduce a different kind of pricing structure and, by implication, redistributive politics.

Organizers were clear in terms of the tax conversation they wanted to have: as Brendan Ogle, one of the main union organizers and founders of the union-led Right2Water movement said, the Irish pay close to EU average income taxes and consumption taxes such as VAT and excise duties, while employers and corporations "pay just about one-third of the EU average in Employer's Social Insurance. In 2012, they paid 7.7 percent while the EU average was 20.5 percent." The result is a public service system that is woefully inadequate, with Irish citizens paying for basic services out of their net incomes—services that in other countries are paid for by large employers through tax. As the EU put it, Ireland would have to increase spending on public services, income supports, and investment by 11 billion euros a year to reach the EU average (Ogle 2016, 184–87).

Protestors were thus insisting not naively on nonpayment, but for a reimagination of a politics of redistribution and social contract mediated by the state.[31] Regressive fees, so the protesters' fiscal argument went, symbolized something akin to the quasicolonial bondage to European banks and, by implication, global financial markets (as one commentator put it on Facebook, Irish Water "will only take our money off-shore—like food during the famine . . . !"). The commentator was here referencing the fact that the mid-nineteenth-century British colonial government argued that the laissez-faire free market would allow for the adequate distribution of food. The Irish nationalist argument has since been that millions of Irish men, women, and children starved because the British exported it.[32] In the 1915–1916 water insurgency, payment through government tax was thus widely understood to be an act of nation building and collective solidarity that would keep wealth circulating within the body politic. Payment through individual household bills would, in contrast, set the stage for another round of foreign value extraction. Brendon Ogle (2016) used that resonant language, too, when he spoke of the need to "reclaim our Republic" after Ireland had lost its "economic independence and sovereignty" through "economic imperialism" (7).

The popular juxtaposition of a national commonwealth versus slavery and colonial dispossession came to life in the way people spoke to me about the meters themselves, pointing them out as we walked through their neighborhoods. Like the old water fountains in Italy that many of my interlocutors had a special affection for, some people pointed out older water meters to me as well, remarking on their beauty and comparing them to the "soulless" new water meters right next to them.

Adorned with the ancient Celtic triple spiral symbol and with the Gaelic word for water (uisce), these old, cast-iron meters were "little beauties" that had been used to measure water on a district level and not at the point of household use. They were thus not only potent symbols of earlier welfare

2.2         A beloved "little beauty" (*left*) next to a maligned new meter (*right*). (Photo: Andrea Muehlebach.)

state efforts to guarantee water as a social good, but of a different mode of valuing and calculating water price altogether. Some activists took pictures of the beauties and serially archived images of them on Facebook, lamenting that they had been "looted and replaced with ugly plastic." The new meter, a faceless technical device that simply said "water" in English, was flimsy and easy to break—something that the many meter fairies, who appeared around the time of the protests, mockingly appreciated as they removed hundreds of them in a matter of only a few days (Trommer 2019).

Many of these fairies were still around when I arrived in 2016. They came in all shapes and sizes—men and women, old and young, clad in tutus, masks, all black, or in ordinary clothes, operating both during the day and at night, all over the country. Like the "struggle electricians" and water activists described by Antina von Schnitzler (2016) in her description of South African battles over energy and water democracy, and like the Italian "Super Marios" I describe in chapter 4 of this book, the water fairies used meters as a technopolitical vehicle to assert their small sovereignties over this extractive device. As one meter fairy whom I met in a Dublin McDonalds put it to me, "We've had the IMF in here, we've capitulated to everything. And we just said no, no more. You're not taking our water. I mean, we'll go along with any conservation measure and all that, but privatizing our water? It's like somebody owning our human right, you know what I mean?" As he took me out to his car to proudly show me the tools he used to remove them, the fairy told me tales of how he and a good friend had the time of their lives advertising their services on Facebook ("Give us a shout if you want them out!"). He grinned when he said that they received more requests for meter removal than they could handle. He and his friend were only one of dozens of groups all over Ireland who posted pictures and videos of themselves removing meters. The fairies laughed uproariously as they told me how they threw water meters over the gates of the Dáil (the Irish parliament), transported dozens of meters to the seaside and lined them up in the sand, or took selfies with them, wearing balaclavas or t-shirts over their faces and mockingly circulated these portraits on Facebook. This was a carnivalesque overturning and creative repurposing of the hated meter—a collective showing of the finger to politicians and their nefarious devices. Laughter, here, was a "free weapon" in people's hands, an expression of triumphant "popular truths" in the face of laughing bankers and politicians (Bakhtin 1984, 94; Weston 2017, 166–67).

This insurgent laughter and bawdiness was met with stern reproach on the part of politicians, who called the fairies "disgraceful" organizations who were "willingly breaking the law, destroying public property," and attacking "the very fabric of the State." Warning that fairies would be made subject to criminal proceedings and fined up to 5,000 euros or imprisoned for up to three months, or both (Healy 2015), government officials were met with derision by people who thought of their activities as noble since they were ultimately engaged in the ethical task of removing the infrastructure of an unjust extractivism. Juxtaposing the two types of meters was thus like juxtaposing two eras—one characterized by what many people thought of as an age of national resource sovereignty, and one characterized as an age of nonsovereignty to finance capital. Some people I met went so far as to argue that the new meters were toxic, emitting radiation that was harmful to humans, possibly even driving them mad. The meters were thus uncanny signs of a merciless austerity regime that both literally and figuratively had the capacity to render invisible unseen damage onto their worlds (Lepselter 2016). Like the anonymous force of finance, the newer plastic meters symbolized the invisible powers that preyed on national wealth and left only injury and injustice behind.

None of these critiques came out of the blue. In cities like Dublin, many people had long struggled against various charges and fees. When I asked about water, they explained their anger to me by referencing the 2008 bin charges, which had seen the city privatize waste management services and spark off a series of small-scale revolts. As one water fairy put it, "First, they transformed the public service into a public limited company. Then they introduced charges: five euros per bin at first. Within two years of having introduced the bin charges, the service was privatized. By now [2016], it's gone up 100 percent—10 euros!—and there's a standing charge for each bin now as well every year. This is the same model they're trying to bring in with water too. So we knew straight away what was going to happen." It was, already then, working-class neighborhoods who protested vehemently against these charges. For them, government had become nothing much more than an extractive machine, burdening the poor with layers of taxes and fees.

### Police

Little of this argument about taxation and fiscal justice was heard by the mainstream political classes. Even water activists from other parts of Europe initially misunderstood the Irish struggle for water. As David Gibney said to me in an interview over coffee in Dublin in 2016, he was flummoxed when attending a meeting by the European Water Movement in Marseille in 2015, when one Italian water activist noted that "the Irish do not want to pay for their water; it seems that Catholics believe water should be free." It took Gibney a while to explain that "we were already paying for water!" Back in Ireland, Irish activists similarly described their frustration with attempting to convey their political message through the mainstream media. How could they, if Denis O'Brien—an Irish billionaire who owns such extensive Irish newspaper and radio holdings that he has been able to create one of the "most concentrated media markets of any democracy" (Leahy 2016)—was also awarded the contract to install the water meters for Irish Water by the Irish Minister of the Environment (O'Halloran 2014)?[33]

Instead, protestors were called "anarchists," "dissidents," and "lazy nationalists" by the press, "implying we were terrorists" who "don't want to pay for anything" (Ogle 2016, 110).[34] Indeed, arguments by protesters often only register as "noise" in the press, not as coherent discourse or "voice." This registering of arguments as noise is not a question of "mutual incomprehension," as Erik Swyngedouw (2018, 28) puts it, but an active process whereby dissent is rendered incomprehensible and nonsensical, reducing those who disagree to the political margins and leaving them politically mute. This muting occurred not only through the actively produced erroneous assumption that water activists refuse to pay for water and instead insist that it ought to be "free," but also through criminalization—the consistent conflation of political protest with delinquency and mob rule.

Trim resident Tony Rochford was the first person to be arrested and charged under the 1994 Criminal Justice and Public Order Act. He had used his car to block an Irish Water vehicle from exiting a cul-de-sac in his estate on May 28, 2014. Images of him being arrested, and of others involved in scuffles with police, were closely watched in Ireland, with pictures and articles shared on social media soon receiving tens of thousands of views. This level of public attention and the ability of new social media to "command the center of a news cycle" and build novel "structures of addressivity" (Cody 2020, 59) contrasted starkly with the bin charges protests that had also attracted significant support in working-class areas of cities like Dublin but had been less visible in the then much less developed social media landscape of the early 2000s (McGee 2015). By 2014, viewers on YouTube were able not only to watch Tony calmly explain to the police why he was blocking his street, and subsequently being arrested as his wife filmed him (over 40,000 views) but to watch hundreds of other protestors—older men holding kids, women with cigarettes in hand, young people blocking machines—insist that they never gave consent to Irish Water and never signed a contract.

Then Jobstown happened. On November 15, 2014, Joan Burton, the Labor Party leader at the time, visited the working-class suburb of Jobstown on the outskirts of Dublin to attend a graduation ceremony. She was met with hostility; anger at the Labor Party was at an all-time high. Ireland's largest conservative political parties, Fianna Fáil and Fine Gael, had embraced the Troika program during their 2011 election campaigns. Labor, in contrast, had promised to renegotiate the bailout and repeatedly expressed its rejection of the looming water tax. It was rewarded for this stance by an increase of its vote share by almost 10 percent during the election of 2011. But as soon as it entered into a Fine-Gael-led coalition, it performed an about-face, moving from opposition to water charges and from insisting that water was "a basic and fundamental need [which] should not be treated like a market commodity" to arguing that the Irish ought to "give Irish Water a chance" since "things change" (Eagleton 2017). As one interlocutor put it to me, "They basically turned their backs on the poor and crucified the working classes."

When Burton entered Jobstown, she found herself in a suburb where 61 percent of all families were single-headed households, many of whose state allowance had been slashed by her Social Welfare and Pensions Bill—one of Labor's "earliest capitulations to the austerity program" (Eagleton 2017). Water charges, however small, were thus met with fury. Dozens of people, including recently elected Anti-Austerity Alliance (AAA) politician Paul Murphy as well as members of the Republican-Socialist party Éirígí, began a sit-down protest in front of the Labor leader's car, then surrounded it and prevented her from leaving for about three hours. While accounts of what happened that day differ starkly, with many news outlets reporting the car being surrounded and banged on with fists, protestors argued that the protest had been peaceful, that Burton was not scared, and that "she was in fact laughing at us" while "checking her cell phone," as I heard people say over and over. The next day at dawn, more than forty Jobstown protesters were arrested in raids conducted by police. Three of those apprehended were prominent AAA politicians; seven were juveniles between the ages of thirteen and seventeen. Twenty-three were eventually indicted with charges ranging from "criminal damage" to "false imprisonment"—an offense that in Ireland carries the maximum sentence of life in prison.

The Jobstown event soon became a lightning rod for discussions over the nature of anti–water charges protests and of whether Jobstown was a political or criminal event. A number of politicians took the opportunity to call protestors "sinister," warning that "they break the law," "engaged in violence," and that "it is only a matter of time before someone gets hurt" (*Independent* 2014). Such characterizations of social protest heightened the legitimacy of police presence in working-class neighborhoods. The media followed suit, describing in detail the supposed violence and delinquency of protestors who "incited hatred." Clearly, an article went on to note, there was a "fine line between peaceful protest and mob rule" (McGee 2015).

This language rehearsed a long-standing, routinized, and highly racialized demonization of the protesting poor across Irish history. In the late nineteenth century, when the Irish Land League mobilized vast segments of the population to engage in the boycotting of existing, high-rent land tenure systems, British critics described protesters as "primitive men" and "savages in our midst" who were propelled by a "mob mentality" and spreading a "reign of terror" (Phemister 2019, 36–42). Jobstown protestors were almost identically described as engaging in "acts of violence and terrorism" (Eagleton 2017). This is not surprising given the colonial origins of policing in Ireland, which always implicitly hinged on protecting English elites and on controlling a rebellious populace (Manning 2012, 351; see also Arextaga 2000). Indeed, even though the Irish Gardai represent the Irish state as "the first new democracy in the twentieth century—a "quasi-democratic force mandated to protect the interests of the emergent [postcolonial] state"—it also still bears a "shadowy resemblance" to its colonial precursors, notably the Irish Constabulary founded in 1836 and then renamed the Royal Irish Constabulary (RIC) in 1867 (Manning 2012, 351–52). The Irish Constabulary's original role was that of "an imposer of force on the people" and a constant reminder that "Ireland could only be governed by force." While becoming more "domesticated" by the end of the nineteenth century, the current Irish police must be understood from within this longue durée mentality: that local populations needed to be policed with a force that is, at times, highly militarized (Sinclair 2008, 173–74).[35]

Until today, everyday enforcement emphasized the authority of the individual Garda who often operate in discretionary ways. Modestly trained and rarely supervised or reviewed when dealing with complex incidents, the officer often works independently of "supervision, direction, general public opinion, or policy" (Manning 2012, 356). The law thus not only confers "a wide range of coercive powers (and duties) directly on each individual police officer," but also "affords the officer exceptionally broad discretion over how or whether to exercise that power in any law enforcement situation" (Walsh 2018, 625). The discretionary actions by Irish police were compounded by the intimidation tactics of the private security company Guardex that some people I met rumored Irish Water had hired. As residents in the Dublin neighborhood of Stoneybatter put it in a Facebook post, Guardex employees were "hiding their faces with gaiters, sunglasses, and hats, and when we ask them to show us some ID, they refuse. It's awful what they do, hanging around our communities with their faces covered all day." Here, specters of illicit state-mediated violence filled social-media networks; neighborhoods were haunted by the persecutory power of the state (Aretxaga 2003, 402).

Soon, a court injunction banned all protests within twenty yards of meter installation, prompting even more arrests. The images of police violence against water protestors that circulated so widely on social media contributed significantly to a "huge drain in public confidence in the Garda" (Walsh 2018, 622). It did not help that five Dublin protestors were given jail sentences ranging from twenty-eight to fifty-six days (Eagleton 2017). Two of the jailed, Derek Byrne and Pauly Moore, engaged in the tried-and-true strategy of Irish Republican opposition to colonial rule: the hunger strike. By February 21, 2015, several thousand protestors rallied in Dublin in support of the two jailed protesters, all under the auspices of the growing

"Jobstown Not Guilty" campaign. Holding up signs in English and Gaelic, protestors chanted "From the River to the See, Irish Water will be Free!" and "You cannot Tax a God Given Gift!"

In addition to these jailings and new sets of protests, courts issued injunctions to mandate an increased police presence at protests, with up to forty officers overseeing Irish Water metering work in some Dublin neighborhoods. A similar "special force" of twenty-five officers was established in Cork with the mandate to protect meter installation. Many arrests were made, including of protestors in Wicklow in East Cork who formed blockades at depots where Irish Water meter materials were stored. Like late nineteenth-century judicial statements that hinged on concerns over the protection of private property and social order (Phemister 2019, 39), a number of protestors who stood within the barriers set up by Irish Water on the sidewalks reported being accused of "trespassing" on private property. Protestors instead insisted that protests were their civil right and that they could not be removed. Others were detained and accused of causing "apprehension for the safety of persons and property" by "loitering in a public place." As is often the case in frontier situations, the legal situation on the ground was extraordinarily indeterminate, with questions raised whether this was public or private property and whether protestors were "trespassing" on private property or "loitering" in a public space.

The financial frontier, in short, here revealed itself to be not only a zone of violence and political repression, but a zone where the status of property—private or common or public—was put to question. For a moment, public sidewalks hovered indeterminately between attempts at their conversion (from public land into the "private property" of Irish Water—hence, the accusation of "trespassing") and their continued public nature (hence the accusation of "loitering"). Both of these attempts at criminalization were challenged by those who insisted that this was not a question of property (or crime) at all, but of rights—the civil right to protest. In some cases, I heard that lone protestors sitting or standing in holes dug by Irish Water were arrested and charged with "incitement to riot." Soon, the twenty-three facing trial for the Jobstown event became international causes célèbres, receiving statements of support from international trade unions and public intellectuals including Angela Davis, Ken Loach, Yanis Varoufakis, and Jean-Luc Mélenchon. Noam Chomsky noted that convictions against the Jobstown activists "would have the effect of criminalizing protest and sending a chilling message to all those who would seek to protest in the coming years."[36]

By mid-2015, less than 50 percent of people were paying their bills, which meant that Irish Water soon after failed the Eurostat test. While the government responded by insisting that this was a minor setback, it quickly took out more short-term loans from commercial banks in an attempt to pass. In the meantime, "passing the test" entailed more than mere fiscal and managerial work. It also entailed demonstrating that the state was able to protect and secure its critical infrastructures from disruptive populations (Pasternak and Dafnos 2018). As Peterson put it for the case of Nigeria under structural adjustment in the 1980s, austerity and its attendant financialized debt-economies form "a necessary intimacy" with violence—a violence that sees both unruly local populations and global investors as their primary addressees (Peterson 2014, 63).[37]

When police began to accompany Irish Water workers and formed rings around the holes in the ground to physically ward off protestors, some protestors in Cork began to appear on the streets wearing the same bright yellow reflective vests that the Garda (and many Irish Water workers) came in. This gave rise to scenarios where Gardai, donning their yellow reflective vests, were filmed arresting protestors donning the very same vests.[38] The protestors thus conjured more than a generic body of solidarity at the financial frontier—a barrier against the expropriation of a common good. They performatively asserted a public that both mimicked and critiqued the police, laying bare its violence while attempting to hail it back into guardianship. After all, the Garda Síochána are, as much as they emerge out of colonial Ireland's shadowy past, simultaneously also iconic of new, postcolonial beginnings: "They stand for authority of an indigenous sort, in some sense for an Ireland free of England, and an organization intrinsically and originally Irish" (Manning 2012, 354). Composed historically of "young, strong, modestly educated, white, Catholic men" (McNiffe 1997), the Garda "represented Irish social values" and was thus held sacred (Manning 2012, 353).

To be sure, a number of my interlocutors recognized that the Garda were not always violent and that they "were just doing their jobs," noting that new recruits in particular were faced with "shite" salaries and that they were probably not only in full agreement with the antiwater meter campaign but also struggling to pay their mortgages and water bills, just like everybody else. But many still confronted the Gardaí for siding with a government that was handing over their water and its metering to one of the richest and most unpopular entrepreneurs in the country. Some evoked the oath all Gardaí make upon entering the force, namely, to "faithfully discharge the duties of a member of the Garda Síochána with fairness, integrity, regard for human rights, diligence, and impartiality, upholding the Constitution and the laws and according equal respect to all people." Instead, many argued that the police were not a neutral force but stood accused of what AAA politician Paul Murphy called "political policing," thus aligning the Garda with a "long-standing perception [in Ireland] of a police-government relationship in which the immediate political and institutional interests of the latter prevail to the prejudice of a professional and publicly accountable police service" (Walsh 2018, 623). The police, in short, were for many of my interlocutors nothing much more than executioners of a faraway, unjust system.

During his court trial, sixty-six-year-old Sean Doyle, jailed for protesting the water-meter installation program in Wicklow, stated the following:

> I did not come here voluntarily. I was summoned here by your court of law. Our struggle for justice, equality, and fair distribution of wealth and our natural resources is constantly at variance and impeded by your laws. . . . Criminal to me is homelessness, children sleeping on the streets. Criminal to me is bailing out banks while people are being evicted from their homes. Criminal to me is the robbery of our natural resources while children go hungry. Criminal to me is the Leinster House committee embarrassed and reluctant to collect billions of corporate taxes from Apple and others while the health and other services crumble with a half a million on waiting lists to see specialists. Criminal to me is to stand by and allow our water to be privatized. Every meter in the ground is a meter closer to privatization. Criminal to me is when all our resources are being robbed and our rights as citizens eroded and enforced by your laws.

Doyle was declared not guilty.

## On Social and Other Contracts

In April 2016, after attending a meeting by Ballyphehane Says No, I took a walk in Cork and meandered along the long lanes of brownstone houses in the town's working-class neighborhoods. I was struck by the many posters that still stuck in the windows of many of the homes—thousands that had been printed and circulated a year earlier. Printed in striking whites and reds, they read "NO CONSENT. NO CONTRACT. NO TO WATER PRIVATIZATION. NO

2.3    "No Consent, No Contract." Cork, 2016. (Photo: Andrea Muehlebach.)

WATER METERS HERE." These posters were the remnants of the second leg of the Irish water campaign in 2014 and 2015, when people whose water meters had already been installed insisted on nonpayment.

The nonpayment of water bills was a key tactic of the campaign, with many people insisting that they would be willing to go to prison "rather than pay for a fundamental human right" (Murphy 2019). The Irish here drew on their venerable tradition of the boycott that they had invented in the late nineteenth century as a nonviolent form of political protest against landowners' collection of exorbitant rents and that has, in the century since, globally circulated as a political tactic.[39] While there were tensions and disagreements in the water movement over boycotts as a political strategy (Ogle 2016, 145–46), the nonpayment campaign was successful, with less than 50 percent of the population paying their bills by April 2015 (Bresnihan 2016, 6).[40] The Irish government responded by amending the original 1872 Debtor's Act, passing a new Civil Debt (Procedures) Act in November of 2015. Though less draconian than the power originally granted to Irish Water under the 2013 Water Services (No.2) Act, which allowed for the reduction of water supply to households with unpaid bills (a provision removed in the Water Services Act of 2014), the 2015 Act introduced measures that levied late payment charges on unpaid bills and enforced debt repayment through automatic deductions to social welfare payments or wages.

Some activists noted that this cruel tactic had its legal loopholes. One pamphlet circulating on the internet that year stated that Irish Water would have to prove that debtors were in breach of contract—something they could not do if the debtor had never explicitly consented to being Irish Water's client. It also called upon Irish Water's purported debtors to send Irish Water letters by registered post, noting that they were not Irish Water's customers and that the installed meter or any readings taken from it "will not be construed as a contract either explicit or implied" (O'Rourke 2015). Contrary to the presumption underlying privately financed infrastructure projects, where investors think of themselves as contracting with "consumers" (Langley 2018, 178), the Irish refused this presumption outright.

While it is difficult to say how many protestors were actually prepared to go to court for nonpayment, my point here is to foreground the ways in which this simple red-and-white poster, with hundreds stuck in people's windows, raised provocative questions regarding contracts—social and otherwise. Cutting right into the heart of liberal capitalist fantasy, which holds that a contract occurs between two freely contracting parties who both voluntarily and intentionally consent to contractual duties and obligations (Appel 2019, 140), protestors turned this presumption on its head. Instead, thousands insisted that they had never given their free consent to Irish Water and that they were, in essence, nonconsenting third parties in an illegitimate contractual exchange. The question they raised was whether a government could sign contracts on behalf of the people, thus wittingly binding nonconsenting households to Irish Water.

The originality of this tactic lies in its politicization of contracts as such. Turning to liberal market ideology and insisting on its foundational core—the contractual individual—protestors used their demonstrated lack of consent as a means to critique the illiberal character of this supposedly liberal market. What appeared as a rational transition to a new, more efficient, and ecologically sound national company was revealed to be not just profoundly undemocratic because of the foregoing of consumer consent, but also a de-facto act of expropriation of the right to contractual freedom. Like the Italians, the Irish asked whether the state had the right to sign a contract on behalf of the people, or whether it was the people who needed to consent to what appeared as the inevitable privatization of their commonwealth. Recall the Italian lawyers I cited in the previous chapter, who argued that privatization there had consisted of purely discretionary governmental choices "with things that were taken to be its property." There, the government was accused of freely disposing of property that was in fact "the property of the people," behaving "like a private individual badly in debt." When Irish families stuck that poster in their windows, they similarly implied that the establishment of Irish Water represented a kind of privatistic "eminent domain," whereby their rights as citizens had been unilaterally seized (Radin 2012, 14). The fundamental challenge raised here was what collective property is, how it should be held, and who the proper contracting parties ought to be.

This argument about contracts has been used in different guises by water movements all over Europe. In Italy, as I describe in chapter 4, numerous small court cases have been won by water consumers on the grounds that a proper contract was never stipulated between the relevant parties. GORI in Campania, for example, lost some cases on these grounds, with lawyers politicizing the question of contract just like their Irish counterparts did. In France, the country's third largest multinational water corporation, the Société d'Aménagement Urbain et Rural, SAUR, shut off a client's water for twenty months after he failed to pay his 218 euro bill. When the client brought the case to France's Constitutional Council, it ruled that no water provider may cut off water from primary residences, even in the case of nonpayment. SAUR challenged this ruling, arguing that the Constitutional Council violated SAUR's "freedom to engage in private contracts and its freedom to do business" (Public Services International 2015). Yet the argument about the binding nature of private contractual law turned out to be the weakness of SAUR's argument, for it allowed the plaintiff's lawyer to argue that private contract law did not apply, given that the user never had the ability to choose between different water service providers or negotiate its terms or price. Private contract law, the plaintiff's lawyer argued, was subordinated to public law and the French state's commitment to the public service responsibilities of private water providers. The French Constitutional Council thus ruled against SAUR, establishing a ruling that is "final, without appeal" and that until today prohibits water shutoffs (Public Services International 2015).[41] This ruling was at least in part achieved because of the politicization of contract and the question of whether private contract law should prevail in the case of a public service. Who are the contracting parties here? Is it governments or "consumers" who contract with private providers? And what if consumers do not consent to being treated as such, but insist on their right, as citizens, to access publicly provided water?

What, then, does it mean to refuse the bill altogether and to insist on paying through general progressive taxation? This is a question about social versus other kinds of contracts, and of Irish Water being caught between the two. On the one hand, Irish Water had begun to ready itself vis-à-vis a beckoning horizon of global financial investment that would one day contract with Irish Water under the condition that the company demonstrate its profitability and capacity to secure, if necessary with violence, its profitability. On the other hand, there was a horizon of soon-to-be customers who think of themselves as rights-bearing citizens and who never consented to this potential future of Irish Water. Instead, the Irish water movement appealed to the state to mend what has become a broken social contract. Its insistence on general progressive taxation attempted to hail the state into drawing on the population and businesses, especially large corporations, to pay their fair share. Rather than pledging its tax base to investors, protestors argued that the state ought to use this tax base to borrow at significantly lower rates than the private sector can. The barriers that became the hallmark of the Irish water insurgency were thus not only symptomatic of the shape that the political is taking as vital goods are privatized and households see themselves struggle to pay bills at the end of the month. These barriers also performatively asserted the collective body of a citizenry that attempted to protect the neighborhood while seeking to keep the reach of predatory capitalism at bay. It also attempted to hail the state back into being—a state that would express itself not through austerity, law, and order, but through collective prosperity and collective thriving (Collins 2017, 112).

The Irish government retracted its plans on several fronts. In 2014, it promised to guarantee fixed-level water charges until the end of 2018. It also granted a one hundred euro water allowance for every household (Bresnihan 2016). But many protestors called for the abolition of Irish Water altogether and feared future privatization. Their message was clear in the 2016 general election, where water charges were the central political issue. The Right2Water trade unions had brought together organized labor, political parties, and community activists in an effort to funnel the massive groundswell of protest around meters into a more mainstream critique of austerity (Murphy 2019). By the time the 2016 election was over, two-thirds of all members voted into the Irish parliament were elected on an anti–water charges platform. The two previously governing parties, Fine Gael and Fianna Fáil, were voted out. Almost 100 of 158 seats were filled by candidates who had campaigned on an anti–water charges platform, which meant that numerous policy changes on domestic water charges could soon be achieved (Ogle 2016, 238). The Irish water movement has since also called for a referendum that would enshrine the public ownership of water in the Irish Constitution.

Some of my interlocutors insisted that the water insurgency had woken a whole generation into questioning the neoliberal status quo and into thinking of themselves as capable of pursuing change through concrete action. In 2016, when I traveled across Ireland, it was clear that the energies of the water insurgency had transitioned into the many battles currently underway over housing and homelessness. People made clear connections between the extractive nature of water metering and the extractive nature of rents, following the fault lines as they cracked open along the frontiers of financial expansion.

The Irish water insurgency thus looks back on victories. As Karen Doyle asked me during a pandemic Zoom conversation in March of 2021, "Can you imagine what it would have been like had we had those [water] bills coming in the door?" But many are also disillusioned. The new water treatment plant in Cork is a public-private partnership financed through a guaranteed income over the next twenty-five years. Veolia has been put in charge of reading water meters, even though these readings are currently not used for billing (Bieler 2021, 146). Noreen Murphy has rightly noted that none of the water movement's demands have really been met: the complete abolition of domestic water charges, an end to domestic water meters, the disbanding of Irish Water, and a water referendum (Murphy 2019). Meanwhile, investors lie in wait. In 2019, Global Water Intelligence published a global water tariff survey. One of its highlights included a specific singling out of Ireland and Northern Ireland as the only countries in 2019 to not charge directly for water. As if to titillate its clients, GWI notes that the "national utility in the Republic is proposing charges for high usage in the future." Investors, in short, are expecting the possibility of a slowly opening market. But the Irish people remain vigilant as well. As Karen Doyle put it, "I look back onto such great memories, but also that possibilities still exist for the future. . . . There's no saying what this government will introduce because somebody has to pay for the pandemic, is what they keep telling us. And so we know that they will come after everything again. Irish Water is there. It festers over there and investors [are there too]. I know they're there. But they also know that we're here, too. I would say that we will be ready. All of us, again, so that sense hasn't gone away. You know, they can take us on at their peril, and we will win again."

# 3

## We Berliners
## Want Our Water Back!

IN 2016, while cycling through Berlin, I noticed a number of billboards announcing that the city's remunicipalized water utility (Berliner Wasser Betriebe; BWB) had launched an unusual campaign called "Our Water Speaks for Itself" (*Unser Wasser Spricht für Sich*). I was immediately intrigued by how the campaign had water directly address Berliners in the first person singular, with quips like "I'm more strictly controlled than you are in Berlin's clubs." The BWB's Facebook page also suddenly began to feature water as the protagonist, as in, "Hi, it's me again, Berlin's water! As an Ur-Berliner, the health and wealth of the city are close to my heart. I've been making myself comfortable here in Berlin's river valley since the Ice Age. Man, was I glad when I saw the light of day for the first time!" And so on.[1] What held my attention was the campaign's double entendre: that the city's exceptional water quality was represented as speaking for itself (insofar as it spoke for the BWBs exceptional stewardship of its water and water infrastructure), and that water began to address Berliners directly. I wondered about the curious way in which water presented itself as an anthropomorphized figure in dialogue with Berliners, a friendly associate whose registers of address performatively reproduced the intimacy with which human bodies are made through and with water. This intimacy was enhanced by the fact that people could ask Berlin's water questions on Facebook. In May 2016, for example, a woman called Marion Schwarz asked, "How calcified is our water and can we really still drink it?" Within minutes, Berlin's water answered: "Hello Marion! I am indeed water of a 'harder sort.' My colleagues have listed all substances I contain on an internet page. Why don't you check them out? And of course, you can continue to enjoy me without hesitation [smile emoticon]."

I begin this chapter with this scene of intimacy and transparency because I read it as a poignant finale to the lengthy battle that engulfed Berlin's partially privatized public water utility for many years. The intimacy with which the BWB today presents water is the result of a long process whereby a small and relentlessly stubborn group that calls itself the Berlin Water Table (Berliner Wassertisch) managed to move Berlin's water utility away from being partially privatized and utterly opaque to Berliners, toward becoming a common good (*Gemeingut*) that strives to be directly accessible, accountable, and transparent to the city's inhabitants. The activist group did so through a sensational citywide referendum that shook Berlin to the core in 2011. The Berlin Water Table had worked for years—conceptualized a campaign, collected tens of thousands of signatures, written a popular law, fought the Berlin Senate in court, and ultimately won a referendum (*Volksentscheid*)—to force the city to buy Berlin's water utility back after it was partially privatized in 1999. The point made by the Berlin Water Table was that the processes through which Berlin's privatized water utility were managed and priced lay hidden behind opaque veils (what my interlocutors called *Schleier*) of money and secret corporate contract, and that it was only through the disclosure of this secret contract that clarity could be gained and justice attained.

The referendum was thus a practical and highly consequential critique of John Maynard Keynes's point that finance always introduces "veils of money" between the "real asset" (in this case, water infrastructures) and the "wealth owner" (in this case, the investor or shareholder in a utility), and that "the economy would be more and more hostage to speculation over the paper claims to wealth, generating [not only] high volatility and instability," but opacity and "veiling" as a direct result (Foster and Magdoff 2009, 16). The sudden public visibility of the secret contract as a result of the referendum had the effect of tearing these veils down, with enormous political repercussions. The victorious referendum became not only a precedent-setting case in Germany, but also a globally circulating paradigm for direct democratic citizens' action in the struggle for public water. The end effect was a BWB chastened by the widely held public assumption that it was really nothing but a financial predator (*Abzocker*), an opaque force that hid its nefarious inclinations behind the sacred veil of the corporate secret. Hence the rise of anthropomorphized water, speaking to Berliners as if it were their best friend: accessible, transparent, unveiled. And a hyperintimacy arose—a fantasy of immediacy between Berliners and the water they drink. The remunicipalized BWB today insists that the provisioning of water is a *hoheitliche Aufgabe*—the sovereign duty to provide public services to its citizenry and on the strength of public law (the term *hoheitlich* in German has a particular ring to it, denoting not just sovereignty but a quasi-kingly, even "sceptered," public duty). Its Facebook page and Twitter and Instagram feeds are filled with what looks like an attempt to turn its innermost self inside out: picture after picture laying bare its pipes and wires and canals as it attempts to charm Berliners back into trusting that their water, once again, is theirs.

This chapter examines struggles over contract and law and over both illegibility and clarity at the financial frontier, asking what forms of contract and what kinds of law ought to govern common goods. This struggle over opacity and revelation illuminates two points many of my interlocutors made across Europe: that the involvement of faraway financial actors introduced a level of heightened secrecy into previously public (and at least in theory more accessible and transparent) utilities, and that the financialization of public goods opens up a constitutive contradiction between public democratic oversight and private confidentiality and nondisclosure (Whiteside 2018, 8). My interlocutors asked whether water utilities should be governed by private contracts barely accessible to parliamentary oversight and subject to nondisclosure agreements or whether they should be governed under the aegis of public law (*öffentliches Recht*), which, at least in theory, can be laid open to the scrutiny of the public. They asked who ought to write the law at the fault line of the frontier—the "market," the "state," the "people"? This chapter argues that the financial frontier is a space where different legalities and forms of sovereignty come into conflict, a zone where boundaries between kinds of property, law, and sovereignty are constantly (re)drawn (see Cooper and Mitropoulos 2009, 363).

Of course, such stark distinctions between public and private or markets and states are profoundly simplistic. They force us to ask whether contracts written under the aegis of public law are really always accessible and transparent (they, of course, are not); whether public institutions are not also replete with their own secrecies, opacities, and exclusions (they, of course, are);[2] and whether the clear-cut distinction between public and private is not in itself a ruse after decades of neoliberalization, which has long introduced new public management and new public financial management regimes into all institutions of government (it is). These points were often made by the people I met. As I show, their struggle against the inherent secrecy of private contracts pushed not for a facile "return" to a supposedly transparent public; rather, their struggle for a public utility also hailed a particular public and a particular state—a demand not for a state that actually was, but for one *that ought to be*. Peoples' struggle against opacity and secrecy, in short, were struggles to push the state and Berlin's population into a commitment to treat their water as a truly public good—that is to say, to manage it through a specific institutional form, public law, and direct democratic citizens' participation. They thus tried to force the state to commit to a redefinition of what the public truly ought to mean and do.

I here make contracts into a primary object of ethnographic inquiry by asking not only what the effects of tools like contracts are in the world, but how contracts render predatory practices legal while being veiled in the liberal fantasy of contractual equality (Appel 2019, 142; Graeber 2011, 102–8). I explore both the content of the contracts (in fact, there was not only one, but many—a legal proliferation that reveals that financialization "pushes the law beyond its own limits, inventing ever more arcane, baroque variations on the contract-form itself" [Cooper and Mitropoulos 2009, 366]), as well as their social life as documents full of proprietary information, contracts that were essentially written by and for the market even as they governed the management of a still nominally public resource.[3] This indeterminacy meant that the contract operated not just as a fetish of purported equality (when it in fact contained a very detailed expropriatory formula in the form of state-backed long-term profits for investors—the famous Paragraph 23.7 that I describe below). It also set in motion particular modes of governmentality and desire in that it bound politicians, no matter what their political disposition, to the market in nonnegotiable ways. In effect, the contracts helped set up a tributary structure whereby the dividend, as Max Weber put it in his analysis of stock markets, becomes a vehicle through which governments pay tribute to capital (Weber [1894] (2000), 316; Birla 2009, 21).[4] The contracts thus created a public whose fiscal and political life would orbit around the fulfillment of incurred financial debts rather than around a collective obligation toward water, the infrastructures through which water flows, and the life that is thereby sustained. Not surprisingly, these contracts became objects of obsession among critics (If only we could see and read them!); objects of wonder and wild rumor (Is it true that the contracts are hundreds, perhaps even thousands of pages long? What exactly do these pages say? Have you seen them?); objects of secrecy and subterfuge as well as of antagonism, intense politicization, and litigation over its perceived illegitimate powers. Such antagonisms are not particular to Berlin. The contracts that govern public-private partnerships have been called "diabolical," "crazy," and "ruinous" elsewhere, too.[5]

What was revealed in the now famous referendum was not merely the predatory contractual content undersigned by the city and private investors—the act of theft (*Raubzug* [Lederer 2010]) that lay anchored in the contract itself—but rather, capitalism's foundational secret, so clear for all to see at the frontier: it relies on expropriation and exploitation, not free markets organized around contractual equals, as its true sources of surplus value. This secret of accumulation by dispossession must always go unremarked (Morris 2016, 34). Berliners' insistence that they had the right to see the contracts revealed not just the injustice of proprietary corporate information when it comes to common goods like water, but the compulsive ways in which capitalism and its allies insist on secrecy and are prepared to defend this secrecy via recourse to the law.

This chapter also makes private contracts—indispensable linchpins in the recursive cycles of accumulation by dispossession—into an object of historical inquiry (see also Appel 2019). It turns out that this was not the first time that Berlin had signed a badly prepared contract over its water works (Mohajeri 2006, 178). In fact, Berlin already had a history of signing contracts with private investors in the mid-nineteenth century and of breaking contractual agreements with these same investors because the private management of water soon created what politicians already then called "a massive crisis for the public good." I offer this early history because there is much to be learned from looking back to these early forms of speculation—not only to understand the striking recurrence with which wealth is extracted by private investors in complicity with the state (see also Elyachar 2012), but also to understand the recurrence with which these financial frontiers repeatedly also see the flourishing of a politics of remunicipalization and a reassertion of the public.

The central protagonists of this chapter are a group of activists who came together in 2006 as the Berliner Wassertisch. They gave themselves this name after founding-member Dorothea Härlin visited Venezuela and began to think of the local "water tables" (*mesas de aguas*) there as direct inspiration.[6] Together, they worked for years on a campaign they called "We're done with Secret Contracts! We Berliners Want Our Water Back!" (*Schluss mit den Geheimverträgen! Wir Berliner Wollen Unser Wasser Zurück!*). Soon, the group managed to convince a majority of Berlin's population that the city's privatized water utility was a vehicle through which opaque forms of predatory accumulation were occurring through "shadowy" deals with the state. Water, as they put it in their first pamphlet in 2006, was the property of Berliners that had been alienated from them in a profoundly undemocratic process—a sell-off rendered invisible by the secret contract signed by their senate with the global water corporation Veolia and the German energy utility Rheinisch-Westfälisches Elektrizitätswerk AG (RWE).[7] The Wassertisch was already then banking on a more general mainstream cultural tendency to think of finance as highly secretive (Ho 2009, 27), a point made also by Tommaso Fattori, now an elected representative in Tuscany (whom I cited in chapter 1). As Fattori put it, "The locked board rooms of the public-private 'mixed' joint stock companies are tables where opaque consultations take place, where cartels of private businessmen and figures of public power sit, whose choices are . . . removed from any possible democratic accountability." The privatization of public goods thus goes hand in hand with the "privatization of decision making" as well (Fattori 2011). This European realization comes at the tail end of critiques long articulated from the vantage point of the Global South. As one parliamentarian put it when explaining the secretive history of oil legislation and contracting in Equatorial Guinea to anthropologist Hannah Appel, "In the early years, when American companies started production, the contract negotiations were done in a very private way [*de una forma muy reservada*], almost confidential. . . . It was as if they were dealing with private property, to such an extent that *no one knows what was in the first contracts*. What are the most important clauses? No one knew. No one even knew about the state's [percentage take] on each barrel of oil. And this has remained opaque until now" (2019, 146).

In Berlin, the problem of secrecy became a "generative mechanism" that rendered visible the fact that the BWB (and, by implication, the city) was totally beholden to the spiraling debt that the agreement with private investors precipitated (Jones 2014, 54). The BWB had become not unlike state institutions in the Global South under structural adjustment, where informal relations began to override formal ones and where the public became evermore privatized and the private "publicized" (Peterson 2014, 90). It was also because of this intense secrecy that profound clarity was ultimately reached: it turned out that secrecy had no place in the management of a city's most vital good. The Water Table was able to insist that water ought to be directly accessible—and its utility fully accountable and transparent—to the city's inhabitants.

### On Opacity, Revelation, and Recursion

Berlin's watery history must be understood as a tale of financial predation as well as permanent political provocation. Let me start in the late seventeenth century, when the wells and the river Spree in the growing city had become so sullied with sewage and animal waste that people complained about the terrible smell creating "infected air" and "sticky illnesses" (Schug et al. 2014, 17). By 1877, when the city housed around two million people, naturalist Carl von Linné wrote that one could smell the stink of Berlin from a nine kilometer range. The tale of Berlin's water utility thus begins with the problem of sewage and its public-health implications. During the long arc of the nineteenth century, devastating cholera epidemics swept across European cities, killing hundreds of thousands of people (Schug et al. 2014, 41). The question was how the sewage problem ought to be governed; whether Berlin households should in the process also be provided with safe drinking water; and who should pay for, build, and manage this undertaking (Mohajeri 2005, 39).

The answer to this question was not immediately apparent at a time when Berliners were ruled by a panoply of often rivaling institutions and figures (see also Anand 2017, 69). There was a Kurfürst, backed by the Prussian monarchical government, a local magistrate, and a self-governing city council peopled with upper-class citizens. But it was the chief of police, Carl Ludwig von Hinckeldey, an envoy of the Prussian King and a representative of the Prussian Ministry of the Interior, who was responsible both for matters of public order and for infrastructure (electrification, streets, firefighting, and, as it turns out, water). Soon, von Hinckeldey decided to have Berlin's water works built by two British railway engineers and entrepreneurs, Sir Charles Fox and Thomas Russell Crampton (Schug et al. 2014, 34).[8] Berlin's infrastructural history thus occurred parallel to the building of Egypt's Suez Canal that I recounted in the introduction. It anticipated the infrastructural histories that would unfold in other major global cities, where modern water infrastructures were also built in the mid- to late-nineteenth century by British engineers and funded by both British and French investors.

Von Hinckeldey had wrangled with the city for years over the building and financing of a modern, centralized water supply system. He eventually moved to sign a hastily negotiated contract with the Englishmen in 1852. This was a controversial decision because the city parliament had not been granted oversight or any say in the process (Mohajeri 2005, 47–48)—a velocity and mode of contract making that would be repeated over a hundred years later when Berlin's water was partially privatized in 1999. The contract awarded Fox and Crampton the exclusive right to supply Berlin with water for twenty-nine years. They founded the Berlin Water Works Company as a London-based joint stock company in 1853. The members of its board of directors were rich British traders and aristocrats—an "aristocracy of money," as Max Weber put it ([1894] 2000, 327)—and pioneers at a financial frontier where no international consensus yet existed on the regulation of speculation. Questions such as what would happen in the case of the failure of actual delivery, among other things, were still being debated (Birla 2009, 147–48). The Berlin Water Works Company was tasked mainly with providing water for the cleaning of Berlin's filthy streets, with building water hydrants, and with building and maintaining five public water fountains. The contract also specified that the Englishmen were to lay 60.3 kilometers of piping for the provisioning of Berlin's households with running water. The number of households that were to be provisioned with water was not specified.

By 1860, confidence in private provisioning began to flounder. The Berlin Waterworks Company had slowly been reaping profit from Berlin's water and showed little interest in investing in expensive infrastructure in the rapidly growing city (Mohajeri 2006, 174). Its investment in water hydrants and public fountains had also been "very modest" (Mohajeri 2005, 60). The city government was soon flooded with complaints by urbanites who received running water in their homes, especially about low water pressure in the upper floors of apartment buildings since the Berlin Water Works Company had installed only the cheapest (that is to say, narrowest) pipes (Mohajeri 2005, 98). Many people were never connected to the system at all. Indeed, the contractually stipulated 60.3 kilometers of piping were never meant to provide running water universally, and since the contract had guaranteed monopoly to the British corporation, the city was barred from extending the pipes even if it wanted to. Just like the case of colonial Mumbai, where the water system was built by the British colonial government and "designed to discriminate" between the colonial elite and those to whom the privileges of liberal citizenship were denied (Anand 2017, 14; Gandy 2008, 112), investors in Berlin never extended the pipes as needed and barely invested in the management of sewage, which in practice meant that the city's groundwater and rivers continued to be contaminated. Nor did the city have much say in the pricing of water, which meant that water prices soared. In the midst of this floundering urban system, the Berlin Waterworks Company was still paying its shareholders—only about 1 percent in dividends by 1860, but 12.25 percent by 1872 (Schug et al. 2014, 38). Clearly, as Prussian Minister of Trade put it as early as 1857, the "Berlin Water Company's interests did not overlap with the public interest" (Mohajeri 2005, 93). On the contrary, the contract had "created a massive crisis in public health and a massive crisis for the public good" (Schug et al. 2014, 48).

The magistrate began to negotiate with the Berlin Water Works Company in 1868; it was a difficult undertaking because the contract stipulated that a buyback would only become possible in 1881. After five years of negotiations and eight years before the official end of the contract, Berlin initiated an early buyback in 1873. Negotiations ended with the city paying the British corporation the enormous sum of 8.3 million taler, made up of the real-estate (land) value and the value of the infrastructure built by the British corporation, as well as the dividends that the corporation projected that it would lose between 1873 and 1881 when the contract would have formally ended. Despite this nominal defeat, the company managed to extract the sum total of future projected revenue from the city and its current and future inhabitants. One might say that the grammar of the conditional perfect ("we would have earned profits had you not terminated the contract") came to propel the negotiation itself, extracting profits to be earned from the present (Mitchell 2020).

While the municipalization of its water utility caused enormous financial difficulties for Berlin, it allowed the city to form the "Berliner Städtische Wasserwerke AG" in 1873. From then on, the now German-owned joint stock company dedicated itself to communal provisioning and communal care (*kommunale Fürsorge*), refusing all offers on the part of international private investors. By 1893, all households were connected to Berlin's sewage system. Berlin's water prices were soon one of the lowest in Germany (Schug 2014, 117). The city thereby engaged in the classical grand infrastructural gesture that was meant to signal modernity, efficiency, and public health (see also Gandy 2014). By October 1923 and after a series of municipal agglomerations, the Berliner Städtischen Wasserwerke AG became one of the largest unified drinking water utilities in Europe (Schug et al. 2014, 115). While still a joint stock company, its six million *Reichsmark* were completely in German hands.

But by 1937, the National Socialists were in power. In the name of what they called "resource freedom" (*Rohstofffreiheit*), the Nazis liquidated the shareholder corporation and bought back all shares owned by Jewish investors (paying, of course, way below market value). Fascist nationalization occurred in Berlin in the way that it occurred in Naples, too, where the Fascists "Italianized" the city water utility by handing it over to an Italian businessman, only to soon after place it squarely into the hands of Italian national banks (De Majo and Vitale 2004, 65). By 1937, Berlin's joint stock company was dissolved, its shares "Aryanized" and handed over to the city. From now on, Berlin managed its utility as an owner-operated municipal enterprise (*Eigenbetrieb*) called Berliner Städtische Wasserwerke.[9] The municipal enterprise, borne out of a moment of right-wing resource nationalism, would become the dominant form that most water management utilities took on for much of the twentieth century. These enterprises are publicly owned and generate revenue for cities, a form of community wealth that is collectively held—until the 1990s, that is, when things again began to change.

### The Locusts Are Coming!

Berlin's water quality is a "stroke of luck," perhaps even a "gift of God," said Michael Splawski, a shift manager at Friedrichshagen, one of Berlin's nine water works. The water is so clean that babies can drink it, he waxed poetically in a 2011 interview with Berlin's *Morgenpost*: "It's like that with us humans, too. Some are beautiful, some are ugly." Other cities like Munich or Bremen have to transport their water from far away. But not Berlin: almost all of Berlin's water is abstracted from its extensive groundwater aquifers filtered naturally through a unique bank filtrate (*Uferfiltrat*). It is what some commentators have called a milestone in biological water abstraction that relies not on technical fixes but on the care of the whole hydrological cycle (Mohajeri 2006, 177).[10] The largest communal water and sewage utility in Europe, Berlin's water flows in a subterranean network of well-maintained pipes that are almost eight-thousand kilometers long ("as far as the distance between Berlin and Shanghai," as Splawski puts it). The city's water quality exceeds the requirements of the German drinking water ordinance and is unchlorinated. Only the American tourists living in hotels in the Mitte neighborhood want their water chlorinated, some of the members of the Wassertisch snickered, which is why some hotels apparently add chlorine into their water stream (a fact I was unable to confirm). Small wonder, then, that everybody bid on Berlin's water utility in 1998, when 49.9 percent of its shares were put up for sale. Everyone from Enron to the French water corporations Suez and Veolia wanted to sink their teeth into this well-maintained infrastructure and its beautiful water.

But why would a city want to sell off what people like Gerlinde Schermer, a prominent Social-Democratic (SPD) politician and incessant critic of the utility's partial privatization, called the city's *Tafelsilber* ("silverware" or better, "crown jewels")? It was the late 1990s. Berlin was broke and sitting on a mountain of debt. German unification had seen to it that Berlin, long the showcase for the successes of capitalism vis-à-vis its Socialist counterpart on the other side of the wall, suddenly received four billion euro less in federal subventions. The deindustrialization of the city's East and its unanticipated population decline and rising unemployment also didn't help (Beveridge and Naumann 2014, 282), nor did the fact that it now faced the costly task of amalgamating its previously segregated halves. This included the amalgamation of the city's separate utilities, including the East German Water Works Company (VEB WAB), which had been taken over by its Western counterpart shortly after the fall of the wall. A series of massive investments were made, especially into the corroded East German infrastructure. Sixty thousand meters were installed into unmetered East German households (Schug et al. 2014, 207).[11] Soon, the German National Audit Office criticized the city for being $46 billion in arrears (Beveridge and Naumann 2014, 282). Debt (*Schulden/Schuld*), as Gerlinde Schermer reminded me, denotes both debt and guilt in the German language and signals a moral taintedness, even sinfulness (Lazzarato 2012, 30, Graeber 2011). Schermer was convinced that it was this double entendre that allowed for austerity measures to be implemented particularly easily and without much social upheaval in Germany.

But what really brought Berlin to its knees financially was the so-called *Bankenskandal*, a banking scandal involving the previously public Berlin Bank, the Berliner Bankgesellschaft, which was partially privatized in 1994. Now a public-private partnership, the bank had offered preferential loans to friends and supporters of leading politicians (mainly Christian Democrats) and was so wracked with corruption and incompetence that it soon incurred huge debts. By 2001, the bank declared bankruptcy. The key, as members of the Wassertisch repeated in disbelief, was that the bank was partially privatized via a complex holding structure—an almost exact replica of which the city later again used to partially privatize its water utility in 1999.[12]

Both the Christian Democrats (CDU) and the Social Democrats(SPD), the ruling coalition at the time, were united in their commitment to austerity and the *Schwarze Null* (the "black zero," German for "balanced budgets"). Led by the SPD's soon-to-be widely maligned Senator of Finance Annette Fugmann-Heesing, then also known as Berlin's "iron lady," politicians fantasized about transforming Berlin's water utility into a global corporate player. German technology, high-quality engineering, and efficiency would soon compete against megacorporations such as Vivendi and Suez (Schug et al. 2014, 221). After one hundred years of provisioning water publicly during two world wars and a city divided by the Cold War (Moss 2020), Berlin began to look for private investors.

The ground for this had already been prepared in 1994, with the commercialization of some of BWB's functions (Beveridge, Hüesker, and Naumann 2014, 70; Passadakis 2006, 17). This occurred through the transformation of the BWB's legal structure, away from its municipal enterprise (*Eigenbetrieb*) structure into a public law corporation (*Anstalt öffentlichen Rechts*, or AöR). The latter allowed for the BWB to enter into commercial activities, access the necessary funds for the massive infrastructural investments needed mainly in the East, and to reduce the workforce directly employed by the city (Lanz and Eitner 2005, 10). What the management of the BWB at the time really wanted to do was turn the BWB into a joint stock company (*Aktiengesellschaft*, or AG)—a vision that was strongly resisted by unions (Lanz and Eitner 2005, 10; Passadakis 2006, 17–22).

Characteristic of the tense choreography that so often happens at financial frontiers (Muniesa 2012), this union pushback was met with the Berlin Senate's 1998 creation of a politically more palatable nested corporate structure that enclosed the BWB, still a public law company, within a complicated shareholder corporation called Berlinwasser Holding AG. This superordinate holding structure was a joint stock company, which allowed for Veolia and RWE to partake in the BWB while denying that privatization had actually taken place. Yet the opposite was the case. Veolia and RWE immediately invested in the holding and thus indirectly into the BWB via so-called silent partnerships (*stille Gesellschaften*). Both corporations also held key positions in the holding's board of directors and supervisory boards (Schug et al. 2014, 227; Passadakis 2006, 12). When RWE bought London-based Thames Water a year after it acquired shares in BWB, Thames Water—the corporation responsible for the privatization of London's water—represented RWE's interests in Berlin (Passadakis 2006, 13). This Berlin variant of the public-private partnership was a particularly complex version of what people all over Europe referred to as "Russian dolls" (in Ireland) and "Chinese boxes" (*scatole cinesi*) (in Italy)—an endless series of nested structures whose contours and exact mechanisms were almost impossible to trace.

As soon became clear, the subsumption of a public law company under a joint stock company (Lanz and Eitner 2005, 9) meant that the public law to which the BWB was subject could be circumvented by private contract law, notably through the framework agreement that regulated the relationship between the BWB and the two major shareholders. Clearly, the Berlinwasser Holding AG was not a symmetrical partnership, but rather an attempt to subsume a public system of law within the logics of private law; one kind of public (of common property) with another (the shareholder public); and one contract (the social contract) with another (the private contract).

The holding's corporate structure was the brainchild of a partial privatization law (*Gesetz zur Teilprivatisierung der Berliner Wasserbetriebe*; TprvG) that was passed by Berlin's parliament in May 1999. Drafted by a lawyer with close ties to Veolia (Lanz and Eitner 2005, 9), the law made sure that Veolia and RWE were guaranteed what the law's Paragraph 3 called the "appropriate calculatory returns on invested operating capital." This is the identical language used in Italian contracts that guaranteed an "*adeguato remunerazione del capital investito*" and that Italians struck from their laws in their extraordinary 2011 referendum. "Appropriate return of investment? But what is appropriate?" Gerlinde fumed, still incensed many years later. De facto, the Berlin contract guaranteed similar annual profit rates to those enjoyed by the privatized water companies in England and Wales—around 8 percent (Beveridge and Naumann 2014, 282; Lobina 2014, 33). By June 1999, Berlin signed a twenty-nine-year contract (*Konsortialvertrag*) with RWE and the French corporation Vivendi (now Véolia)[13]—a "pilot project" for Germany and a supposed "motor of growth" for the city of Berlin (Passadakis 2006, 16). "Twenty-nine years!" as activists exclaimed; "That's longer than the life of the Berlin Wall!"

The contract for what was then the largest public-private partnership project in Europe was not only long but incredibly complex: as a BWB employee who spoke to me under condition of anonymity put it, the contract was so complicated that "the small legal department of our local water utility was completely overwhelmed with it." This comes of no surprise, since the process leading up to the partnership involved no fewer than thirteen consultancies and lawyers' offices (Beveridge 2014, 56). Their presence, not unlike the middlemen so vividly described by E. P. Thompson (1993, 202), rendered the "partnership" profoundly nontransparent, smothered by layers and layers of baroque legal provisions. Once again, the ruse of the partnership was laid bare, insofar as one of the partners envelopes the other with an excess recourse to law; it was an example of the sovereign power of finance articulating itself through the law's proliferation.

This is a common occurrence in the contractual world of public-private partnerships, where the length of contracts (in Germany at least) routinely sits between eight hundred and thirty-six thousand pages since they contain both framework agreements and partnership agreements as well as a panoply of additional individual contracts. Of course, contractual proliferation is a form of risk management (Bear, Birla, and Puri 2015, 394) insofar as they need to hedge against the myriad potential uncertainties that might arise over the length of a duration that is often almost a human generation long. They must also do justice to a multiplicity of investors bound together into a consortium of corporations (Rügemer 2018, 167). Called "contract of trust" (*Vertrag des Vertrauens*), the Berlin contracts came with promises of job security for workers, a guaranteed minimum investment in the infrastructure over the course of the next decade, and price stability for four years until the end of 2003. The goal was to have the Berlinwasser Holding AG emerge as a global model rivalling both Veolia and RWE's efficiency and management skills.

For critics, in contrast, the "locusts" (*Heuschrecken*) had arrived like a plague of Biblical proportions, initiating what appeared like a "permanent transfer of public infrastructures to the private sector (Rügemer 2018, 8). They would then presumably move on, like locusts, once all wealth and value had been extracted.[14] By October of 1999, Berlin's Leftist opposition initiated a judicial review (*abstrakte Normenkontrollklage*) with Berlin's Constitutional Court[15] demanding that the court review the partial privatization law since the contract itself was, of course, secret. The law, to put it simply, had guaranteed investors a rate of return that the Court eventually ruled was unconstitutional. This rate of return was fixed via the formula R+2 percent, which consisted of the average return on ten-year old German federal bonds over the course of twenty years, plus 2 percent. The

2 percent represented a "risk surcharge" that investors had added to their calculations ("A fixed *risk surcharge* in a risk-free enterprise?" members of the Wassertisch scoffed in disbelief). The court similarly ruled that the risk surcharge relied on "arbitrary" pricing that stood in little relation to actual costs—a cost that would ultimately weigh on end users' bills.

Investors had further been promised additional profits in an "efficiency enhancement clause" (*Effizienzsteigerungsklausel*), which guaranteed that all profits garnered out of "improved efficiency" (which de facto meant a wave of early retirement) would for the first three years after privatization go entirely to private investors.[16] Berlin's Constitutional Court ruled that this clause, like the risk surcharge, was unconstitutional. As the Court put it, the BWB was dealing with the "vital state duty of public service provisioning" (*lebensnotwendige Staatsaufgabe im Bereich der Daseinsvorsorge*) and should therefore not adopt private sector profit maximization uncritically. The Court, in short, sought to erect its own legal barriers against financial incursion, pitting public law against the law of the market. Little did it know that Berlin's Senate was willing to proceed as if this ruling had never occurred.

### The State as Guarantor

One of the very few people who had seen the initial private contract was Gerlinde Schermer, Berlin's parliamentary deputy chairperson (*stellvertretende Landesvorsitzende*) at the time. She was one of only five elected officials who voted that day against the privatization of Berlin's water. Schermer had grown up in the Socialist German Democratic Republic (DDR) as the daughter of a self-employed small businessman and described herself as having done her homework around the kitchen table while her father conducted his business. Never afraid of big numbers, she ended up studying finance, graduating in business economics, and eventually worked for one of the DDR's large energy corporations. She remembers "hungrily lapping up democracy" when the wall fell and "learning something new every day." It seemed strange to her, a parliamentary delegate born and raised in the Socialist East, that she was experiencing something of a déja vu when she was not granted automatic insight into a contract that governed the management of the city's water—a public good that Wassertisch Press Secretary Ulrike von Wiesenau repeatedly referred to as the "crown jewel of democracy." "Those of us from the DDR simply had better sensors when it came to the infringement of our democratic rights," Schermer put it to me, "the folks from the West simply did not notice, like frogs slowly being cooked in hot water."

Schermer had received the right to view the secret contract from Berlin's Constitutional Court after the opposition's abstract judicial review in 1999.[17] She found that the Senate had quickly amended the contract in 1999 with what was bluntly called a "circumvention paragraph" (*Umgehungsparagraph*)—Paragraph 23.7, which the Senate had inserted into the contract with the explicit aim of circumventing the negative ruling by Berlin's Constitutional Court. As Paragraph 23.7. states, any losses incurred by investors due to a court ruling would be offset by the city—and this for the next twenty-eight years. Berlin's Senate had thus contractually entrenched the sacred principle of guaranteed returns in the secret contract—and this in blatant disregard of the Court.

The scandal of Paragraph 23.7 lay in the fact that it in essence was a state pledge to the market—that it would either renounce its own profits if investor profits were to fall short, or make up for lost profits through recourse to Berlin's state budget. It could do so because it, like all states, can pledge its tax base as collateral—a tax base pledged on behalf of Berlin's citizenry. By stressing the principle of *pacta sunt servanda* (that private contracts must in their nonnegotiability be adhered to and can under no circumstances be breached), it took another contract—the social contract—for granted. There was only one "higher ranking law" (*höherrangiges Recht*)—and that was the law of the market. Paragraph 23.7. was, as I quote Marco Bersani saying in chapter 1, precisely the moment where "politicians and parties consented to being expropriated of their political function." Gerlinde Schermer put it identically to me when she said that "politicians have deprived themselves of the capacity to make political decisions" (*Politiker haben selber ihrer eigenen Entmündigung zugestimmt*).

By 2003, Berlin's now Leftist Senate passed a revised partial privatization law that included new amortization rules. To the fury of critics, these amendments were initiated by then Senator of Economics Harald Wolf from the Leftist Party Die Linke, a politician who while in opposition had explicitly fought against the privatization of the BWB. These legal amendments allowed for the Senate to raise interest rates regularly and raise the water price in order to satisfy the guaranteed return of investment (Lanz and Eitner 2005, 11). While Leftist politicians were explicit about the fact that this move represented a "fiscal catastrophe," they were loath to confront Veolia and RWE (Passadakis 2006, 29). By 2004, Berlin revised the secret contracts again to reintroduce the original formula (R+2 percent) with the guaranteed returns that the Constitutional Court had declared unconstitutional. The scandal that lay at the heart of the secret contract, in short, was that it had completely preempted due legal process (Beveridge and Naumann 2014, 283). It was as if the Constitutional Court's ruling had never happened.

The critique, coming from Schermer, was hard to make. She was routinely ridiculed by fellow politicians for "wanting Socialism back." "They called me crazy," she said to me. It did not exactly help that the only newspaper willing to print Schermer's arguments and the accompanying, often exquisitely written articles by Wassertisch Press Secretary Ulrike von Wiesenau, was the *Neue Rheinische Zeitung*—a now obscure online news source that emerged out of the newspaper originally founded by Karl Marx in 1848.[18] "I constantly talked about the content of the contract, but no one listened to me," Schermer explained. But Schermer insisted, arguing year after year that Berlin had been tricked about the consequences of the public-private partnership and that the reversal of the whole construct would be cheaper than its continuation. She did the numbers; produced pages and pages of graphs, statistics, and financial projections; and showed her fellow elected officials how the utility calculated water tariffs and interest rates, how Berlin's senate had justified the city's increased water tariffs (which had shot up by around 30 percent by 2009 and were by then the highest in Germany (Behnis 2009, 2020),[19] and how the high interest rate allowed for private investors to cash in 73 percent of all profits even though they only owned 49.9 percent of the shares. This meant not only that Veolia and RWE were being paid through water tariffs, but that Berlin had partially forgone its own profits in order to ensure the profits promised to private investors: 41.2 million euros in 2004 alone, to be exact. It also meant that Berlin, not unlike the Egyptian government I describe in the introduction, eventually had to scramble to come up with money to furnish its debts. At that point, Berliners were incensed by their water bills and the injustice that lay behind the hidden veils of the contract. It seemed that politicians had banded together with private investors into a single "predatory mob" (*Beutegemeinschaft*) (Von Wiesenau 2011). By 2010, Schermer's SPD colleagues were rolling their eyes at the mere mention of her name. Schermer, who speaks (or better, rants) with exquisite passion and eloquence, had spoken out against the issue for ten consecutive years at every single yearly SPD party congress, a fact that, so Berlin's *Morgenpost*, "sunk her political career" (Fahrun 2010). Until the referendum, Schermer was not able to prove her point that the secret contract contained that secret pledge of the state to the market and in circumvention of the law—Paragraph 23.7. Try as she might, the ruling parties denied all of her accusations, cloaking everything under heavy veils of silence.

Soon, however, Gerlinde Schermer was joined by a group of activists increasingly critical of the privatization of Berlin's water and of the Senate's tendency to behave like a "lord of the manor" (*Gutsherr*), with Berlin as its estate, as Hermann Wollner, affiliated with the Berlin Wasserrat, put it to me in early 2016. Many of the early members of the soon-to-be-founded Wassertisch were members of *Attac*, the Association for the Taxation of Financial Transactions and for Citizen's Action, a Europe-wide group that is the intellectual home to several well-known water activists in Europe. Others came from all walks of life—from academia and high-school teaching, journalism, Berlin's pirate party, its art and circus scene, and from a group of property owners who had gone to court about their high water prices in 2004 and won.[20] They were joined by Carl Waßmuth, an engineer who had come to the realization that public-private partnerships made no fiscal or infrastructural sense and who, as researcher for an organization called Gemeingut in BürgerInnenhand (Common Goods in Citizen Hands), also became an ally. Once the Wassertisch was founded in 2006, it immediately resolved to campaign for a popular referendum that would call for the contracts' disclosure.[21]

Others also worked to render visible the obscure inner workings of Berlin's water utility. They did so from within a context where the national mood had significantly changed. By 2006, Germany had seen around twenty-five citizens' initiatives that had prevented the partial privatization of their water utilities (the German city of Potsdam, for example, where water had been partially privatized in 1997 and became even more costly than in Berlin, the city annulled the contract by 2000 and bought its utility back). Berlin-Brandenburg's association of housing companies (Verband Berlin-Brandenburgische Wohnungsunternehmen; BBU) sought insight into how *exactly* their water tariffs were calculated. They were initially rebuffed by both the BWB and the Senate, again on the grounds that corporate secrets and confidential corporate data had to be protected.[22] Berlin's consumer rights center had also called upon Berlin's water users to send protest letters to the BWB when prices were again increased in 2006 (Passadakis 2006, 38). Like the Italians I describe in chapter 4, critics showed that BWB's calculated water price was a ruse, arguing that while it appeared to reflect *actual* costs it in fact did not. Rather, their water price included *projected* costs—costs that the company predicted it would accrue through future infrastructural investments—charging Berliners for these theoretical future expenses in the present while in fact significantly reducing them (Mitchell 2020).[23] The Wassertisch, like other activists I talked to, insisted that its members were prepared to pay for the real costs of water provisioning but not for returns on investment—thus signaling like the Irish that they were prepared to pay once for water but not twice.[24] "It's not that we wanted water to be cheap," as Mathias Behnis put it to me in ways reminiscent of many Italians I spoke to, "But that the price we pay is reflected in actual infrastructural maintenance rather than in profits that get pocketed by global investors."

### The Trial

The unification of Germany in 1990 is commonly understood as a major incision in the European political landscape. But it was also, in Berlin at least, a major infrastructural event in that it brought together not just the two halves of the city, but two separate water utilities as well. Berlin was divided in different ways over time. Initially, after World War II, it was separated into an Eastern (Russian) and three Western (American, British, and French) sectors and eventually consolidated into East and West Berlin—a fractured cityscape characterized by many infrastructural segregations (Schug et al. 2014, 169).[25] Berlin's water utility was divided into two administrative entities and separately expanded and maintained during the Cold War, despite having originally consisted of one unified infrastructure. By 1961, Berlin's infamous wall was built, sealing the East off from the West for twenty-eight years. Even the waters of the divided city tasted different: East Berlin's water utility chlorinated its water until the fall of the wall, while the West had ceased to do so in the 1970s (Schug et al. 2014, 200). For East Berliners, then, it was not just their political universe that was revolutionized with unification, but also things as mundane as the taste of water after their water's chemical composition was aligned with that of the West.[26]

Yet Berlin remained indivisible in one crucial way: the original water canals that undergirded the city remained a single technical whole connecting the East to the West. It was through these subterranean canals, many of which were walkable, that people began to flee from the East beginning in the 1950s. They did this so relentlessly that the Ministry for State Security (Ministerium für Staatssicherheit) had steel bars placed into the canals long before the sectoral borders were fully closed in 1961. The BWB estimates that about eight hundred East Germans fled to West Berlin under the riskiest of conditions, even after 1962 (Schug et al. 2014, 180–81). To do so they had to walk, crawl, or swim through stinking sewage and break or saw open the bars. Police had to guard the utility holes at night but were so overwhelmed with the task that the Ministry completed the securitization of Berlin's underbelly by using thicker steel bars and all sorts of clever technological tricks, including simulated alarm systems. By the late 1960s, the state security service (Stasi) perfected the system by using thick steel train tracks as barriers, and utility holes were covered with extra lids. By the 1980s, some of the individual canals were secured with up to three consecutive barriers. As one BWB employee said to me, chuckling as she recalled the utter disbelief of BWB workers, the last of these underground barriers was mounted on the *very* day, in 1989, that the Berlin Wall fell.

I tell this story here because it mirrors the ways in which Berlin's postunification senate sought to similarly obstruct citizens free access—this time to information regarding their public goods. The years leading up to the referendum were littered with obstructionist attempts on the part of the senate as citizens sought to make inroads into the disclosure of the contract. As was the case with the saga of the divided city and the lengths it went to prevent people from penetrating the subterranean water infrastructure during the Cold War, so did the neoliberal senate go to lengths to prevent citizens from revealing the secret that lay at the heart of the contracts it had signed with private investors. Just as the DDR government attempted to erect barriers between the subterranean infrastructure and people fleeing the East, so did the postunification government erect barrier after barrier against citizens who sought to access the content of the contracts hidden behind veils of private contract law. Let me elaborate how this tug-of-war unfolded over time.

In January 2008, the Wassertisch submitted 39,679 valid signatures to the Berlin Senate with the slogan "We're done with Secret Contracts! We Berliners Want Our Water Back!"—a first leg in their popular initiative (*Volksbegehren*) which they passed with ease. In ways reminiscent of the popular lawmaking that I describe for Italy in chapter 1, members of the Wassertisch wrote a draft people's law (*Volksgesetz*). None of them had proper law degrees. "Our goal," as Claus Kittsteiner explained, "was not to beg for anything, but to write our own law." Hermann Wollner, an agricultural specialist from East Germany who had joined the Wassertisch at a later stage, noted with pride that Berlin's constitution differs from German federal law in that it enshrines the right of citizens to write their own laws and have the population vote on them through public referenda.[27] Berlin's constitution is thus quite unusual within the German juridical landscape in that it explicitly foregrounds the people as sovereign and as makers of law. This constitution is a product of the city's particular political history after the fall of the Berlin Wall, where a political commitment to democracy and the rights of the people took precedent. After all, the German Socialist Republic had been brought to its knees amidst mass demonstrations in the name of "We are the People" (*Wir sind das Volk*). The right of the people to write laws and initiate referenda gave juridical expression to that sentiment. As Herrmann Wollner put it, "This is not a constitution that just lies around in some lawyer's cupboard, but a constitution that is read once in a while by the people! Do you understand?" It was the Berlin Senate itself that had initiated what the Constitutional Court calls a "paradigm shift," entrusting "the people of Berlin with the capacity to engage in direct democratic processes" and thus strengthening the "self-determining capacity of the voting population" (*Stärkung der eigenverantwortlichen Entscheidung des Wahlvolks*) (Verfassungsgerichtshof des Landes Berlin 2009, 19–20).

The Water Table's draft law, which they called a "disclosure law" (*Offenlegungsgesetz*), would go far beyond the already existing freedom of information act in that it demanded the immediate disclosure of all agreements pertaining to the partial privatization of Berlin's water, both in the past and in the future. It also insisted that any future contract or contractual amendments regarding Berlin's ongoing public budget (*Landeshaushalt*) would have to be approved by the Berlin parliament, whose representatives were to be given at least six months to review said contracts or contractual amendments. Such "contracts and agreements demand extensive public examination and discussion," the disclosure law stated, and should automatically become void if they are not made subject to public debate. The Berlin Water Table thus explicitly sought to slow down the accelerated lawmaking characteristic of our financialized epoch. Against the speed of executive command, the Wassertisch insisted on time, deliberation, and a slowness of public discussion and accountability.

The Berlin Senate immediately declared the popular initiative unconstitutional. Once again, it marshalled the full weight of the liberal argumentative arsenal, arguing that a disclosure of contracts would represent a string of violations: of corporate freedom of competition and freedom of contract; of the corporate right to informational self-determination (*informationelle Selbstbestimmung*); of their freedom of profession (*Berufsfreiheit*) and right of ownership (*Eigentumsrecht*). The Senate sought to stage this as a battle between different orders of law, arguing that private contract law (enshrined in German federal law) represented a "higher ranking form of law" (*höherrangiges Recht*) than the rights of Berlin's population. It also argued that the proposed disclosure law would "dispossess" (*enteignen*) shareholders and infringe upon the constitutional rights of private investors.[28]

The Wassertisch launched an appeal against this decision with the Berlin Constitutional Court and was granted a court date on July 14, 2009. At stake was a foundational question that touched directly on the hidden secret of the liberal democratic state: that the political sphere made up of nominal equals is de facto a "Republic of Property" organized around the protection of private property (Hardt and Negri 2009; see also Macpherson 2011). The Wassertisch's challenge thus raised a number of questions that fundamentally challenged this order: Which law ranks higher? The right of private investors not to be "dispossessed" of their property, or the rights of citizens to preside over their common goods and write their own laws to do so? Put differently, who was the sovereign when it came to the provisioning of vital services? Who was the sovereign when it came to collectively held forms of property? And who was the sovereign when it came to the writing of laws?

The court was bursting at the seams on the day of the hearing. The very publicity of the event performatively asserted what was at stake—public law, accessible and visible to the populace, against private law, the contractual contents of which were treated as proprietary and thus remained hidden. The Wassertisch had scraped together some money and was represented in court by Professor Kessler, the then president of Berlin's consumer service center. Outside the court house stood one of the Wassertisch's members, Joanna Erdmann, dressed up as *Justizia*, with a glass of water in her one hand and a scale in the other. The specter of justice carried special weight in the context of this particular courthouse, which is haunted by the ghosts of its history. A number of members of the Wassertisch mentioned to me that Berlin's Constitutional Court had during the Third Reich been presided over by one of the most notorious of Nazi judges, Roland Freisler. Until today, a cursory look on Google reveals chilling movie footage of him in this "people's court" (*Volksgerichtshof*), interrogating a broad array of political offenders in his high-pitched voice; it was a façade of justice where the accused were always already assumed to be guilty before proceedings had even begun. It was under his reign that the court turned into a scene of totalitarian terror: Freisler sentenced five thousand people to death between 1942 and 1945, most famously the members of the White Rose resistance group who were beheaded by guillotine for distributing antiwar pamphlets. Graf Claus von Stauffenberg, a member of a failed assassination plot against Hitler, was also executed by firing squad because of Freisler's sentencing.

The history of the court is crucial here because it never reconvened again for the entire duration of the Cold War. It was only in 1992, after the fall of Communism, that it resumed its work—a freshly constituted Court of Justice in a new democratic era. It thus resumed work precisely at a historical moment when the liberal democratic state needed to reassert itself in light of a city haunted and by both its Nazi *and* Socialist ghosts (Shoshan 2016). The Constitutional Court, as a *Festschrift* published in 2012 put it, understood itself not only as a "symbol and guarantor for the united city of Berlin" (Schudoma 2012, 2), but also as the "jewel in the crown" (*Krönung*) of the liberal democratic constitutional state and as the guarantor of the state under the rule of law (*Rechtsstaat*) (11). Even today, the court sees itself as "the guarantor of the fact that all citizens can trust that justice will be served when confronted with injustice" (3–4). The Court's primary role lies in its capacity to check laws produced by the legislature itself and to thus hold lawmakers themselves accountable (14).

Kessler made a number of arguments in the name of the Wassertisch: That whoever provides distinct public services (*originäre öffentliche Aufgaben*) must be considered part of the public administration; that citizens' rights to information ranked higher than the right to corporate confidentiality; that the "formation of political will" (*politische Willensbildung*) must be transparent to the population; and that secret contracts dealing with the provisioning of public services undermine both elected politicians' capacity to exercise their public function and citizens' capacity to engage in the "formation of their own political will" (Verfassungsgerichthof des Landes Berlin 2009, 6). The Senate, as if on autopilot, insisted again on the primacy of constitutionally guaranteed right of ownership (*Eigentumsrecht*).

The ruling produced by the Berlin Constitutional Court on October 6, 2009, in favor of the Wassertisch was remarkable. First, it privileged the right of Berlin's population to engage in direct democratic processes through the writing of law, and it did so over and above the private property rights asserted by the Senate and enshrined in the federal German constitution. The court thus implicitly argued that the rights of the people of Berlin should, initially at least, be treated as equal to federal law. As the court put it, the democratic process—that moment in which the people were still unfolding their "inner will as popular legislator" (*innere Willensbildung des Volksgesetzgebers*)—must always be allowed to come to fruition even if their demands might later be deemed unconstitutional. The process of popular lawmaking, the court insisted, needed to be given equal weight to the laws made by parliamentarians. Any attempt to rescind that right, as was attempted by the Senate, would "endanger the political peace" and "test the constitutional order" (Verfassungsgerichtshof des Landes Berlin 2009, 25–27). It did not hurt that the politicians who showed up in court displayed a singular arrogance and self-righteousness, "driving the judges nuts," as Johanna Erdmann put it to me (*Die Selbstherrlichkeit der Politiker, das bringt die Richter so richtig auf die Palme*). The court case thus rendered visible not just the people's attempt to assert sovereignty over their collective property, but the ways in which politicians met this attempt with profound condescension.

Second, the court made clear that the law that ought to govern the provisioning of core public services must be public law (*öffentliches Recht*), not private law (*bürgerliches Recht*).[29] It thus implicitly ruled on what kind of a juridical thing the public provisioning of water ought to be. The court insisted on explicitly distinguishing between the private laws (*bürgerliches Recht*) that govern relations between private individuals and the public laws (*öffentliches Recht*) that govern the relations between individuals and the state. Water provisioning, core to public service provisioning (*Kernbereich der öffentlichen Daseinsvorsorge*), should not be understood as being subject to private law; indeed, to treat it as such would represent a category mistake. As the court put it, the governance of water cannot steal itself out of public law. This moment, in short, threw into stark relief the question of what bodies of law ought to govern public provisioning. Clear boundaries between kinds of property, kinds of law, and kinds of sovereignty were drawn.

Both aspects of the ruling were sensational and precedent setting. Never before had Berlin's Constitutional Court made such clear-cut statements regarding the value and dignity of popular democracy. Nor had it ever as explicitly stated the primacy of public law when it comes to the governance of collective goods. Its ruling thus stands in direct contradiction to the global wave of public-private partnerships, all of which are governed by private law and secret contracts. The difference between the two lies in more than the question of transparency and access to information. It lies also in the question of what a public and the public provisioning of vital services are. The danger with public-private partnerships, like the colonial models of the public described by Ritu Birla (2009) in her study of British colonial law in India, is that the joint stock company and its implied model of association becomes an "associational template for civil society" more generally (26–28). The joint stock company as associational template thus implies a public of business partners who all own shares in a "resource" that is, as the Constitutional Court insisted, in fact a commonwealth. This collective good ought to be collectively shared, not divided into shares that are individually owned. The court's ruling thus gave life to the possibility of a public orbiting around the indivisible care of a commons, ruled over by public laws, and mediated by a democratically accountable state.

Meanwhile, in 2007, a politician from the Green Party and member of the Berlin house of representatives, Heidi Kosche, launched another spectacular lawsuit against the city. A biochemist with a wicked sense of humor and enormous amounts of chutzpah, Kosche also wanted to see the contract and wrote to the city's financial authority to gain full access. Citing her right of control as a parliamentarian, she was immediately rebuffed: "What do you want to control? This is a corporate secret! They asked me that. What a cheek!" As was the case with the Wassertisch trial, the Senate again argued in favor of corporate confidentiality and against Kosche's right of access to information. As Kosche put it to me, a breach of trust on the part of Berlin would "make the city appear unreliable in the eyes of potential investors."

Kosche bravely sued in the name of the Green Party—a lawsuit she won after a dramatic trial that was closely watched by Berlin's political establishment. Kosche's court case was again a moment when the smugness of Berlin's politicians was on full display, as was the Constitutional Court's urge to establish itself as an authority in the battle over legal sovereignty at the financial frontier. Once again, Kosche indignantly told me, "the other side" slouched in their seats during the hearing, bored, checking their phones, utterly confident that they would win the trial. Clearly, she said to me, the court "was not really taken seriously by the political establishment at the time." The sitting judge and then president of the constitutional court, Margret Diwell, was irritated and insisted that if a parliamentarian was taking the city to court in order to exercise her rights of control, "the city would have to send more than just a random lawyer! Herr State Secretary, Herr Mayor, you are to appear in court in person!" This was a moment when the Constitutional Court again attempted to assert its full legal authority over Berlin's political scene—the law itself putting state legislators in their place, hailing them as citizens before the law.

Kosche won, and the Senate begrudgingly began to release the contract and its numerous subcontracts, bit by bit, folder by folder—180 in total, I was told. These folders were released at such a slow pace that one newspaper calculated that it would have taken Kosche three years to see all the documents. Kosche went to court for a second time to force their immediate release. By July 2010, she won again. At that point, the city mediascape was awash with intrigue about the fact that folder after folder suddenly started to be leaked, anonymously, in boxes, in front of Kosche's office at Berlin's House of Representatives. Every morning, Kosche recounted to me with glee, a box was left at her office door—a delicious process of revelation that allowed Kosche and the Wassertisch to release the contract's contents at their own pace. When asked where they had gotten the contact from, Kosche would shrug her shoulders. As Mathias Behnis, another Wassertisch stalwart put it to me with not a little bit of *Schadenfreude*, "we just said we found the contract on the subway. Or was it the bus?" At that point, the Wassertisch had just jumped the second hurdle of its popular initiative, which was an official application to proceed with the referendum (*Volksbegehren*). On June 14, 2010, its members handed in 280,000 valid signatures, far above the 170,000 needed. The pressure on the Senate was immense.

### The *Volksentscheid*

Below is the iconic image created by the Wassertisch, made in the lead-up to their referendum in February of 2011. Striking is the depiction of a mundane infrastructure (a tap), an ordinary resource (a drop of water), and a vociferous shark, euro-sign gracing its eye. The image renders visible the predatory process that lay embedded within the secret contract that the Senate refused to publish.[30]

At this point, the mood in the city had reached a boiling point, and the political establishment began to fear the vehemence of citizens' anger. By the end of October 2010, Berlin's *Tageszeitung* had leaked the entire contract on its website, taking its readers through its main contents and confirming what Schermer had been saying since 1999: that the government had guaranteed profits to private shareholders—profits that not even a ruling by the Constitutional Court could overturn. They also showed how RWE and French corporation Veolia had made hundreds of millions of euros off Germany's capital on a yearly basis—all paid for by Berliners. Heidi Kosche and other members of the Wassertisch loudly criticized the BWB's pricing structure, among other things. As Kosche would later write, Berlin's price had been successively raised in improper ways (*missbräuchlich*

3.1      "Water Privatization? No Thank You!" (Photo courtesy of Berliner Wassertisch.)

*erhöht*) (2014, 3). A plethora of graphs and flyers helped Berlin's population understand that 45 percent of Berlin's water costs were made up of what came to be widely known as "fictive costs" (Kosche 2014, 4). They showed, for example, that the BWB consistently overestimated the rate at which Berlin's water infrastructure would depreciate, so much so that it stood in "crass disproportion" to the actual life span of the infrastructure. The BWB had estimated that the city's sewage pipes would last only thirty-five to fifty years (which is why the utility's pricing would have to reflect this apparently rapid deterioration and the many future investments the utility would supposedly have to make). In reality, the life span of sewage pipes was more like one-hundred years. The difference in estimated life span was reflected in an accumulated depreciation of 264 million euros (versus the 40 million euros that activists said were necessary).[31]

By November, the pressure was so intense that Berlin's Senate, Veolia, and RWE decided to publish the contracts—a full seven-hundred pages—with Senator of Finance Ulrich Nussbaum noting that transparency was a central feature of good politics. Revelation followed revelation after years of secrecy, a proliferation of "transparency" that suddenly burst forth after years of silence and denial. The Senate insisted that the upcoming *Volksentscheid* had been made redundant by its disclosure of contracts. But its reputation lay in tatters. For Berliners, the Senate was nothing but a cheap hustler engaging in fraudulent tactics. Why would anyone in Berlin trust the Senate? And how could Berliners really be sure that the seven-hundred contractual pages published by the city were really everything there was to see? No, said Rainer Heinrich from the Wassertisch, "these seven-hundred pages are only a fraction of the truth." As Claus Kittsteiner put it to me in a conversation in 2016, "the Senate screwed us over and over. Seven-hundred pages? For all we know, the contracts could consist of five-thousand, even nine-thousand pages!"

Yet even if the contract had been published in its entirety, the point of the referendum was another: to render visible the popular will and to generate a "show of force by the people" (*Machtdemonstration des Volkes*) as Gerlinde Schermer put it (Schermer 2011). What was at stake, then, was the "performative power of unmasking and the revelation of that which was already known" (Cody 2011, 44)—a public dramatization, not of contractual information (the content of which was already an open secret) but of the popular will, a staging of a public that stood diametrically opposed to the public that Berlin's Senate had contractually conjured over the years.

On February 13, 2011, a total of 666,235 Berliners voted in favor of the Wassertisch's proposition, for the disclosure of all secret contracts, and for the implementation of their self-written law. This was the first time that a popular referendum had ever been successful in Berlin. No one, not even the members of the Wassertisch, thought it would happen. The quorum they had to reach seemed almost impossibly high, since they had to mobilize 25 percent of the voting population to the urns. In the end, 27.5 percent of Berliners turned up, 98 percent of whom voted in favor of the disclosure of the contract. This was, as Schermer put it to me jubilantly years later, an "exemplary exercise of sovereignty on the part of the people!" In subsequent events, and strongly reminiscent of the small sovereignties that I describe previously, members of the Wassertisch at times wore golden paper crowns on their heads, under a banner they had written, "We are the sovereign!" (*Der Souverän sind wir!*).

The contracts, once rendered visible, failed to impress those members of the Wassertisch who ended up reading it in its entirety, like Ulrike Kölver. "We had no idea what that thing would look like," she explained in hindsight. "It wasn't something you could just quickly scroll up and down; instead, we found a bunch of endless notarized documents, a whole procession of names, everything translated, certified and accredited. . . . The most important part of the contract is only about sixty to seventy pages; well, maybe two hundred. The rest was just frills; lists of the properties that belonged to BWB's inventory, lists of city fountains. . . ." Regardless of whether the contract (and all its subcontracts) were read at all by Berliners (they presumably hardly were), the mere act of revelation represented a public event so humiliating that the ruling Leftist coalition agreed to buy Berlin's water back. Once again, as had happened a bit more than one-hundred years earlier, Berlin spent an enormous sum of money doing so. The Wassertisch had argued for unilateral cancellation of the contract because of its unconstitutional guarantee of profits, but the Senate responded that the only option was an expensive buyback that ultimately cost 1.3 billion euros—double the amount that investors spent in 1999 when they bought themselves into the utility. Once again, as had been the case more than one-hundred years ago, private investors insisted on being compensated, not only for the initial sum they had spent buying Berlin's water utility shares, but for the dividends that they were projected to lose between 2011 and 2028 when the contract would have formally ended. Once again, investors were able to lay claim to not just present but future wealth—a rent they will receive from Berliners for years to come (Mitchell 2020; Appel 2019).[32] A betrayal, the Wassertisch has argued, of both the present and the future.

### A Social Infrastructure

One of the Wassertisch's unusual achievements was that it was able to render visible the secret that constitutes all financialized public utilities, or indeed, capitalism as such: that it must render invisible the fact that it relies foundationally on mechanisms of state-backed predation. For Marx, "primitive" or original accumulation was always secretive insofar as it had to be cloaked in the illusion of idyllic contract and equilibrated exchange (Appel 2019, 140). Yet nothing could be further from the truth. The revelation of the contract, with the scandalous Article 23.7 at its center, showed not only that the famed "partnership" was anything but, but that the state had guaranteed the market a rate of profit over the course of a human generation. The state, in short, was laid bare as guarantor of a predatory tributary structure, a willing executioner of expropriation no matter what the cost.

This revelation and, more importantly, the dogged process that led to this revelatory act—the Wassertisch's campaign, its writing of the law, the court cases, the referendum—fundamentally changed the democratic culture of Berlin for years to come. As Michael Efler, then an elected representative in Berlin's parliament put it to me in an interview in 2016, the Wassertisch has become a charismatic example of how remunicipalization might actually occur through concerted, sometimes almost quixotic, political mobilizations. Social movements all over the country began to emulate the Wassertisch's tactics, and Berlin has—since the successful referendum—seen a proliferation of movements utilize this legal tool. "A very important breakthrough for the utilization of direct democracy," as Efler put it, with clear effects since it created the conditions for an avalanche of popular referenda that followed the model of the Wassertisch.[33] "And it's not only Berlin's citizens who learned something," as Mathias Behnis put it to me, "Berlin's Senate also learned that it cannot block referenda via recourse to the Constitutional Court." Rather, it had to acknowledge the sovereignty of the people, acknowledged within Berlin's constitution. The financial frontier's fault line, in short, gave life to the mutual coconstitution of the law, and to the recognition of multiple sovereigns and their capacities and limits as well.

But challenges remain. The disambiguation of the holding took years and was extremely complex. As David Hartmann, a collaborator in Heidi Kosche's office explained to me in an interview in 2016, a large amount of profits still lay ensconced in the holding's many subsidiary companies, and questions regarding the movement of these profits from one subsidiary to the other were complicated because of implications for taxation. This meant that the holding continued to exist for years even as the Wassertisch repeatedly called for its transformation back into a public law corporation or, even better, an owner-operated municipal enterprise. This battle over the legal form of the utility mirrors others that are fought all over Europe as water utilities continue to be remunicipalized.[34] It is often also accompanied by a critique of the fact that nominally public utilities often continue to be run like profit-oriented corporations. In Berlin, where Jörg Simon, the previous chairman of the BWB's executive board was CEO of its remunicipalized iteration until 2021, water prices continue to be unusually high. While the Federal Cartel Office ordered a price reduction of 15 percent in 2014, the water utility's high price and high returns continue to service high debts—not just those of the BWB but those of the city more generally. Critics thus continue to accuse the BWB of secrecy and veiling—just like the partially privatized utility obscured its de-facto profits, so too does the remunicipalized utility obscure the fact that its high water prices include a "hidden water tax" that is used to service ongoing city debt (Von Wiesenau 2012).

But many of my interlocutors in Berlin also speak of a deeply cultural problem that remunicipalized utilities face: how to rid an organizational culture of its corporate ethos after years of private management and control. This was a question of business culture that could, as the Wassertisch continues to argue, only be solved through proper democratization. The Wassertisch founded the Wasserrat in 2013 as a forum for all those interested in promoting the democratic participation of Berlin's citizens in the newly remunicipalized BWB. It has repeatedly reiterated its slogan as it seeks meaningful participation in the utility's governance structure: "First remunicipalization, then democratization!"[35] One important step was taken in 2018, when the newly elected Leftist coalition declared the BWB to be a "blue community" (admittedly after some dogged nudging on the part of two Wassertisch stalwarts Dorothea Härlin and Johanna Erdmann).

The political fault line that emerged in Berlin gave vitality not just to the question of democracy and transparency but to very different visions of what infrastructure is and what forms of futurity ought to be expressed by it. After all, "infrastructures are always concrete instantiations of visions of the future," with investments into infrastructure always involving a calculation of future returns that in the case of public utilities are often uncertain or hard to measure in mere numbers (Gupta 2018, 62–63). Max Weber, writing about railroads, similarly noted that it is never just the present generation that uses the railroad, but that a given population's heirs will, too. The burdens of paying for this infrastructure must thus be justly distributed across generations and not burden one at the cost of the other (Weber 2000 [1894], 314). Current infrastructural arrangements expressed through public-private partnerships do the opposite—burden current but especially future generations with often unsustainable debt, a pernicious inheritance current generations are placing on the shoulders of the next. After all, Berlin's buyback of the BWB, financed through yet another thirty-year loan that the city secured for itself at local taxpayers' expense, is a good example of the kinds of debts accumulated now and in the future: Veolia's shares alone cost Berlin 590 million euros. RWE's shares cost an additional 618 million euros. All of this was the result of the city having sought out a quick financial fix in light of huge public debt in 1999—the original sin of the quick financial fix that was soon replaced with the longue durée of debt repayment.

What remains is not only a demand for democracy but for an infrastructure that a number of my interlocutors called a "social infrastructure." There is a need, as the engineer Carl Waßmuth put it to me in a conversation in 2016, to understand more broadly the ways in which "our social life is intimately intertwined with infrastructure; we cannot exist and would be quite vulnerable without it." Would it be possible, he mused, to develop a new poetics around infrastructure—an infrastructure we might appreciate, even cherish again, because of its foundational contribution to social life? How to escape austerity-era Germany's worshipping on the "altar of debt"? Waßmuth spoke of an expressionist poem by Georg Heym's titled "God of the City" (*Gott der Stadt*), written at the beginning of the twentieth century—a poem centered on a smokestack sitting in the middle of the city and around which all city life is assembled as if kneeling in prayer, offering itself up to this central piece of modernist infrastructure with even church bells chiming in the smokestack's honor. Here, Waßmuth conjured a kind of tributary structure that seems diametrically opposed to the one set up by the payment of dividends. Rather than pay tribute to the market, he implied, society should pay tribute to that which socially and materially holds it together—its vital (today often called "essential") infrastructures. This tribute ought to translate into long-term maintenance and care—not just of material systems but of the humans and nonhumans that make them work. After all, vital infrastructures are continuously used and thus continuously used up: "They need investments that are furnished regularly, not in sudden bursts because infrastructure has been depleted after years of neglect!" What Berlin needs, in short, is a social infrastructure through which durable wealth is regrounded and not extracted, an infrastructure that is the material expression of a social contract in that its collective use extends itself across space and time.

# 4

## Just Price

CASTELLAMMARE DI STABIA is a small town nestled in the Bay of Naples, just outside the city of Naples in Southern Italy. It lies close to the ancient Roman cities of Stabiae and Pompeii, both of which were destroyed by the eruption of the Vesuvio volcano in AD 79. As I drove around with Ferruccio, a local school teacher and lover of all things related to his town, I remarked on the stunning vegetation. It was early February 2016 and the land was lush with dark-leaved trees dripping with oranges and lemons, thick palm trees, and cacti plants rimmed with bright pink fruit. Ferruccio explained that this land was one of the most fertile in the world, enriched with minerals accumulated through the mixing of volcanic ash with soil.

"A paradise inhabited by devils," he said.

The fertility is not only agricultural. There are many wondrous treasures that erupt from that abundant soil. Castellammare, also called Città delle Acque (City of Waters), is famous for its thermal waters that emerge out of the ground from the town's twenty-eight springs (Squillace 2015). "Water is in our blood"; "Water is part of our DNA"; "Water is our heart"; "Water is our medicine"; the people of Castellammare would say to me, noting with some pride that the water flowing from their taps was heavily mineralized and ever-so-slightly fizzy. Castellammare's springs produce mineral water with distinct chemical compositions; they contain magnesium, calcium, sulfur, iron, bicarbonate, hydrocarbon, chloride, and sodium. The thermal bathing culture of Castellammare goes back four millennia and was set in a landscape that was then teaming with hot mineral springs. These therapeutic springs, which were thought of as miraculously regenerative, brought forth many cults honoring the gods and nymphs often associated with springs in Ancient Greece and Rome. Indeed, Naples' ancient coinage was populated with figures central to local water cults, such as the Siren Parthenopē, who threw herself in the water and drowned after she failed to seduce Odysseus. Her dead body, Greek myth has it, washed ashore on the Bay of Naples and to this day adorns many fountains in the city, water sprouting from her breasts.[1] Catholicism would draw vociferously on this already existing cornucopia of religious belief. Until today, the springs in Castellammare are named not just after the Madonna, but also after a series of saints. They are used for a wide range of therapeutic purposes. People come in droves to fill their plastic canisters with "miraculous" water, especially the waters of the Madonna (*aqua della Madonna*), also referred to as mariners' or sailors' water (*acqua dei navigatori*). Some have called this water one of Castellammare's principal forms of wealth; it was once sold, after all, to as faraway places as the United States (Fusco 2014).

I had come to Castellammare in early 2016 because I was hoping to meet members of its local water committee, well known in the area for their struggle against what Italians call *bollette pazze* or "crazy bills"—bills that were so crazily high that people were unable to pay them. The people of Castellammare shared their predicament with the other seventy-four towns and villages that straddled the province of Naples and Salerno in the Sarnese-Vesuviano district of Campania. GORI SpA, the integrated water service (S.I.I.) provider for the Sarnese-Vesuviano District Area of the Campania Region, had entered into a long-term agreement with the Campania Region and the Campania Water Authority (Ente Idrico Campano) and served 1.7 million people in the area, an agreement that was last renewed in 2018.[2] Castellammare's water, so valuable to the local population, found itself flowing through a utility that had become complexly embedded within the nested ownership structures so typical of public-private partnerships: 37 percent of GORI's shares are owned by the powerful Rome-based multiutility ACEA through its subsidiary, Sarnese Vesuviano Srl. ACEA, in turn, is listed on Milan's stock exchange. A total of 23.333 percent of its shares are in turn owned by Suez, the French water corporation whose history I outlined in the introduction.[3]

I had heard about these *bollette pazze* elsewhere in and around Naples as I visited the towns in the Sarnese-Vesuviano district where water was being managed by GORI. Here, 45 percent of households were in arrears by the time I visited in 2016—up from 25 percent in 2005 (Gemma 2016, 9). Everywhere I went, people complained about the fact that their water bills had gone up with the "regularity of a Swiss watch"—67 percent between 2011 and 2016; another 9 percent in 2015; and another projected 31 percent between 2016 and 2019 (*Corriere della Sera* 2016). The people from the water committees in towns like Castellammare, Nocera Inferiore, and Casalnuovo recounted how GORI was always finding new billing tricks, new language, new ways to manipulate price. As one interlocutor put it, "And what form is better than a monopoly form? Once they have monopoly, they determine price!" During the time of my research, GORI (or *diavolo gori*, "devil gori" as some refer to the utility), had begun to retroactively charge people for water that they had consumed between 2006 and 2011 and for which they had supposedly underpaid.[4] Some had been sent retroactive water bills (*partite pregresse*, as they were called) that were 1,000, 2,000, even 3,000 euros high—bills that I could not believe existed until I saw them with my own eyes because they had been photocopied, carefully kept in folders, or held up and publicly burned in demonstrations.

*Bollette pazze* were proliferating all over the Italian utilities sector. They introduced new volatilities into often already impoverished households— the everyday dread of opening up the next envelope containing the next bill, and of having what should normally be a mundane act be laced with vertiginous anxiety (see also Knight 2021). Television programs reported on retirees living in tiny apartments on monthly pensions of 630 euros whom the electrical company had charged 4000 euros within the span of three months. They reported on housewives whose hands shook every time they opened an envelope containing a gas bill that could be hundreds, even thousands of euros high. Some Italian regions had seen demonstrations against crazy water bills, sometimes with hundreds of people protesting with burning torches, their blue water referendum flags held high in the air. In Frosinone in the region of Lazio in May 2016, protestors gathered in front of the government prefecture, shouting that they would not pay and ending their protest by burning their bills on a blazing wood pyre while police looked on. "I just received an 800 euro bill—that is almost double the amount of my monthly pension!" one man yelled. Another shouted, "I am here to protest against whoever speculates on a primary good—a good that is *not* their property because water is a common good!" (Redirossi and Ferazzoli 2016).

In the Sarnese-Vesuviano district, people similarly viewed bills with suspicion. As one interlocutor put it to me, "These bills hide the global scam that we've been subjected to" (*Le bollette nascondono la truffa globale che stiamo subendo*). Holding her hand high up into the air she noted, almost in disbelief, that "our water is being traded on the stock market in Japan!" For many, these bills made manifest an economy that was the result of a particular kind of madness—that of global market actors who knew nothing about their local water, its histories, local meanings, and particular taste, and who were invested only in stripping it of its qualities in order to price and trade it. Water, their *bene comune*, had been transformed from an inimitable local treasure into a global commodity embedded within an abstract, rationalized pricing system, that is to say, into a vehicle for the extraction of profits by a few (Besky 2016, 8; Elyachar 2012). For the people I met, price was not at all a pristine signal that perfectly communicated value—an efficient and simple market tool that transparently conveys people's wants (Ballestero 2019, 58). Rather, prices were a sign of the distortions that had come about because market actors both near and far—the "mafias," as people called them—had taken an interest in their water. These forces were hidden and mysterious and thus subject to much rumor and speculation. After all, as some put it, GORI was an "illusionist magician" (*un mago dell'illusionismo*) who managed to render invisible the process of expropriation. "There's never any proper explanation for this," people said, pointing to their bills. The price breakdown offered by GORI on its bills was such that any meaningful relationship between goods, price, and service rendered had broken down. The *bollette pazze*, in short, had to be fought; crazy prices had to be replaced with a just price.

While the protagonists of this chapter mostly include my interlocutors in Castellammare di Stabia and members of the vibrant No Gori Civic Network (Rete Civica No Gori) that has been battling GORI since 2011 in the region's Sarnese-Vesuviano district, the object of this chapter are the crazy bills—the financial frontier's most emblematic material artifact. These bills became the arena within which battles over different kinds of value were fought. The numbers on the bill, in short, meant something very different to the people I met than they did for GORI. Long ago, John Maynard Keynes noted that the advent of finance always creates two different pricing structures that operate separately from each other—the pricing of physical output and the pricing of financial assets. Against the abstract pricing of financial assets and the logics of valuation it is embedded in, my interlocutors posited that this mode of pricing did not reflect the proper ethical price that a commonly held form of wealth such as water should have. Wealth, for them, far exceeded domains of commodity circulation and instead included things that are not globally transactable precisely because they are essential to social reproduction (Foster 2018, 292). Their wealth, in short, should be priced, but in ways that stood in relation to the sacrality of the good. I thus read these struggles over crazy bills as a congealment of these differently scaled and situated regimes of valuation, an "encounter" (Ballestero 2019, 49) between citizens and utilities, and between utilities and the complex global forms of valuation and wealth making within which they are embedded.

Here, I explore how the water movement in Campania moved from a campaign of "civil obedience" that the national Italian water movement launched after the referendum in 2012, to a refusal to pay their crazy bills to GORI when their attempts at civil obedience failed. Along the way, I track different regimes of valuation as they are constituted "on scales both intimate and epochal" (Kalb 2020, 2). From the vantage point of regulators, the pricing of water in ways that allows for the full recovery of costs seems necessary and intuitive. The people I met in Campania, in contrast, thought of these pricing schemes as forms of madness, incapable of understanding the sanctity and meaning of life's most precious gift.

This foundational incommensurability was exacerbated by the fact that pricing in the water sector is highly localized—a city like Naples, which is furnished with its own remunicipalized water utility and until recently drew its water from the Serino spring in Irpinia, can price water differently than GORI, for example. Even after Naples' remunicipalized water utility Napoli ABC (Napoli Acqua Bene Comune, or Naples Water as Commons) lost direct access to the Serino spring and aqueduct (thus having to buy water from the region), its water prices were still significantly lower than those of GORI. Napoli ABC was frequently in the news for its relatively low water prices—a provocation not just to GORI but to all the other private providers in Italy who have insisted that remunicipalization was impossible because of the high costs of water infrastructure maintenance. GORI's price hikes were thus a constant point of tension in Campania since Naples' prices were not only more affordable, but also transparently rendered—a pattern found also among other publicly held Italian water utilities such as in the province of Verona, where the mechanism of water tariff calculations are publicly available and below regional and national averages (see Guerrini and Romano 2013, 81).[5]

GORI's price setting was thus not just inordinately high but also profoundly obscure.[6] As one critic put it to me, people in impoverished Campanian towns were paying double of what people in Naples' were paying with their infamous *partite pregresse*, and eight times more than people in the wealthy northern city of Milan. How could it be, people asked, that one of the poorest Italian regions with one of the country's lowest per-capita incomes would also sport one of the most exorbitant water prices on the Italian peninsula? "Those companies behave like colonizers," Marco Bersani from the Italian Forum for Water Movements said to me in Rome in February of 2016, "especially in the provinces."

GORI attempted to make the argument that the provisioning of water was expensive and consisted of multiple complex components (including risks, which are increasingly incorporated into calculations of price all over the world [Guyer 2009]). The people I met instead argued that GORI's price composition—that is to say, the way the company broke down the price into its component parts—did not render mechanisms of pricing more transparent but instead hid a simple truth behind numbers: that illegitimate profits were being extracted and pocketed by predatory mafias both near and far. Predation, while hiding behind the smooth veneer of the technically rendered bill, was in fact visible for all to see. The task of water movements was to render that truth visible and to return to a calculation of just price. They did so by insisting on a system of pricing grounded in highly territorialized valuations of water as a commons rather than as a resource from which investors extract vast wealth. Unlike global investors who insist that "the true value of water is not recognized," by which the mean that prices are set too low (Yang 2020; see also Besky 2016, 17), my interlocutors all insisted the opposite: that their commonwealth ought to be affordable precisely because it was so precious. Water, they argued, ought to be priced by accountable public authorities because it should never be made subject to the cold qualities of pure number.

Highly localized battles such as the ones documented here do not go unnoticed by global investors like Allianz Global Water. On the one hand, they have noted that water affordability is their top priority since "water is a human right." Such rights-based language clearly is not incommensurate with the financing and management of water supply systems by the private sector; it is, on the contrary, eminently compatible with it (Bakker 2007, 438). At the same time, Allianz Global Water also notes that "social pressures against water tariff inflation are . . . mounting" since "almost every dollar that is spent on improving water assets will have to be financed by higher bills." Allianz argues that these mounting pressures from below can be managed through "more efficient capital management," notably by having water utilities improve the efficiency of their operations (with "efficiency" usually translating into the reduction of labor costs through smart-water devices including smart meters; remote management controls; and specialized software systems for network monitoring, management, and planning—technical fixes, in short, to a social problem).

Investments firms like Allianz Global Water also position themselves as the best kind of stakeholder capable of implementing necessary innovations. Contrary to politicians, who as Allianz Global Water puts it "fear popularity loss from an increase of water fees to finance long-term [infrastructural] projects," global finance represents itself as impartial because it is unhinged from these local political strictures and therefore more capable of intervening into them. According to this view, it is local relationships, attachments, and accountabilities that sabotage the proper valuation of water and its price, and thus proper infrastructural "innovation."[7] The water struggles in Campania, however, were relentless in their politicization of price, mobilizing every political and legal tactic available.

### A Short History of Pricing

Italian lawmaking regarding water governance and pricing has been highly volatile over the years. The legal frameworks governing Italy's water pricing systems have been repeatedly replaced, with the country seeing no fewer than four different water pricing methods between 1996 and 2019. In part, the volatile legal situation emerged out of the desperate need for regulation in a country that had no national regulatory framework for groundwater until 1994, when it was first made part of the public domain (Massarutto 2015, 208). Italy is relatively well endowed with freshwater resources but has exhibited increasingly severe water stress (Massarutto 2015, 202; Romano and Guerrini 2019). Freshwater abstraction currently exceeds 40 percent of the country's renewable resources. Water scarcity is increasing in some parts of the country, as is inefficient water use, with average water leakages being 41.4 percent in 2015 and in some regions even 50 percent or more, although exact leakage rates are, of course, always notoriously difficult to come by (Anand 2017, 166–67; Björkman 2015, 38–39). Sixty percent of Italy's rivers and lakes are polluted with industrial waste, pesticides, and microplastics (Legambiente 2020). The European Community has launched several infringement proceedings against Italy for not meeting wastewater treatment standards (Guerrini and Romano 2014, 5). The investments required to meet infrastructural needs range in the tens of billions of euros—costs that the EU Stability Pact has insisted ought to be recovered through user fees. Put differently, the turn toward full cost recovery came precisely at a moment when water utilities were tasked with huge expenditures arising out of massive infrastructural need while simultaneously faced with increasingly stringent European water quality legislations.

Full cost recovery was inaugurated by the 1994 Galli Law, the same law that first regulated groundwater use and integrated water and wastewater systems. A general framework for the management of water was created as regions were tasked with integrating Italy's highly fragmented water and wastewater systems through the identification of "optimal management areas" (Ambito Territoriale Ottimale, or ATO) and authorities (AATO; Autorità d'Ambito Territoriale Ottimale). The AATO (recently renamed EGA [Romano and Guerrini 2019, 4]), were to delegate the operation of water services to either public, public-private, or fully private companies (Guerrini and Romano 2014, 7). While the tariff structure was left untouched in 1994, the law made clear that subsidies from the general budget would dramatically diminish and ultimately disappear, thus necessitating loans from private capital markets. Water tariffs were to generate sufficient margins to repay ensuing debts and thus began to include an investment remuneration component—the famed "adequate remuneration of invested capital" (*adeguatezza della remunerazione del capitale investito*) discussed in chapter 1 (Massarutto 2015, 211). By 1996, a ministerial decree introduced the so-called Normalized Method (MTN), a tariff-setting method that allowed utilities to cover operational costs and depreciation, as well as interest and taxes based on *planned* investments, or what was called the ex-ante regulation (Guerrini and Romano 2014, 11).

The "adequate return on investment" provisionally capped returns at 7 percent—what later came to be known as the "7 percent rule" (Romano, Guerrini, and Campedelli 2015, 46; Marotta 2012, 659).[8] In 2006, an Environmental Code (DM 152/2006) reinforced the principle of adequate remuneration of invested capital. In some regions like Tuscany and Emilia-

Romagna, prices soon doubled (Massarutto 2015, 212–13). These laws (and the "normalized" pricing methods they introduced) thus marked a period where water pricing moved from being almost entirely subsidized by the public budget, with households paying very little or sometimes nothing for water (Massarutto 2015, 211),[9] toward what is neoclassically defined as economic equity, that is, a system where "consumers" pay relative to the cost they "impose" on systems (Bakker 2001, 149).

The 7 percent rule was to be implemented across the board all over the country, regardless of costs of living and regardless of how unaffordable water would become to the poor. Politicians and lawmakers were thus responding primarily to creditors rather than to the larger question of what a just water price would mean from a household perspective. As Bakker has argued for the case of 1990s England and Wales, the rapid price hikes occurring within the privatized water sector there were distributed highly unequally, with the proportion of income that lower-income families spent on water and sewerage rising much faster than for higher-income families. By 2004 and 2005, the proportion required to cover the combined cost of water and sewerage bills for a single pensioner's income could in some regions be as high as 14 percent (Bakker 2001, 151).[10] Water debt in England and Wales thus increased faster than any other household expense, especially for low-income families. In Campania, many of the people I met asked simple questions. How do I pay for water if it takes up such a significant part of my household budget? How do we manage if we are already paying so much for gas, electricity, and rent? The question of just price is one of proportions (that is to say, of how high a proportion of household income is spent on water) and relationality (how expenses for water relate to other vital household expenses [Ballestero 2019, 51–52]).

By 2009, the government issued the Ronchi decree, which introduced the compulsory privatization of all social utilities, including water and wastewater services. All AATO were now obliged to entrust the management of local public services to either public-private partnerships or full private ownership. As joint stock companies, these fully or partially privatized corporations now had to have at least 40 percent of their shares owned by a private partner who would be guaranteed a 7 percent return (Guerrini and Romano 2014, 10; Mattei 2013, 368). The "adequate return on invested capital" was a phrase I heard over and over again, with people incessantly repeating the phrase both as a reminder of foundational betrayal (how could the government commit to being a guarantor of private profits rather than a guarantor of rights?) and of victory. After all, it was precisely this wording that was abrogated by the 2011 referendum. From now on, the remuneration of the invested capital component in the calculation of water tariffs was, in theory at least, forbidden.

Yet after the referendum, Prime Minister Berlusconi tasked the AEEG—Italy's regulatory authority for gas and electricity—to design a new tariff method in the water industry. Now called AEEGSI (Autority per l'Energia Elettrica, il Gas ed il Servizio Idrico) and since 2018, ARERA (Autorità di Regolazione per Energia, Reti e Ambiente), this authority was already notorious among many of the people I met since it had overseen the price hikes that led to the crazy bills in the gas and electricity sector, with Italians receiving some of the highest bills in OECD countries (Finanza Repubblica 2020). When regulators argue that Italian water prices are the lowest in Europe and that prices should therefore be raised, they fail to recognize that water price stands *in relation* to a whole panoply of other vital necessities that Italian households are already paying for. Unlike the delicate balancing act performed by Costa Rican public regulators who exhibited an exquisitely contextualized ethic of water pricing as they related the price of water to the price of other necessary household goods (Ballestero 2019, 151–52), AEEGSI's water price setting seemed to occur as if in a vacuum, not as part of a holistic consideration of household needs and with nothing more than full-cost recovery in mind. Pricing, in short, became an "adjunct" to the market and ceased to be a social exercise (Block 2001, xxiv), an economy "directed by prices and nothing but market prices" (Polanyi 2001, 45).

By 2012, AEEGSI had introduced a transitional pricing method, the MTT, only to replace it with another "definitive" pricing method called MTI for 2014 and 2015. Water bills that had previously consisted of operating costs, depreciation and amortization costs, and the return of investment, now consisted of a much higher number of cost items that included tax and interest expenses for invested capital, cost of new investments, environmental and resource costs, and adjustments for the prior years' tariff (Romano, Guerrini, and Campanelli 2015, 46). This proliferation of cost items—that is to say, the increase in the number of variables that now composed price—made water bills not less, but more obscure to people as they asked where their water prices came from and how price was composed.[11] For them, the new pricing method simply used a barrage of new cost items to cleverly mask what were de facto profits, hidden from view through a highly technical formula. They argued that these obscurities of price composition were simply the concrete manifestation of the more general opacity that marked the ways their water was currently being governed. As associations like the Rete Civica argued, a more comprehensible bill should let users understand their real consumption of water relative to actual costs.

Some authors argue that the new pricing formula respected the 2011 referendum by eliminating the guaranteed return of investment (Romano, Guerrini, and Campedelli 2015, 48; Guerrini and Romano 2014, 11–12). While the old "normalized method" had included the costs of planned investments (the ex-ante regulation), regardless of whether these investments were actually ever implemented (Italian water utilities had realized only 56 percent of planned investments by 2009 and only 49 percent in the previous year [Romano and Guerrini 2019, 4]), the new method supposedly did away with a water pricing trick by insisting on the ex-post regulation, which includes only those costs related to actual investments (Guerrini and Romano 2014, 11).[12]

Others have since noted that the new pricing method did nothing to improve the situation. Indeed, even authors who had initially lauded the post-2011 pricing method by pointing to the fact that companies must now determine tariffs based on real rather than projected costs (Guerrini and Romano 2014, 11–12), wrote a year later that companies managed to preserve this very practice (Romano, Guerrini, and Campanelli 2015, 51–52; see also Bieler 2021, 64).[13] ARERA confirmed this suspicion by recently reporting that the gap between promised and actually realized investments is in fact widening, especially in Italy's south (81.9 percent of planned investments were implemented in 2014, while only 77.6 percent were implemented in 2015 [Romano and Guerrini 2019, 4]). By 2020, critics lamented the fact that Italy lagged far behind the European standard in infrastructural investments—an average of thirty-two euros per year and per inhabitant, versus an average of one hundred euros in the rest of Europe. For them, this massive imbalance is the result of the entry of private investors into the Italian water market and not the fault of a supposedly incompetent public sector (Maraini 2020). The bill, in short, continues to be a reflection of projected further costs, many of which are never actually implemented— the predatory future perfect ("money will have been invested") embedded into the very grammar of the bill.

My interlocutors were also furious that the new pricing method simply reintroduced profits through other means. This is confirmed by the literature, which has found, for example, that a new tariff component called the FNI (the tariff component for new investments) has users pay for expected investments twice: once before their realization and then again two years later in the form of depreciation and amortization costs (Romano, Guerrini, and Campedelli 2015, 46). New cost items on Italian bills, in short, allowed for companies to extract value for infrastructural investments twice—once before and once after their realization, a trick reminiscent once again of the Irish situation, where protestors were furious about the fact that they were being "taxed twice." In addition, a study of 128 Italian water utilities noted that 42 are still privately owned, despite the referendum. Many pay significant dividends to investors. Indeed, the number of Italian water utilities that pay dividends to shareholders increased with the new national tariff method (Romano and Guerrini 2019, 7) because dividends are today paid to both private *and* public shareholders such as municipalities and other public bodies, many of which are indebted and in urgent need of cash. The publicly owned water utility in the wealthy northeastern city of Verona, for example, continues to apply the 7 percent rule to their tariff calculations even despite the referendum, since it would otherwise not be able to repay debts or realize necessary investments (Guerrini and Romano 2013, 82). The designation of utilities as either public or private thus has much rhetorical value but tells us little about how these utilities and their accounting sheets are actually managed.

This practice of deriving profits from water provisioning in explicit contravention of the referendum remains common in Italy today and is supported by the national association of ATO authorities (ANEA), which argues that infrastructural investments could otherwise not be made. The Italian National Forum on Water Movements argued, in contrast, that the question of infrastructural repairs is one of political will, since water utilities, especially in wealthier regions, make huge annual surpluses above and beyond the guaranteed returns of investment: in 2010, ACEA ATO 2 in Lazio made 59 million euros surplus; Acque SpA ATO 2 in Tuscany made almost 13 million surplus; Publiacqua ATO 3 in Tuscany made almost 15 million, and so on (Forum Italiano dei Movimenti per l'Acqua 2012, 4). The issue, the forum argued, are undercapitalized public utilities that cannot get bank loans, especially if they are located in smaller towns where the procurement of loans is often hindered by a smaller tax base (see also Humphreys, van der Kerk, and Fonsecca 2018, 107). Rather than make debt financing and capital remuneration necessary by starving poorer utilities, other more equitable models of public financing must be sought (see also Whiteside 2018). As previously noted, public institutions can borrow at significantly cheaper rates than the private sector can, thus significantly reducing capital costs (Massarutto 2020, 8). It is mainly the smaller, poorer utilities in impoverished regions that are penalized the most since they are forced to extract increased tariffs from the poor (Marotta 2012, 664).

In April 2014, an AEEGSI ruling forced water utilities to reimburse citizens for the undue tariffs collected before the adoption of the MTT. Water firms consequently returned about 55 million euros to 11 million Italian households (Romano, Guerrini, and Campedelli 2015, 48). Yet Italians today pay more for their water than ever before (Romano, Guerrini, and Campanelli 2015, 52–53; Massarutto 2015, 221–22). The newest water tariff calculation method, the MTI 2016–2019, only deepens these trends and ignores the Italian Forum for Water Movement's demand that water bills be reduced by a sum at least equal to the interest on invested capital, if not more (Marotta 2012, 658). Indeed, while middle- to upper-class households spend less than 3 percent of the household budget on water today, and thus below what is defined as the "affordability threshold," there is some "disquieting information" regarding the impact of these novel pricing methods on Italy's poor. Today, families with poverty-line incomes spend 1.5 percent of their basic income on water and waste services. This might not appear very much if viewed in isolation, but it can be devastating if viewed against the backdrop of significant price increases for other vital goods like electricity, gas, and transportation (Massarutto 2015, 221–22). The pricing of vital services is projected to further increase as all investment costs are fully transferred to consumers (Massarutto 2015, 228). The predatory mechanisms that the referendum aimed to do away with, in short, have in many cases remained intact.

For the Italian water movement, the price that should be paid for water was, strictly speaking, not a price at all but a fee. A long line of thinkers including Karl Polanyi have kept these two concepts separate. Fees compensate for the provisioning of a service, the calculated costs of which cannot exceed the costs necessary for its maintenance. Fees are paid by citizens in order to maintain a necessary service and are paid in exchange for quantifiable obligations that arise out of social relations. Price, in contrast, comes into play with "the acquisition . . . of desired goods" (Polanyi 2001, 104) and reflects the forms of valuation set in motion by market exchange (Guyer 2009, 2015). Water is "priced" once consumers are figured as "imposing" costs on a system—a system that must be priced in ways to produce surplus value so that the investors who carry it get their share (Bakker 2001, 149).

The difference between fees and price is also one of implicit ownership. With prices, people are thought of as users making demands on a service. With fees, citizens are thought of as having built the service through taxation, the material results of which they then, by implication, own. The past president of the German Alliance for Public Water Management (AöW) Christa Hecht put it to me particularly clearly during a conversation in 2016 when she made a similar distinction between fees (*Gebühren*) and price (*Preis*): "The law governing fee structures is clear," she said. "Citizens have paid for water systems with their fees. This means that these infrastructures cannot simply be sold off without their permission."

### The Mafias

Back in Castellammare, I spent the afternoon with Ferruccio, who is something of a melancholic town historian who keeps a website containing loving eulogies to Castellammare's past beauties, including many self-authored poems and dozens of scanned old postcards of the town, reminders of its past life as a tourist attraction as well as of its lamentable decline. His tour of his beloved town before our meeting with the local water committee was tinged with sadness as well as anger about the politicians who had ruined it. Gone were the thermal baths, the *terme di stabia* that had flourished in the past, bringing tourists and work. The baths and its hotels, nestled in the hills overlooking the sea, are now shuttered ruins overgrown with weeds. Gone, also, are parts of the beautiful seaside promenade. Much was crumbling, fenced off, or under construction during the time of my visit, with stray dogs lazing at the doors of quiet seaside cafes. Youth unemployment has soared well above national average—over 60 percent—and so it was no wonder that "the mayors were bought by the privates," as I heard locals say. My interlocutors were incensed by the fact that when GORI first came to Sarnese-Vesuviano district in 2006–2007, it not only began to raise water tariffs but also offered hundreds of jobs to (usually unqualified) family members of local politicians. While it is crucial to mention that publicly owned water utilities all over Italy tend to have significantly more employees than other public utilities do (Romano and Guerrini 2014, 15), my interlocutors were incensed that the clientelism of their previously public water utilities had been relocated into GORI and increased, not decreased, under the supposedly more "efficient" corporation.

This was not only the case in Campania. The EU Stability Pact subjected municipalities all over Europe to massive budgetary constraints and hiring freezes, which meant that mayors, particularly in impoverished Italian towns, had access to less and less money that would have allowed for infrastructural repairs or the hiring of municipal workers. In some towns, the effects of austerity-induced budget cuts inhibited older clientelistic networks by making it impossible for mayors to dole out jobs to voters. But the ensuing privatization of public services, like water utilities, did little to halt these trends. Rather than render water provisioning more efficient and transparent, it at times even exacerbated these clientelistic systems by offering new opportunities for collusion. Joint stock companies like GORI did not fall under the stringent parameters of the Stability Pact, which meant that they controlled money and were able to offer (sometimes sell) jobs and contracts to friends and acquaintances or, worse, to companies affiliated with the Camorra, the Campanian mafia-like criminal organization. It was privatized utilities like GORI that became the "real powers that controlled the vote," as some of my interlocutors explained, with mayors intensely interested in these public-private partnerships and the pork-barrel politics (*voto di scambio*) they enabled. If mayors managed to transfer their network of personal enrichment from the municipality to the joint stock company, they went from being "no one" to being "the person who gave this or that other person a job." In fact, having a stake in GORI or, better, sitting on one of its boards, was today worth more than being in political office.

Many of my interlocutors in and around Naples but also in Rome and the northern city of Turin were able to track the routes taken by local politicians as they worked their way up through the hierarchies of water utilities (see also Portelli 2017). Many of them came from the hated PD (*Partito Democratico*), the party that had evolved out of what was originally Italy's Communist Party and that had overseen what many of my interlocutors see as a total sell-off—*la svendita totale*—of Italy's public assets. One of Castellammare's town vice mayors, Alberto Irace, as the district attorney confirmed, was in office when the town's water utility was privatized and promptly became the ATO 3's first president, only to take the position of consultant for an ACEA satellite in Toscana, Pubbliacqua. He eventually became the CEO of the Roman multinational ACEA that today serves six million users and has a budget of hundreds of millions of euros—all of it derived out of the much-maligned *remunerazione del capitale investito* that ACEA, contrary to the outcome of the referendum, had accumulated over the years (Palladino 2016). Figures like Irace, ever more distant and alienated from the towns they came from, were thus directly implicated in GORI's "thievery" (see also Alliegro 2012, 163).[14]

The injustice of price was thus sought in the predatory actions of both faraway and much more intimately known actors. For many, the mysterious numbers on their bills were a manifestation of the open secret that was there for all to see—a universe of personal favors and backdoor deals that had proliferated with the arrival of supposedly more efficient and transparent corporate actors—a feature that others have already noted is more generally constitutive of financialized government (Vogl 2017). High water prices paid not for urgent infrastructural repairs or for the proper management of sewage, but for the "systems" of private personal enrichment, both near and far. Many of the people I spent time with in the Sarnese-Vesuviano district thus closely watched GORI and its employees, as did the Guardia di Finanza, the Italian financial police that investigated GORI in 2016 for its excessive spending on everything from salaries to costly consultancies (Gemma 2016, 9). For my interlocutors, every new GORI car, every GORI employee in the small towns of Campania, was read as an unnecessary expense that would end up on people's bills. "We're not their ATM machines!" I repeatedly heard people say. Ferruccio, driving around Castellammare's streets, would occasionally point to a white little GORI car. Was the employee simply sitting there, chatting on his cell phone? "There they are," Ferruccio growled. "Can you see these GORI employees, driving around in their cars all day long, doing what? All of this ends up in our bills!" Or, "GORI hired two consultants for some TV spot, all of which cost 2 million euros . . . and where does this get reflected? In our bill!" Mayors were also closely watched. Was he spotted talking to or shaking the hand of a GORI employee? If so, why?

People discussed not just GORI's clientelistic networks but also the profound inefficiencies built into the purportedly more efficient private company. Why else would GORI employees install new water meters in the chronological order of client numbers, rather than according to a pattern of geographical proximity ("they drive to one apartment building and install one meter and then ten kilometers somewhere else and install the next meter and then back again!")? Why else would GORI dismantle water meters entirely if a client was in arrears rather than simply close the meter off with a seal? Sure, some people might break the seal, but the real reason could only lie in the fact that the dismantling and reinstallation of water meters was a costly affair for which GORI could charge additional fees (50–60 euros for the dismantling of the meter and another 120–30 euros for its reinstallation). This overly complicated technical procedure made sure that the hundreds of excess people it had hired had something to do.

Meanwhile, water leakages had increased from an already astronomical 52 to 58 percent while water tariffs had soared by 49 percent in the four years between 2011 and 2015 (Gemma 2016, 10). Local media outlets regularly reported on water provisioning being reduced to a trickle or halted altogether, sometimes for hours and without warning.

Everywhere I went in the towns of ATO 3—San Giorgio, Nocera Inferiore, Casalnuovo, Portici, and others—people pointed out broken infrastructures, too. Here was a burst pipe that GORI did not fix for days; there was a pipe that was emitting untreated sewage sludge into a river. Facebook pages abounded with images of infrastructural neglect and ruination—archives of betrayal by the water utility and the politicians who had sold it off. Reminiscent of Mumbai's residents who complained about the fact that regardless of whether they got water, "the bills always come" (Anand 2017, 198; Anand 2011), many people in the Campanian villages and towns complained about how they were charged more and more for water despite visible infrastructural ruination. Most scandalously, GORI had removed a number of old public water fountains or let them run dry, as was the case in Nocera Inferiore when citizens protested the dismantling of several older water fountains during a particularly hot July in 2016, leaving nothing but holes in the ground (*RTA Live* 2016). To them, GORI was playing a "pipe politics" (Björkman 2015, 12) that left nothing but dry deserts behind—barren endpoints of neoliberalism's culture of death (*RTA Live* 2016).[15]

The fountains' disappearance came in the wake of GORI's installation of dozens of "case dell'acqua" (*houses of water*) in many municipalities of the ATO 3, where people could buy carbonated and noncarbonated water for five cents per liter. GORI represented these *case* as "the modern version of the public water fountain" that would allow people to access carbonated water cheaply and without buying plastic bottles (Gara 2015). Towns like Cimitile, Acerra, Anacapri, Camposano, and Pomigliano ceremoniously inaugurated the *case dell'acqua*, with one mayor triumphantly announcing that the *case* would allow these towns to recuperate "the collective spirit that will take us back to the origins, when public water fountains in the *piazze* represented a moment of encounter and socialization" (Lipari 2015). My interlocutors scoffed at these claims. For them, the rise of the shiny new *case* and the concomitant dereliction of their humble older water fountains (some of which were prominently featured in the posters people had made in the lead-up to the 2011 referendum) were nothing more than a sign of the breakdown of the social contract (see also Schwenkel 2015, 521). What previously stood as a towering example of the centrality of free water to public life now had to be bought, for a fee, from *diavolo* GORI. It did not matter that the water sold at the *case* was affordable or that they allowed people to use less plastic. What mattered was that this water was priced and flowed directly into the coffers of the hated privatized utility.

All of these accusations—the secret that was open for everyone to see—were confirmed in 2019 by the district attorney of Torre Annunziata after a ten-year long investigation. ACEA had knowingly let GORI's costs balloon abnormally by filling it up with "recommended" personnel (that is to say, people with "connections" [Zinn 2001]), around twelve hundred instead of the requisite six hundred. GORI had furthermore doctored its budgets in order to maintain ACEA's status on the stock market. It did so with the approval of politicians who were part of the water district and who had been bought with the promise of jobs. Because of the statute of limitations, none of the twenty-six investigated politicians were charged.

These logics of predation and enrichment were, however, never just a Campanian or even Southern Italian story. On the contrary, my interlocutors were clear in their insistence that these backdoor deals and predatory patterns were a systemic feature of the privatization of public water utilities both near and far, local and global. This argument is confirmed by others who have commented on the universe of political and economic favors, illicit reciprocal relations, and opaque "friendships" that lie at the heart of contemporary forms of shifting neoliberal government, which "emphasizes working with, and through, existing social networks of the market" (Bear 2015, 101; see also Calderone and Arlacchi 1993, 20; Elyachar 2012; Schneider 2016, 7; Rakopoulos 2020; Watts 2016, 88). Here, the illicit relations and backdoor deals that were set in motion by the entanglement of public and private actors and institutions are a feature of financialized governmentality *tout court*. They emerge out of "liminal situations" and rely on the temporary suspension of clearly defined ties, rights, and obligations (Bear 2015, 102).

The story of Berlin is a case in point, in that it made visible the gray zones of illicit favoritism that govern the privatization of public infrastructures. Berlins' senate, recall, had—in a backdoor deal—contractually guaranteed private investors their return on investment even as Berlin's Constitutional Court ruled against it—thus including in the secret contract an addendum that explicitly flaunted the law. When German critics referred to this senatorial guarantee as the "Sicilianization of profits" (Boewe 2009), they incorrectly associated these illicit deals with tired Southern Italian stereotypes rather than understanding these mechanisms as intrinsic to all financial frontiers. After all, frontiers are always marked by the interpenetration of legality and illegality as the boundaries between public, private, and sometimes even criminal enterprise become unclear (Tsing 2003, 5103). These illegibilities, already exacerbated with a market fundamentalism blurring the lines between licit and illicit business and "formal" and "informal" production (Comaroff and Comaroff 2006, 25; Schneider and Schneider 2008, 359; Schneider 2016),[16] have reached an apex with informalized styles of financialized government (Vogl 2017, 4).

This is not to say that these predatory backdoor deals are the same everywhere. The opportunity opened up by the informal entanglements between public and private actors could, in a region like Campania, very well end in Camorristic infiltrations (*infiltrazioni camorristiche*) as some people mentioned, often very obliquely and in whispers. There were many reasons to believe that this network of illicit favors within the water sector could intersect with the realms of organized crime, which has been shown to increasingly use public procurement as a way to launder money before it enters the financial system (Caneppele, Calderoni, and Martocchia 2009).[17] Such worries were legitimized when people like Amedeo Laboccetta, a noted gambling lobbyist who had been ejected from political office after coming under investigation for illicit financial deals, became the president of GORI in 2014. He was supported not just by Carlo Sarro, the emergency manager of the ATO 3 of the Sarnese-Vesuviano district and a politician who was rumored to have rigged a number of public tenders to favor of the Camorra, but also by many mayors from the Sarnese-Vesuviano district, including the mayor of Castellammare di Stabia (Sannino 2014). The rumors were further confirmed when PD-politician Vincenzo de Luca became governor of the region of Campania in 2015 after having been officially deemed unfit for public office by Italy's parliamentary Antimafia Commission. DeLuca had immediately passed a law that significantly reduced the power of the ATOs by grouping them under one single entity (Ente Idrico Campano, the institution that mayors were protesting against in the scene I describe at the beginning of the book). Activists feared that this "technocratic and authoritarian" move toward a more centralized regional structure would not only "expropriate" local communities of their capacity to influence water politics via their mayors (Napolitano 2015) but allow the region and its Camorra-sponsored representatives to take control of all springs; all strategic planning; and all regional, national, and European funds (Montalto 2018).

And yet, I was struck by how many of the people I met never just spoke of the mafia in the singular, but more often in the plural. After all, people were not simply referring to bounded local networks. Rather, their use of the term *mafie* referred to a logic of predation that recurs across scales, a form of rent seeking that functions as a capillary networked system that extracts value for personal gain both near and far (Li and Semedi 2021, 40–41).[18] The Camorra in Campania was thus understood not as a bounded institution but as a predatory mode of conduct that saturates public life and that includes a logic of secrecy and obfuscation; a Darwinistic attraction to money; parasitic sinews of clientelism; protectionism between public officials and private business; and a complete disregard for basic constitutional rights, law, and life (Giusto 2020). This mafia and its predatory features, in short, overlap with and bear strong resemblance to the "most advanced types of capitalism" (Giusto 2019, 5), a "predatory mode of distribution" that does nothing but syphon off wealth (Li and Semedi 2021, 79; see also Weston 2017, 158). As a hydraulic engineer put it to me over lunch one day at Napoli ABC, the *malavita* [*bad life*; i.e., organized crime] was "the purest expression of the free market." Why, I asked? "They always have the most money, the most resources. Stacks and stacks of money." Referring to the bidding processes that accompany the outsourcing of public services, he notes that "They will always outbid others. It's pure Darwinism."

This is why many people's use of *mafie* in the plural seemed significant to me: there is not just one. Rather, the *mafie* were not just a set of Southern Italian institutions but a mode of comportment that can be found everywhere where one finds these predatory practices—in GORI, in the mayoral office in towns like Castellammare, in ACEA in Rome, in the Italian regulatory authority AEEGSI that managed to smuggle the logics of extraction back into the pricing formula even after the referendum, and among faraway investors who knew nothing about Castellammare's waters—except that they wanted to drain life and wealth from them. Frontiers, Tsing has put it, are never a simple "neighborhood storm." A frontier always "gathers force" from afar, engaging multiple local-to-global scales" (2003, 5106). Similarly, the water bill and its crazy price was the expression of multiple scales of predation, of *mafie* both near and far.

### The Necropolitics of Privatization

The transition of people like Laboccetta from political office into GORI was more than just worrisome to the people I met. It was terrifying because it seemed like the exact reiteration of the catastrophic collusion that occurred over several decades between Northern Italian industrialists, local politicians, and the Camorra after the lucrative waste disposal business was outsourced to private companies in the 1980s (Caneppele, Calderoni, and Martocchia 2009; Armiero and D'Alisa 2013, 8–9; De Biase 2015, 49–50). This collusion resulted in what came to be known as Campania's infamous "triangle of death," a 1076 km$^2$ area north of Naples that had become the site of massive illegal toxic waste dumping. It is estimated that ten million tons of illegal waste, including asbestos and radioactive sludge, were trucked into this area and buried or burned, mostly during the 1980s and 1990s. By 2016, Italy's National Institute of Health officially recognized the connection between illegal waste dumping and the alarming rates of cancer and other illnesses in the area. Campania's environmental agency, ARPAC, found two thousand contaminated sites and lists fifty-seven affected municipalities—poisoned water, air, and agricultural terrains (D'Alisa and Armiero 2013, 41). Doctors have reported that some municipalities have seen cancer rates double in as little as the last five years and birth defects go up 80 percent above the national norm (Di Costanzo and Ferraro 2013, 25–26), a killing "in small doses" as Achille Mbembe would put it (2019, 35). Local farmers have produced grainy YouTube videos of their animals dropping dead, one by one, over a matter of weeks. Similar environmental crimes have proliferated over Italy (Baccaro and Musella 2013), reaching far beyond the confines of an "ecomafia" and deep into the workings of large Italian industries (Trocchia 2017).

The people I spoke to in Campania were terrified that this pattern of total disregard for life would be repeated with the privatization of water. As Padre Zanotelli, a Catholic priest and central figure in the Neapolitan water movement put it to me, "First it's the trash, now the water. Wherever there is money, they go," lowering his voice as he said it, as if the walls of the little bell tower where he lived had ears. Many of the people involved in the Campanian water movement had roots in the Stop Biocidio (Stop Biocide) movement that had arisen out of the Campanian toxic waste scandal (Capone 2013). They had a sharp eye and excellent knowledge of the longue durée of these necropolitical networks of predation.[19] All knew about the decades-long collusion between northerners, local politicians, and the Camorra. The story of a Camorra boss, secretly recorded as saying "they can drink bottled water" when asked what would happen to people if toxic waste trickled down into Campania's aquifers, was well known and circulating widely in the water movement there (Alliegro 2020; Giusto 2018). The idea that water was simply the latest vital substance that local people were being dispossessed of deeply animated their activities. After the violation of their collective bodily health, the *mafie* were now coming for their water as well—a fact that was articulated by some local water committees on banners, flyers, and T-shirts, flaming red and written in dialect: *"C'at accis pur acqua"* (Even water you've killed!).[20] The choice of wording is, of course, deliberate, in that it accuses the Camorra not simply of robbing people of their health, but of deliberately murdering their water as well.

This battle against necropolitical networks of enrichment was performed with particular theatricality in 2016, when Luigi de Magistris, then major of Naples and a noted antimafia magistrate, inaugurated two new public water fountains in Naples, together with then director of Napoli ABC Maurizio Montalto. For Montalto, the very substance and culture of the newly remunicipalized utility had to be changed into something that was more transparent, more accountable, *more legal*, as he put it at a conference in Rome in 2016. Both water fountains were adorned with commemorative plaques honoring victims of the Camorra, allowing for the mayor and director to declare that Napoli ABC provided water that was "clean in every sense of the word." Soon after, Napoli ABC sent out water bills to all Neapolitan households and attached to each a copy of an article on these two water fountains, entitled "Memory and Commitment to the Water of Legality." Napoli ABC was being transparent, Montalto explained, by informing Naples' citizens about its "managerial and ethical decisions"—all of which were clearly expressed by its affordable price. At Napoli ABC, price gave numerical expression to a politics accountable to people and, ultimately, to life as such.

### Just Price

Castellammare's local water committee was still known in the area for its continued fight against crazy bills, even when I first arrived in 2015. What fascinated me was that they had fervently adhered to an earlier national civil obedience campaign, launched by the Italian water movement on January 1, 2012. The campaign emerged after it became clear that politicians and lawmakers would find ways around implementing the 2011 national referendum, mostly through new pricing mechanisms that obliquely reinstated the returns of investment on peoples' bills. The campaign thus argued that if the political classes refused to implement what should have become law, the people would do so instead: "We are not disobeying the

4.1      "Campaign of Civil Obedience: With the referendum, we cancelled profits from the management of water but politicians and managers don't know how to respect the popular will. Let us do it ourselves. Let us cancel profit-seeking from our water bills." (Photo: Andrea Muehlebach.)

law but simply insisting on its application," wrote the Italian water movement as it announced the campaign.

The term *obedience* was evocative here in that it positioned the government as "disobedient" and as flaunting the law that the referendum ought to have become. This point gained legitimacy after a subsequent ruling Nr. 26/2011 by Italy's Constitutional Court, which insisted that the referendum results were "immediately applicable." The people were therefore abiding by the law by implementing the referendum—the clearest manifestation of which would be the eradication of the proportion on their bill that represented the "remuneration of invested capital."

Significantly, this campaign was not about the refusal to pay bills. Rather, it was about people determining which components of the price were just and which ones were not. In the province of Arezzo in the region of Tuscany, where water was privatized in 1998 and where nearly 50 percent of the water utility's shares belong to a conglomerate of shareholders that includes French corporation Suez and Italian corporation ACEA, local water committees were some of the first to organize against opaque bills and the first to attempt these recalculations. As activist Luca Belloni explained, "We are recalculating our bills, identifying the percentage that is hiding the "remuneration of profits" that we abolished with the referendum. The government is holding onto it until today, but we are only paying what we owe them according to the law." The number that the popular referendum had eliminated was worth 13 percent of the bill, an "autoreduction" implemented by thousands of families in the province of Arezzo (Forum Italiano dei Movimenti per l'Acqua 2014a).[21] The Arezzo campaign was quickly scaled up by the Italian Forum for Public Water, which soon launched a national campaign including very concrete instructions: a *vademecum* (handbook) designed for individual households as well as apartment building managers and owners, small businesses, farmers, and even industry, explained that the "remuneration of invested capital" equaled 7 percent—the calculation of which hinged on both realized and expected investments on a given territory. How this guaranteed return of investment would appear on the bill varied across the country and could make up between 10 and 25 percent of the total water tariff depending on the area plans (*piano d'ambito*) made by respective ATOs. In some egregious cases such as La Spezia, 26 percent of the water bills were composed of the guaranteed remuneration of invested capital, numbers that the Italian water movement urged people to subtract. But the problem was not only that the remuneration of invested capital continued to be part of the way prices were composed—albeit in hidden ways. The scandal also lay in the fact that some utilities *raised* prices, even after the referendum. In Ancona in the region of Marche, for example, the AATO 2 raised water tariffs by another 6.5 percent within weeks of the referendum. The Campaign of Civil Obedience thus urged people to do two things: demand reimbursement for the excess money they paid for illegitimately billed services, and autoreduce the amount that they paid for services after the referendum, starting as soon as they had sent their utility a declaration of intent.

The forum provided people with a printable form with which they could formally inform the utility and the ATO of their intent to autoreduce their payments on water bills while also demanding reimbursement. These forms were to include the exact percentage that the sender intended to subtract from their bill going forward—a percentage that the National Forum calculated for every ATO and every municipality in Italy and made available on its website. By 2012, the forum was able to draw on one of the most important legacies of the referendum—the legion of tiny water committees that remained all over the Italian territory. They helped set up small public help desks all over the country that people could approach as they sought help filling out the two-page long claims forms that they sent to their respective water utilities. People wrote their own postal pay slips containing the "correct number" (*cifra corretta*) that would purge predatory pricing from their water bill. It was through these calculations and the politics of "correct numbers" that people became what they called custodians of the referendum (*custodi del referendum*), implementing the law they had themselves made.[22]

The corrected postal pay slips quickly spread. By 2013, towns like Arezzo saw over three thousand people autoreduce their bills. They also threatened to sue their utility Nuove Acque should it attempt to sabotage their efforts. In Ancona in the region of Marche, hundreds of citizens responded by signing the claims letter provided by the Forum. They presented these forms to the multiutility, Multiservizi SpA, urging it to implement the results of the referendum. In La Spezia, the local water committee presented the president of Acam Acque with the first two thousand signed declarations of intent collected for the campaign. In the province of Reggio Emilia, local water campaigners ceremoniously delivered two hundred declarations of intent directly to the municipality after having also sent them to Iren, the Italian water corporation that was active in their territory. All in all, twelve thousand people from Padova to Puglia autoreduced their bills. Some public institutions followed suit, such as the forty Tuscan towns who vetoed 10 percent price hikes by arguing that it was impossible to continue to ignore the results of the referendum (see chapter 1).[23] The civil obedience campaign got a further (albeit short-lived) boost in March of 2013, when Tuscany's regional court (the Tribunale Amministrativo Regionale, or TAR) ruled in favor of water movements, arguing that postreferendum water bills were "illegitimate" in so far as they contained the "remuneration of invested capital" that the referendum in 2011 had explicitly abolished. As the TAR put it, "The principle of capital remuneration . . . is inevitably overruled by the abrogative capacity of the popular will."[24] By 2016, Arezzo's water corporation began to shut off these families' water. But people again immediately took the water utility to court (Palladino 2016).

The civil obedience campaign was remarkable because it represented a form of insurgent citizen price setting, with citizens taking the law—and the laws regarding pricing—into their own hands. The campaign sought to stabilize and thus render just the unjust pricing of a vital good. When citizens attempted to counter crazy bills through their own countercalculations (see also Muehlmann 2012), they insisted on a world of valuation diametrically opposed to that which characterizes this epoch of financialization: one grounded in highly territorialized valuations of water as a commons. People became "regulators," like those so vividly described in Edward Palmer Thompson's account of the eighteenth century food riots (1971). Like their eighteenth century forebears, the people in Campania engaged in the setting of price in order to "enforce the laws" because the authorities refused to do so.[25] Like eighteenth-century price setters, they bemoaned the vanishing of a system of price setting that was more legitimate to them because it was managed by local authorities and affordable for all. Like the eighteenth-century price setters, they lamented the fact that marketing and pricing procedures had become less and less transparent the more intermediaries and dealers became involved. They also similarly insisted that they were not stealing but engaging in a politics of countercounting to "correct" price, thus inaugurating a more accountable and transparent pricing system. And like their eighteenth-century counterparts, the price setters wielded their own complicated mathematical formulas. This was not, they insisted, simply an economic battle—a matter precipitated by the grumbling of stomachs (Thompson 1971, 79)—but ultimately a moral and ethical question about the moral economy of just price.

The campaign anticipated the ways in which utilities would respond to this coordinated challenge from below—namely, by treating people like run-of-the-mill debtors. The forum predicted that utilities would use the usual tactics of intimidation—serve injunctions against people who were now suddenly in arrears of payment, send debt collection agencies to their homes, or, worst of all, shut off people's water. The campaign thus knew that the battle would have to be won on another front as well—they had to convince people that it was not *they* who were debtors but the utility that was in debt to *them* since it had extracted too much money. They had to convince the population that it was illegitimate, indeed illegal, to continue to charge those hated 7 percent guaranteed returns of investments on water bills. And that it was legal and just for people to correct an unjust composition of price.

## On Civil Disobedience

The Campaign of Civil Obedience emerged out of a moment when the trust in democracy, due process, and of people's capacity to hail institutions back into legality had not entirely dissipated yet. "Immediately after the referendum," Marco Bersani from the Italian Water Forum explained to me, "we were still involved in a battle for the respect of the referendum's outcome, a battle for democracy. We were confident that we could realize democracy through its established institutions." But, he warned during a conversation in 2016, "We have now entered a new phase, not just nationally but internationally . . . with a new juridical landscape where profits prevail over democracy." For Bersani, people could not turn to the law anymore as a reliable institution. The time had come, Bersani seemed to imply, for civil disobedience to prevail.

It was 7:00 p.m. in the evening in the fall of 2015, and Ferruccio had brought me to a small parish common room nestled along the side of one of Castellammare di Stabia's churches. A group of about thirty elderly men and women were waiting for what seemed like hours for a lawyer whom they wanted to consult about nonpayment. I was already acutely aware that the mood had changed from "obedience"—the political tactic that had grown out of the belief in a functioning democracy—to "disobedience" that had grown out of a sense that democracy had been eviscerated and its concomitant institutions undone (Greenberg 2020, 4). I listened to the murmur of conversation: "What are the legal ramifications if we don't pay?" "How are these bills composed anyway?" As I sat there, waiting, I watched these retirees, worries written all over their faces. It was clear that the dread of radical price hikes—of opening up the next envelope containing the next bill—introduced new, highly unpredictable futures into these pensioners and their families' lives, especially since middle- and lower-income households had increasingly been squeezed by mortgages, rising rents, and an everprecarious labor market. I assumed that many of their children and grandchildren were unemployed or underemployed. This meant that extended households, always social rather than mere economic units (Zaloom 2017), are sites where the payment for basic services like water "is no longer shaped by the cyclical temporality of regularly recurring monthly salaries," but instead by an income tempo that is "incremental and ad hoc" (von Schnitzler 2016, 6). The "end of the salary" (Mbembe and Roitman 1995) and its counterpart, the irregular income, coincides with the rise of relentlessly regular taxes and fees—a schizoid household fisc and temporality that generates anxieties over social reproduction often expressed in terms of fraught intergenerational relations (Narotzky and Besnier 2014, 5; Federici 2015; Song 2009; Langley 2020c; Weiss 2022). The retirees I was sitting with were likely to be the only recipients of a stable income that often does not amount to more than a few hundred euros per month. A *bolletta pazza* was thus more than just an individual tragedy. It also severely tested already strained chains of social reproduction and had multiple cascading effects across a generational system in which children and grandchildren already heavily rely on small grandparent gifts of money, food, and other forms of care.

Some of the people in this parish common room had been involved in the civil obedience campaign, and had attempted to counter the predatory tactics of GORI and its investor friends with their own calculative ethic. Yet by the time I arrived, it was clear that the momentum—of the referendum, of the subsequent Campaign of Civil Obedience, of hailing the state back into lawfulness—was impossible to maintain. Instead, the people in the room had explicitly turned to disobeying GORI's injunction to pay. Matters had reached a boiling point once GORI began to send them the infamous *partite pregresse*—bills that charged people retroactively for water for which they had for years supposedly underpaid. This retroactive charge had been itemized explicitly on people's bills (as a *recupero partite pregresse ante 2012*). GORI had justified it on its website as price hikes that had been "recognized by the ATO 3, discussed by the assembly of mayors and applied according to the terms set by AEGSII."

The district was soon awash with protest. The Rete Civica and the local Five Star Movement—the populist political movement founded by comedian Beppe Grillo whose platform consisted of restoring accountability to Italy's political class through, among other things, a return to water as a common good—began to circulate images of bills with that item (*recupero partite pregresse ante 2012*) highlighted in red, urging people not to pay. Consumer rights lawyers did the same, telling their clients to not even acknowledge receipt of the bill, let alone respond. GORI was thus met with a wall of silence or what people there called a fiscal strike (*sciopero fiscale*).[26] What further fueled the strike was the fact that these crazy bills seemed to be transparently connected to the disastrous financial situation of GORI, which since 2002 had paid neither for the water it was procuring from the region of Campania nor for the collection and treatment of sewage in the district's sewage plants. When the region decided to forgive GORI a debt of 157 million euros in 2013, it represented its decision as a historic move since citizens' bills would from now on be less onerous. But for many of the people in the villages and towns of Campania, this seemingly magnanimous act of debt forgiveness was proof only of the fact that the government had sold the people out yet again. This was a highly political debt that could be forgiven at a whim and in discretionary ways; it was a deep embrace of mutual obligation and cyclical debt forgiveness between the corporation and politicians. The peoples' debt, in contrast, was a relentlessly nonnegotiable fiscal debt—a sign of the fact that the social contract between the government and the people had shattered.[27] Meanwhile, as one of my interlocutors fumed, the public "supported the privates while subtracting money from hospitals, schools, and other public institutions!" (see also Sasso and Sironi 2013).

The people in that parish common room that evening were thus all haunted by the specter of debt collection or, worse, the "savage" water shutoffs (distacchi selvaggi) that had proliferated in the district and that continue until today.[28] People who had been radically politicized during the referendum suddenly found themselves sitting uncomfortably close to what looked like delinquency. "They have *made* us into delinquents," one consumer rights advocate said to me at the meeting.[29] Some of the people in that room had initially autoreduced their bills in accordance with the Campaign of Civil Obedience and maintained a sense of defiance. As one man put it to me, "If the municipality wants to come and take my money and invest it in infrastructure, they can have it. But I will not give it to the water thieves." People like him insisted that being in arrears (morosità) was not anything to be ashamed of—after all, this was a morosità politica (political indebtedness) that often also arose out of pure, desperate need (morosità di necessità) (see also Stout 2019, 172). Others, in contrast, were mortified. "We are respectable people" (gente perbene), they insisted, "who are being instigated towards these kinds of actions. We don't feel comfortable doing this." While the civil obedience campaign had envisioned them as self-determining price setters, they were now mere debtors in the eyes of GORI. Their politics of refusal now hovered dangerously between politics and misdemeanor (see also von Schnitzler 2016, 70), with GORI perverting not just their water utilities but their political projects as well.

People in the Sarnese-Vesuviano region regularly went to the streets, holding banners that read "We will not pay GORI's debts!"[30] The tactic of disobedience thus involved other political and legal strategies. The Rete Civica, for example, had pulled together a network of district mayors (Rete dei Sindaci) with the aim of cajoling as many of them as possible into an anti-GORI alliance so that GORI could ultimately be sent away.[31] Mayors technically have the power to do so since about half of them get voted into the district governing council (Consiglio di Distretto) where a decision on the liquidation of GORI could be made. At the time of this writing, almost half of the mayors of the ATO 3 district had joined (or were cajoled or forced) into this network, a number that speaks to relentless organizing from below. So far however, this has not been enough to challenge the power of GORI.[32] Members of the Rete Civica also physically occupied the buildings of the Ente Idrico Campano. They launched a series of court cases against GORI with the help of the Campanian consumer rights agency Confconsumatori Campania and an indefatigable lawyer named Giuseppe Grauso, who later became council member at the Ente Idrico Campano. In March 2014, a total of 2000 GORI clients from the town of Nocera Inferiore launched a class action lawsuit against GORI, contesting the *partite pregresse* and attempting to reclaim the excess money they claimed to have paid. One of the arguments made in court was strikingly similar to the contractual arguments made by the Irish described in a preceding chapter, where plaintiffs insisted that they had not signed a contract and thus never consented to GORI's terms.

At times, these local court cases were won, such as when the justice of the peace in the town of Marigliano just outside of Naples sided with plaintiffs against GORI. A similar lawsuit was launched by consumer rights organizations with the help of numerous citizens and mayors from Castellammare di Stabia at the Tribunale di Torre Annunziata. By 2019, the regional administrative court (Tribunale Amministrativo Regionale; TAR) and the Appeals Court of Naples ruled against the *partite pregresse*, again in response to a lawsuit launched by the Rete Civica, the consumer rights organization Federconsumatori and the towns of Ercolano, Casalnuovo, Angri, Nocera Inferiore, Castel San Giorgio, and Fisciano, all of who are part of the network of anti-GORI mayors. Yet even though the Rete Civica, Campania's Five Star Movement and the Green Party called for the liquidation of GORI, GORI insisted that its calculation of price was valid. The Rete Civica then staged what they called a #*NoGori tour* that began in Castellammare di Stabia in June 2019 and moved from town to town, gathering people in piazzas and churches to protest the continued presence of GORI.

The tour gave mayors yet another opportunity to declare publicly that the water bills extracted wealth and life from the population but did nothing in return, and that "sister water" (*sorella acqua*) ought to be a public good.

## That Rushing Sound of the Flow of Water

I now tell one last story about the politics of disobedience that has grown out of the political mobilizations for just price. Sometime during 2016, I found myself standing on a street corner in a peripheral town on the outskirts of Naples. Two friends had taken me there after our dinner together, very late at night after I had mentioned that I was on my way to Rome to speak to the popular antiwater-shutoff group, GAP (Gruppo Antidistaccho Popolare), which had first formed in Rome in the autumn the year before. These small groups of five to six people, men and women guerilla plumbers dressed in blue overalls and Super Mario masks, had begun to hook people back up to the water supply after their water had been shut off because of nonpayment. As one of them would later explain to me, they had chosen Mario precisely because he was not a superman, but a common plumber, who helps the people by "giving them back their water." Armed with pipes and meters, both of which are usually removed by GORI, these groups organized nightly guerrilla actions to reinstall both. Not unlike the Irish water fairies who were dismantling water meters at exactly the same time, the Super Marios also thought of themselves as engaging in direct action over a fundamental human right.

GAP had also been the acronym of the Gruppi d'Azione Partigiana, the partisans who had so valiantly fought the Fascists during World War II. These contemporary GAP members saw themselves as operating within this long and venerable Leftist tradition of clandestine insurgency, this time against the "dictatorship" of finance. They knew that this act is a major criminal offense in Italy and comes with between three and six years in jail if the person is caught in the act. I thus found myself on this street corner, listening to one of those marvelous orators one so frequently finds in Italy—telling his tale about how he and his collective had long heard about a family in his town, a father, mother, three children, all without work, *gente perbene* who had not been able to pay for water for years, and that everyone knew that it was wrong and that something had to be done. He spoke with dramatic flourishes, his cigarette glowing in the dark as he moved his arms up and down, telling us how they had learned from a real

"Water Is Life: Whoever Shuts It Off Cancels Out a Right." (Photo: Andrea Muehlebach.)

plumber (someone who worked for GORI, no less) to hook up the water system again, how they had bought the right tubes and the right meter, how they had reinstalled both the meter and the pipes in the darkness of the night, and how they all listened intently to how the water again began to flow. "And that sound of water," he said with so much joy that we all laughed out loud, "That rushing sound of the flow of water . . . was the sound of democracy, of rights, of freedom."

EPILOGUE

IN JUNE OF 2017, I paid a visit to the Laboratoire Eau de Paris, the laboratory responsible for analysis and research at Paris's public water utility,
Eau de Paris (Paris's Water). I soon found myself in the company of three
scientists who had invited me to taste Paris's water. All were officially
recognized water tasters (*goûteurs d'eau*) at the public utility's lab (the lab
employs eight of these specialists in total, all of whom taste the water on
a rotating basis two to three times a week). They ushered me into a small
room, asking me to close the door behind me. We waited quietly for a while
since the water had to be at an exact twenty-four degrees Celsius before
its taste would fully unfold in our mouths. I stood, perusing the posters on
the wall, reading one that said, "Eau de Paris: Our Values, Our Common
Identity" (sustainable management, responsibility, solidarity), all of
which were checked with a red checkmark. We each got two wine
glasses—one would be filled up with tap water, the other with
Evian mineral water. Both glasses were swished out with

water, smelled, and swished out again. The scientists explained to me that Paris's tap water approximated Evian water's chemical composition and taste, which is why they always used it as a "reference water" to compare the two tastes to each other. Wearing white lab coats, one of the *goûteurs* poured Evian water into each of our two glasses, and Paris's water into the other. He filled my glasses up, too. We first tried the Evian water: smelled, swirled it around in the glass, swished the Evian around in our mouths, and smelled again. When we were done, we spit the water into a basin. We then proceeded to do the same with Paris's tap water—smell, swirl, swish, smell again, spit. The three men standing next to me had their eyes closed, savoring the qualities of this precious substance. "Nothing out of the ordinary" they said. We tried Paris's water again, this time by adding a drop of sulphate to dissolve the chlorine and achieve an even more unmediated sense of taste. Again, "nothing out of the ordinary." This was a good thing: there was nothing, no strange chemical aftertaste, no unusual whiff that disturbed the palates of these highly trained tasters. Paris's water, savored by these employees and treated as one of the city's most precious collective wealth (a commons [*bien commun*] and hydraulic patrimony [*patrimoine hydraulique*]), tasted exactly as it was supposed to taste.

I had come to Paris that summer to visit Eau de Paris, the largest public water company in France and one of the world's most famous examples of water utility remunicipalization. France, which still delegates about 70 percent of its water management to private providers, has seen a wave of remunicipalizations in the last decade—the largest number in Europe (Moore 2019, 29–30). Paris was in fact not the first, but simply the most famous example of this more general trend. It was the city of Grenoble that initiated what some have called a French water revolution. There, a citizens' coalition fought long battles and staged dramatic protests throughout the 1990s, including televised appearances where residents held up water bills from 1989, when the water utility was still in public hands and when water cost 5.35 francs per $m^3$, versus bills from 1995, when water had been privatized and cost 15 francs per $m^3$ (Binctin 2018). Soon after, Grenoble's mayor was found guilty of corruption and the misuse of public assets related to the water concession and ended up spending two years in prison. By 2001, Grenoble's newly remunicipalized water utility created an advisory body that Eau de Paris would later emulate. Its water is among the cheapest in France until this day (Herzberg and Blanchet 2016; Herzberg 2015).

Paris reverted back to public ownership in 2010 after twenty-five years of private management by Suez, which had full control over water production and distribution on the left bank of the river Seine, and Veolia, which had the same responsibilities on the right bank of the Seine. In part, the take back occurred because a public audit commissioned by the city of Paris had revealed that prices were 25–30 percent higher than justified and that Veolia and Suez managed Paris's water in profoundly untransparent ways (Moore 2019, 29–30). By 2008, a newly elected Leftist mayor, Bertrand Delanoë, decided not to renew both Suez and Veolia's expired contracts. Instead, he tasked Deputy Mayor Anne Le Strat with taking on the chairmanship of Eau de Paris and managing Paris's water supply, sanitation, and canalization system. Deeply committed to water as a public good and to the principle that water should be managed directly by local authorities, Le Strat and her team "liberated" Paris Water and transformed the previously divided water system into a single integrated company (Le Strat 2010). Most notably, Eau de Paris today consists not only of a board of directors but of a Paris Water Observatory (Observatoire Municipal de l'Eau), some members of which sit on the board of directors. The observatory consists of members of the Council of Paris and of Eau de Paris's technical partners, as well as of representatives of the broader Parisian public—trade unions, consumer rights groups, public and private housing management agencies, tenant associations, and environmental groups. The stated goal of the observatory is to place water users at the "heart of the service" (Le Strat 2010).[1] Its members directly elect the observatory's board and president and hold plenary meetings that are open to public participation. Anyone can join in discussions of topics ranging from water service reform to water tariffs, the right to water and sanitation, public drinking fountains, and the elimination of lead pipes in the water network (see also Kishimoto, Lobina, and Petitjean 2015). Eau de Paris is also a prominent member of the European network Aqua Publica Europea, the European Association of Public Water Operators, that was founded in Paris in 2009 to advocate for public management on the European level and to counter corporate water lobbies.

The integration of Eau de Paris's two previously independently managed halves allowed the company to eliminate inefficiencies, cut operating costs by 30 million euros, internalize surpluses that private operators had previously syphoned off as profits, and invest surplus earnings into Paris's water services. Eau de Paris can now make tenders for work public competitive and thus more affordable, rather than be monopolized by either Suez or Veolia, both of whom provided these services in-house, often for a high price. As Anne Le Strat put it immediately after remunicipalization: "There is no need to pay dividends to shareholders and to set aside part of the profits generated by the water services to pay them. All revenue . . . is totally reinvested in the service, and there is complete financial transparency, unlike the previous situation under the private system, where the lack of financial clarity was repeatedly criticized in financial controls" (Le Strat 2010). Or, as one of my interviewees put it to me, "[B]efore, every drop of water went through many different hands; now it's all in our hands."

Eau de Paris is today entirely financed through user tariffs according to the principle "water pays for water," with its budget balancing income with operating and investment costs. While loans can be taken out from banks to build, for example, a water treatment plant, they must be repaid with income generated out of tariffs.[2] "Freed from shareholder pressure and from the constant drive for short-term returns on investment and dividend payments," writes Deputy Mayor of Paris and Eau de Paris's current president Célia Blauel, Eau de Paris's has been able to reduce its water tariffs by 8 percent. They continue to be cheaper than the water managed by Veolia and Suez in the surrounding greater Paris region.[3] Eau de Paris advertises its "just price" (prix juste) and makes the composition of price and the meaning of water bills publicly available.

A return to public accounting meant a return to a different utility temporality as well. As the current head of Eau de Paris put it, "From the point of view of the private entity . . . your horizon as far as time is concerned is the end of your contract. You're not incentivized to develop policies for the long term. And if you look at it from the point of view of the challenges that water utilities have to face now, a lot of them are very long-term challenges, like climate change, or the water cycle" (Polonyi 2020). Eau de Paris's long-term vision also includes a host of solidarity projects, such as when it contributes 500,000 euros annually to a solidarity fund that helps struggling Parisian households pay for household expenses, or when it develops transnational public-public partnerships with water utilities in Morocco, Mauritania, and Cambodia, making its staff, skills, know-how, and funding available as these utilities try to set up "social tariffs" of their own (see Kishimoto, Petitjean, and Steinfort 2017, 172–73; Moore 2019, 50; see also McDonald 2016, 2018).

Eau de Paris's vision articulates itself through a kind of infrastructural publicity, too. Today, it manages twelve hundred public water fountains, at least forty-one of which were installed since remunicipalization and that were the result of a participatory budgeting process.[4] Parisians can now participate in the allocation of Eau de Paris's resources; it was they who tasked Eau de Paris with installing more public water fountains. Today, they range from the iconic Wallace fountains that Englishman Richard Wallace gifted to the city over 150 years ago, to a series of modern fountains devised more recently by Parisian artists and designers. It also installed thirteen fountains that are modeled after the Italian *case dell'acqua* that I describe in the previous chapter, but that differ from the Campanian water dispensers in that they offer water—both sparkling and still, ice cold, and room temperature—for free. I spent an afternoon enjoying the spectacle of people coming in droves to these water dispensers with their own containers, taking liters and liters of ice-cold sparkling water and carting them off to their homes. Many of these fountains are endowed with plaques that say "Water: A Public Service." They inform Parisians not only of where the water comes from (it is supplied by treated water from both the rivers Seine and the Marne and from subterranean sources) but also of its exact mineral content (calcium: 90 mg/liter; magnesium: 6 mg/ liter; potassium: 0.2 mg/liter; and so on). As the president of Eau de Paris writes, "[T]his probably makes Paris the world's best-equipped city in terms of free access to water" (Blauel 2020, 50).

Eau de Paris is one of many remunicipalized utilities that is attempting to reimagine what "the public" or "the common" might mean (Blauel 2020, 48–49; Barlow 2019; Lobina et al. 2014). Such acts of the imagination are crucial at a time where the well-documented failures of public-private partnerships have done little to dislodge the fetish of public-private partnerships, where many public utilities are in fact thoroughly corporatized, and where the question of what a political economy and politics of opposition to the financialization of utilities might look like remains (Whiteside 2018, 4; McDonald and Swyngedouw 2019). At the same time, it is important to caution against the presumption that remunicipalization will inevitably end in the more just, democratic, and participatory management of water resources. In fact, many of my interlocutors were aware of the fact that remunicipalization, like water itself, is a shape-shifter. It can appear as a progressive, even resolutely anticapitalist politics in one location while deeply retrenching market logics in another (McDonald and Swyngedouw 2019, 325). The vigilance that my interlocutors practiced was thus one that grew out of their knowledge that remunicipalized public utilities could in fact also be run like a private business and not at all transparently managed or committed to just price. As Romano and Guerrini (2019) note, publicly owned water utilities can pay dividends to shareholders just like privatized water utilities do (1). Many of the people I met thus closely watched not only their utilities but also the "citizen observatories" that had often sprung up alongside them as well. Were these participatory organs nothing more than paper tigers, or was true democratic input possible (Herzberg 2015)? They asked what democratic participation ought to really look like, what the level of expertise of citizen participants ought to be, and what kind of clout these citizens' observatories would really have in the utility's boards and councils.

If remunicipalization is a form that does not necessarily come with a particular political content, then it can be initiated by local governments on both the left, right, and sometimes even on the extreme right of the political spectrum; it appears as an anticapitalist politics here, or as a social democratic, market managerialist, and even autocratic state capitalist politics there. In Spain, for example, a Leftist Network of Cities for Public Water recently declared water as a common good (*bién común*) that should never be appropriated for the benefit of private profits. A "Declaration for the Public Management of Water," signed by the mayors of Madrid, Barcelona, and eight other Spanish cities in November 2016, explicitly supports remunicipalization, arguing that water is a "natural patrimony" of the planet and that cities have the obligation to protect it in ways that is accountable to both public authorities and citizens. Hungary's current right-wing regime, in contrast, had under Prime Minister Viktor Orbán remunicipalized water (and other) social services in an effort to reverse the waves of post-Socialist privatization in the 1990s. Not unlike the right-wing resource nationalism of the Nazis in 1930s Germany, Orbán bought back shares in privatized companies and demonstratively cut tariffs for water as well as energy and waste management by 25 percent (Horváth 2016, 194; McDonald 2018, 48). Hungary has since veered off into a highly authoritarian, centralized, nationalist, and Eurosceptical model of service provisioning (McDonald 2018, 51; see also Strang 2016, 294) that bears striking resemblance to the rise of populist resource sovereignty movements elsewhere today (see McCarthy 2019; Susser 2017; Mahmud 2020).[5]

The water insurgencies emerging all over the world thus take on many shapes and can veer into many directions over time. But struggles over democracy and the commons, and over transparency and just price, remain. Some cases like Berlin can be described as spectacular victories. Others such as the ones in Ireland and Italy have resulted in victories that are decidedly more ambivalent—a kind of détente or temporary laying down of arms as adversaries retreat or reconstitute the lines of battle. The feelings of many people with whom I spoke to in Italy swerved vehemently from a sense of utter disappointment and betrayal by political elites to a sense of defiant achievement. Tommaso Fattori put it to me as follows:

> I think it's wrong not to see what we have achieved with the referendum. But on the other hand, I also have political reasons to argue that the referendum was partially implemented, in order not to discourage people. Otherwise, they will think that nothing really ever matters. I discuss this all the time with my political colleagues, and yes, the referendum has been . . . betrayed, but we also succeeded in averting a worsening of the situation. If we had not had the referendum, would everything have stayed the same? I would say absolutely not. With the referendum, we were able to block the entry of private corporations into about half of the Italian public utilities. . . . So let's take the case of Milan. It's a joint stock company which is 100 percent public, but if we had not won the referendum, we would definitely have Veolia and Suez in there.

In many cases, then, victories were entirely invisible because they consisted of futures that could have been but did not occur—a series of nonevents that many of my interlocutors interpreted as clear, if often quite invisible, successes. Their sense of historical and political achievement thus hinged on a narration of a sequence of events *and* nonevents. These victories could consist of widely celebrated reversals of privatization, as was the case in Paris and Berlin, but also of the prevention of attempted privatizations and of fates narrowly averted, at least for the time being.

Even with the relentless recursivity of expropriation (recall the recent merger of the two global water giants Suez and Veolia), and even if remunicipalization remains a politically complex and indeterminate process, and even as the water insurgencies documented in this book interpret their political efficacy in indeterminate ways, I end with a reminder of some of the more radical gifts that these water insurgencies have given to the world: to date, there have been 334 successful water sector (drinking and wastewater service) remunicipalizations,[6] many of which have kindled fires at the frontiers of the political and fiscal imagination.

Over and again, my interlocutors argued for a return to properly public expenditure—the Irish in their relentless insistence on more progressive taxation, my German interlocutors for cheap public loans and against the neoliberal fetish of "balanced budgets," Italian water movements on the grounds that many water utilities made huge annual surpluses that could easily be diverted back into projects of remunicipalization. They looked toward the many instances where innovative financing experiments were already occurring, such as when the city of Rennes in France hacked European Union rules on public procurement and ultimately made its water utility remunicipalization financially sustainable (Hopman et al. 2021, 13),[7] or when activists from the city of Thessaloniki proposed to transform the municipal water company into a cooperative by having each household buy company shares. While this model was not taken up in Thessaloniki, it has been implemented by the remuncipalized and now cooperatively owned energy utility in Wolfhagen, Germany (Hopman et al. 2021, 19). Other models of financing are also possible and can include coalitions between municipalities or cities across regions and countries, such as the above-mentioned Spanish "Network of Cities for Public Water" or the international solidarity work already performed by Eau de Paris.

Water movements have also reminded the world that most public water utilities were, for large parts of the twentieth century, mostly funded through a progressive tax system where the cost of capital is zero. They were also funded through the floating of bonds—a "public bond tradition that must be reasserted" despite the fact that fiscal conservatism and the fetish of balanced budgets still reign supreme (Whiteside 2018, 14). The kinds of debt thus incurred were and should again be treated as a political or social debt and as an investment—not a pernicious inheritance current generations are placing on the shoulders of the next, but as a debt that builds infrastructure as intergenerational social property (Bear 2015). In this model, collective wealth is not extracted but regrounded. It is a social contract made and remade materially through continuous infrastructural care, a future built not through global investors but through material obligations to future generations.

Some also spoke of the time when central governments played an important role, such as when they printed public money "for explicitly public purposes" (Whiteside 2018, 12), or when they relied on existing sources of pooled funds.[8] One could, for example, reinvigorate the role of public sector pension funds as ethical investors, given the fact that governments have long utilized this form of capital in service of political and social reproduction (Bear 2017, 3). Rather than invest in privatizing infrastructure projects, including in water utilities in the Global South as Canadian pension funds are currently doing in troubling ways (Skerrett 2018, 124), public sector pension funds could be redirected to support equitable, "definancialized" fiscal projects (Marois 2021; Whiteside 2018,

12). Yet others note the resurgence of public banks, so sidelined and de-funded during 1980s market fundamentalism that their total assets fell from about 40 percent of global banking resources to about 17 percent today (McDonald, Marois, and Spronk 2021, 124). Today, new public banks are being created all over the world—financial institutions owned and controlled by the state or some other public entity, governed under public law, and operating under a public mandate on municipal, national, or even international levels. They have resurged after the 2008 financial crisis as many governments turn back to state-centered solutions that insist that social returns must, at the very least, be on par with financial returns (McDonald, Marois, and Spronk 2021, 118)—or perhaps social and ethical returns are the most important thing of all.

Of course, the designation of a bank as public does not in and of itself guarantee a return to an era in which profit maximization was not the overriding principle. In fact, public banks can be highly commercialized or very much invested in public-private partnerships. But there are numerous examples where this is not the case. The Dutch public bank Nederlandse Waterschapsbank (NV), for example, has the sole mandate of lending to water utilities and of keeping the public sector's financing inexpensive and sustainable. The German Kreditanstalt für Wiederaufbau follows a similar mandate and lends not only to German public water utilities but to lower-income countries worldwide. Unsurprisingly, critics have complained that public banks have "lending rates that are not shaped by market forces" or that public banks deliver lower rates of return than private banks (McDonald, Marois, and Spronk 2021, 125). But that is precisely the point—to devalue financial returns as the only measure of value, worth, and wealth, to reconceptualize what a social infrastructure might be, and to rethink what the public or common might mean.

As I have shown throughout, water movements have wrested open further fault lines, including the question of collectively held property. They force us to ask which collectively held property should ultimately count as inviolable and how one might proceed to render something so—legally, politically, and ethically. Italian lawyers were particularly ambitious in this regard in their attempt to rewrite the Italian Civil Code through their heterodox play with lawmaking. They fought to insert the concept of the commons into the civil code as something that must be held collectively into perpetuity because it is intergenerationally held and "owned." Italy's Commission on Public Goods (Commissione sui Beni Pubblici) published a 2008 report with a searing critique of the very foundations of liberal constitutional law, arguing that the civil code's existing concept of "public property" did not mitigate against the sell-off of the commons. Until today, some of these same lawyers are nationally recognized names and promoters of the concept of the commons in Italy. The concept of *beni comuni* has been introduced into many communal and regional statutes in Italy and used in legal scholarship and many courts of law.

For others, the *form* of the utility was paramount. They passionately argued against the model of the joint stock company and insisted, in Italy and Germany especially, on a return to the *Eigenbetrieb* or the *azienda speciale*, both of which are fully subject to public law. Of course, they knew that public forms do not necessarily guarantee progressive content, but public form and law matter profoundly in that both allow for a transparency and accountability that citizens, at the very least, have the right to demand. In addition to utility form, the question of contract loomed large as well. The Irish story I tell in this book gives astonishing clarity to the foundational challenge posed by water insurgencies when they ask not only what collective property is, but who the proper contracting parties ought to be. These questions have been brought to bear on numerous court cases both large and small. In Italy, some court cases have been won by water consumers on the grounds that a government cannot sign a contract on behalf of a people over a collectively held common good. In France, a precedent-setting case similarly hinged on the argument that private contract law should never supersede public law since even private water providers have public service responsibilities when it comes to the provisioning of collectively held goods. Berlin's "Common Goods in Citizens' Hands" articulates a similar concept of public ownership and social obligation on its website when it says that "[g]enerations have contributed public and private resources, ideas and labor into the creation and advancement of public institutions. Many of these institutions had to be wrested away from the powerful owning class (*den Besitzenden*) through social struggle. They have become key elements in our society and constitute part of our societal inheritance that belongs to us all. It must be the task of each generation to develop these goods and services responsibly and to pass them on to next generations in a good, even better condition."[9] Growing experimentations with collectively owned forms of property abound through experiments in ownership structure, governance and participation, community control, and the self-management of cities' assets, services, and utilities (Hopman et al. 2021; Micciarelli 2021).

Water movements have devised a language that allows for a renewal of critiques of capitalism and of ways through which the world and its life-giving substances can be imagined as inappropriable. After all, capitalism's necropolitical commitment to private property and its insistence that humans appropriate and possess the world runs centuries deep. Recall John Locke's classic frontier argument, made in his 1823 *Two Treatises of Government*, in which he argues that "though the water running in the fountain be everyone's, yet who can doubt but that in the pitcher is his only who drew it out? His labor hath taken it out of the hands of Nature where it was common, and belonged equally to all her children, and hath thereby appropriated it to himself" (Locke 1823, 117). Locke's formulation is one of the most famous examples of the possessive individualism so central to capitalist modernity—a modernity that hinges on the fantasy of a lonely frontier individual who takes from nature's abundance and "appropriates it for himself." This is the moment where a fallacy arises; what is imagined is a world that exists only for the taking. The water insurgencies documented in this book provoke us to think about the world in very different ways: as one that "would never be substantiated into an appropriation," as Giorgio Agamben (2013) put it two years after the Italian water referendum, asking what life could be if it were never given as property but only as common use (xiii).[10] Water movements offer us ways to think outside of the proprietary logics wrought out of recurrent enclosure, challenging us to ask what a relation to the world as inappropriable would look like. At the heart of these movements lies one insurgent question: What would it mean to translate this challenge of inappropriability into an ethos and form of life?

# NOTES

## Introduction: A Vital Frontier

1  I build on already existing work that has long pointed to the neoliberal transformation of water services as a process of accumulation by dispossession as it transfers publicly owned resources and/or services to the private sector. See Bakker (2001, 2003, and 2013); Björkman (2015); De Angelis (2017); Harvey (2004); Roberts (2008); Swyngedouw (2005); and von Schnitzler (2016).

2  I rely on anthropologists who have written about this theme, especially Peterson (2014, 112); Song (2014, 41); Weiss (2018, 463); and Zaloom (2017). The question remains however whether this is speculation at all or simply rent seeking. As Kate Bayliss (2017) has put it, some "highly leveraged corporate structures operate in the absence of financial speculation; these financialized corporate structures are in fact ways for 'rentier transfers' to become normalized" (383).

3  The promises on the part of the World Bank and other institutions often fail to materialize when it comes to expensive water infrastructures, with most middle-income African countries still financing their water works through public sector

finance (Hall and Lobina 2012, 3). Indeed, there exists a wide gap between World Bank ideology, which sees water policy as being driven or led by international donors and the reality of many national governments who are developing their own policies and are, in fact, providing the majority of finance through often more democratic governance structures (Hall and Lobina 2012, 17).

4   Andreas Bieler summarizes five ways in which water has become a frontier of capitalization. First, water is often diverted from local use toward large agribusiness companies as part of the globalized system of industrialized food production. Corporate or state-led land grabs are ultimately a form of water grabbing, as agricultural land would be worthless without access to the water necessary for growing crops. Second, extractive industries such as mining, including hydrocarbon industries such as fracking, tar sands, and the exploration of oil, all significantly burden drinking water resources. Third, large dam constructions for the generation of hydroelectric energy and hydropower development put heavy pressure on local water supplies. Fourth, the bottled water industry is growing and creating acute water stress worldwide (Kaplan 2007, 2012). Fifth, Bieler points to the privatization of water and sanitation services, which has increasingly become a focus for profitable private investment (Bieler 2021, 5–6).

5   As Christa Hecht, former director of the German Alliance for Public Water Works (Allianz der öffentlichen Wasserwirtschaft) put it to me in an interview in 2016, the principle of local use (Örtlichkeitsprinzip) dominates the provisioning of water in countries like Germany. Hecht cited a German saying to me, "Use the water out of your own well. If you poison it, you deprive yourself of your own livelihood."

6   Centralized river-basin institutions have arisen in states that have historically been centralized monarchies—Spain, England/Wales, and France (Juuti, Katko, and University of Tampere 2005, 37).

7   I thank Francis Cody and Shiho Satsuka for pushing me on this point.

8   With enclosure, I mean "enclosure as commodification," i.e., the means through which something is "alienated, unitized, quantified, standardized, and priced" (Kockelman 2016, 5) although my interlocutors also implicitly referenced enclosure as the historical process whereby commons—land, rivers, forests—were turned into private property. To them, "new waves of enclosure" were now reoccurring all over the world (Fattori 2013, 378).

9   I thank Gavin Smith for our ongoing conversations about this topic.

10  Allianz Global Water is part of Allianz Global Investors, a leading global service provider in insurance, banking, and asset management founded in Germany in 1890. Allianz Global Water was founded in April 2008 and invests in equity securities of water-related companies worldwide, emphasizing long-term capital appreciation. Allianz's point that "[w]ater is a defensive investment theme with prospects for high growth" that is "cycle- and politics-immune" and "protected from wider political and economic volatility" can be found

here: https://nordic.allianzgi.com/-/media/allianzgi/eu/luxembourg/documents/water-your-assets-for-growth.pdf (last accessed January 7, 2022).

11 I use *necropolitics* in Achille Mbembe's (2019) sense to define neoliberalism as a "sacrificial economy" of "organized destruction" that cheapens and destroys life (38).

12 Melinda Cooper puts it succinctly when she notes that neoliberalism has reconfigured the relationship between debt and life: "What neoliberalism seeks to impose is not so much the generalized commodification of daily life—the reduction of the extra-economic to the demands of exchange value—as its exchange value. Its imperative is not so much the measurement of biological time as its incorporation into the nonmeasurable, achronological temporality of financial capital accumulation" (2008, 10).

13 The rise of infrastructure as an asset class is well described by Collier (2011, 227–30) and Bear (2015, 2017, 2020). Both have argued that the unitary entity called "infrastructure" emerged in a 1994 World Bank report, where international financial institutions, government committees, global investors, and market consultancies assembled a series of public works as disparate as railways and water works into one, singular category (Bear 2020, 64). At stake was the transformation of public works into privatized infrastructures, with people reconceptualized as users or customers of these systems rather than as citizens who built them through fees and taxes. This was the beginning of a "death foretold of state-run public works and the birth of financialized infrastructure" (Bear 2017, 5).

The water market, in contrast, was for a long time a corporate aspiration rather than an actual reality (Dukelow 2016, 146). Citigroup's chief economist noted years ago that he expects to see a globally integrated market for fresh water within twenty-five to thirty years: "Once the spot markets for water are integrated, futures markets and other derivative water-based financial instruments . . . will follow. There will be different grades and types of fresh water, just as we have light sweet and heavy sour crude oil today. Water as an asset class will . . . become the single most important physical commodity-based asset class, dwarfing oil, copper, agricultural commodities and precious metals" (Bayliss 2014, 302). At the time of this writing, this is exactly what has happened, with water joining gold, oil, and other commodities traded on Wall Street. As CNN reported on December 7, 2020, investors can now, for the first time in the United States, trade water futures and thus hedge against or bet on projected water scarcities in the future. The market has thus moved from letting buyers and sellers buy and sell water rights in the California spot markets in dry years (i.e., in markets where financial instruments or commodities are traded for immediate delivery) to allowing traders to buy and sell water in futures markets on the Chicago Mercantile Exchange. As always, the argument is that a futures market will allow for the better management of risks and a better alignment of supply and demand through transparent pricing practices (Tappe 2020; James and Hing 2021).

14 Many authors have critically interrogated scarcity discourse (Jaffee and Case 2018), with Swyngedouw (2006) arguing that scarcity language has contributed to "the discursive production of the imminence of a hydro-social-ecological disaster" (201). Scarcity is also of course the gravitational center of capitalism's cosmology, which is propelled by the fantasy of endless needs that must be met through more consumption (Sahlins 1974).

15 I build on the important work of many, including Bakker (2003, 442); Anand (2017); Björkman (2015); Ballestero (2019); Illich (1985); Strang (2004); Strang (2015); and Neimanis (2017, 2019). In Polanyian terms, water is a fictitious commodity insofar as it was not produced to be bought and sold on the market, like labor, land, and money. It thus does not behave in the same way as "real" commodities do even as its commodification seems intuitive or natural to investors (Block 2001, xxv).

16 This tendency to insist on life as force and excess outside of capitalist subsumption is found in the insurrectional anarchism and some neovitalist forms of contemporary theory where "life" exceeds and erodes all forms of constraint and representation. Critics have however noted that life and excess operate as "consolatory ideological forms" that overstate their capacity to overturn capital and the state (Noys 2015, 176–80).

17 Bieler (2021) describes authoritarian neoliberalism as a process that is not necessarily inaugurated by nondemocratic means or brute force (although that can be the case, as my chapter on Ireland shows). Rather, it can be observed "in the reconfiguring of state and institutional power in an attempt to insulate certain policies and institutional practices from social and political dissent" (Bieler 2021, 96; see also Boyer 2018; Molé Liston 2020, 25).

18 As Warne notes for the case of New Zealand, however, indigenous critics have argued that the rights-based framework does injustice to the relationship that they actually seek to restore, which is that of relations oriented around mutual obligation, not rights. For more information on this topic, see also the Global Alliance for the Rights of Nature, https://therightsofnature.org/ (last accessed January 7, 2022).

19 See Global Water Summit, "2019 Overview: Disruptive Designs at the https://www.watermeetsmoney.com/2019-overview-2/ (last accessed January 7, 2022).

20 A good example is Veolia, the French multinational corporation, which had revenues of 24.4 billion euros in 2016, assets of 37.9 billion euros, equity of 7.6 billion euros, and more than 163,000 employees (McDonald, Marois, and Spronk 2021, 118). This makes the company a larger economy than almost half of the world's countries.

21 The investor website Investopedia defines the term as a measure of performance. Alpha ($\alpha$) is used when an investment strategy, trader, or portfolio manager "has managed to beat the market return over some period, producing what traders call "excess return" or abnormal return." James Chen, "Alpha: What It Means in Investing, with Examples," Investopedia, March 19, 2022, https://www.investopedia.com/terms/a/alpha.asp.

22 I thank Stefan Leins for pushing me on this point. There is a growing literature on the rise of social finance markets, which offer investors measurable
social impact as well as financial returns on investment. They thus allow
for a proliferation of new forms of social and financial value to coexist and
blend, creating what investors are calling double and triple bottom lines
(Leins 2020; Langley 2020a, 2020c).

23 The role of water in extractive industries such as oil, gas, and mineral exploitation is not just an existing but a growing concern for industry. Recent
moves to financialize water (see note 10) are clearly also linked to this growing
demand on the part of the extractive industries, since the buying and selling
of water rights will allow owners to auction off rights to the highest bidder
in times of scarcity.

24 Water financing varies significantly globally. In many parts of the world,
water utilities continue to be funded out of a mix of domestic resources, tariff
payments, taxes, and international aid. In part, this is the result of the fact
that global water corporations have been hesitant to invest in low-income
countries where opportunities to recover costs are insecure. But they have
also shied away from investments because political backlash in the Global
South has often been strong (although note that in India, the Modi government recently offered loans to federal governments on the condition that they
introduce private water sector provisioning and prepay meters [Bear 2018]).
Both impediments have played less of a role in middle- and high-income
countries so far (McDonald, Marois, and Spronk 2021, 122; Bayliss 2017).

25 For an astute critique of the equally deeply problematic language that has
governed the management of the Colorado River for decades, see Muehlmann's
analysis of "beneficial" versus "inefficient" use (2013, 26).

26 For additional information on how the watermeetsmoney conference framed
these issues, see its 2022 summit agenda: Global Water Summit, "Introducing
the Urban Water Catalyst Fund: The Case for Accelerating Utility Turnaround,"
https://www.watermeetsmoney.com/urban-water-catalyst-fund/ (last accessed
January 7, 2022).

27 For GWI's infographic, see https://globalwaterintel-info.com/p/36G3–5QE
/gwi-2019-water-tariff-infographic-nb?fbclid=IwAR2NQS2dRBhSyUklyXCB
8xo3mUiorhzHmqPlGJBwyAq58qftcy2TiYgWu4Y (last accessed January 7,
2022).

28 As Christophers and Fine have argued, capitalism is at its core a financial
system. The postwar twentieth century with its emphasis on national accounting and the national economy diminished the role afforded to finance
capital, yet this diminishment was abnormal in longue durée terms. This
would mean that there is no such thing as financialization—just different
variants of finance and how and to what degree finance is regulated by the
state (2021, 23).

29 Not surprisingly for the time, Soddy's invectives against bankers and financiers
bordered on anti-Semitism (see Foster 2018; Raffles 2007).

30  In addition, the length of PPP contracts has nothing to do with the infrastructure as such—its technology, engineering, or life span. Rather, these contracts mimic rental contracts—with thirty years being their outer legal limit (Rügemer 2008, 161; see also Mattert et al. 2017).

31  Canadian public pension funds are particularly egregious players in this regard in that they have become indistinguishable from other financial investors. As Kevin Skerrett (2018) from the Canadian Union of Public Employees (CUPE) notes, these "new masters of the neoliberal universe" have become "pioneers in infrastructure investing" and "global leaders in the direct ownership of public infrastructure, primarily in other countries" (122). Canadian pension funds have thus ironically become key beneficiaries of infrastructure privatization while public-sector workers in other parts of the world have seen their employment, wages, and benefits suffer. This model of investment has by now found aggressive support by the G20, OECD, and the World Bank. This means that pension funds from the Global North will further be investing in the acquisition of public infrastructures elsewhere—i.e., precisely the "assets" that trade unions and those on the political left usually demand stay in public hands.

32  For a summary, see Sandra Laville, "England's Privatised Water Firms Paid £57bn in Dividends since 1991," *Guardian*, July 1, 2020, https://www.theguardian.com/environment/2020/jul/01/england-privatised-water-firms-dividends-shareholders.

33  I lean on the work already done by others, including Beggs, Bryan, Rafferty (2014, 982); Song (2014); Stout (2019); Weiss (2018, 463); Zaloom (2019, 201); Leyshon and Thrift (2007, 98); and Kalb (2020).

34  I build on work by Strang (2005); Limbert (2001); Illich (1985); and Ballestero (2019).

35  I use the terms *commons* and *commonwealth* interchangeably even though there is a lively ongoing debate about various possible distinctions, including also between the *common* (singular) and the *commons* (plural). Massimo De Angelis, e.g., has argued that common goods (and commonwealth) ought to be differentiated from the commons insofar as the former are only one element within the larger social system called the *commons* (always in plural). For De Angelis, the social system of the commons includes not just common goods but commoners and the activity of commoning—i.e., "doing in common" (2017, 18). Hardt and Negri, in contrast, include both the Earth's substances and the results of human labor and creativity under the rubric of commonwealth (Hardt 2010, 112), but this commonwealth cannot yet be claimed as such; it is only through an expansion of the commons and of commoning practices, systems, and ecologies, that such a claim to a general commonwealth will be justified (De Angelis 2017, 18–19).

36  Research in Great Britain showed that water bill arrears were higher for women, for households with children, and for single parents (Bayliss 2016, 393).

37  Marx, speaking about land and modern capitalist agriculture, writes that "all progress in capitalist agriculture is a progress in the art not only of robbing

the worker, but of robbing the soil; all progress in increasing the fertility of the soil for a given time is a progress toward ruining the more long-term sources of that fertility" (Federici 2015, 203).

38  For a history of the French water corporation Veolia, see Brown (2019).

39  The merger of Suez with Veolia creates an unprecedented monopoly in the water sector. As Food and Water Watch put it, "[t]his lack of competition will worsen our water affordability crisis, eliminate good union jobs, and open the door to cronyism and corruption" (Food and Water Watch 2021).

40  An early example of speculative wealth accumulated through the building of water infrastructures can be found in the United States in 1801, when the bank of the Manhattan Company established itself as the United States' most powerful financial institution by providing New York City with "pure and wholesome water." The company soon gave up all pretense of doing so since it failed miserably at this attempt, transforming itself into the powerful Chase Manhattan Bank or what is today known as JP Morgan Chase (Salzman 2013, 66).

41  I draw on Arrighi (1994); Badiou (2012); Federici (2004); Hardt (2010); and, above all, Joshua Clover (2016), while recognizing that the cyclicality of capitalist temporality has been the subject of much additional writing, too. As Bill Sewell (2008) writes, the problem of recurrent crises was not only central to Marx's work. Joseph Schumpeter's focus on "business cycles" and Immanuel Wallerstein's focus on longer-term cycles in world system theory are also examples of this line of inquiry into capitalist temporalities (520).

42  Swyngedouw (2005) outlines this history by differentiating between four distinct stages in urban water utilities. The first lasted until the second half of the nineteenth century and was characterized by a number of relatively small private companies that provided services to those who could afford them while excluding those who could not (an inherently exclusionary project that was also erected and mostly maintained in the colonies, where water provisioning was directed toward colonial elites (see also Anand 2017, 14). The second period was the era of "municipalization," when concerns over public health and public access led to the consolidation of water systems and the provisioning of water at a highly subsidized rate. The third stage, beginning around the end of World War I, was characterized by increased Keynesian national regulation, with the expansion of services and subsidized pricing; while the fourth, beginning in the 1980s, saw the neoliberal restructuring of basic services.

43  Note that this was not just a Leftist move. There were plenty of conservative municipalities who have sought a more rationalized form of public government in order to promote overall market growth (McDonald 2018).

44  As Vogl has argued, these entanglements between financier and sovereign have long existed and created the basis for the modern state. He gives as an example the states involved with the wars with the Habsburg Empire, which accepted advance payments and loans with interest in order to cover both exceptional financial requirements and regular and permanent expenses. It

was these debt economies that deeply integrated the emergent modern state into merchant finance and that led to the emergence of stock markets in the first place. Sovereign debt, in short, preceded political sovereignty (2017, 56).

45 In some countries, the public-private partnership is a mere concession where the services provided are paid for by the public. In others, public-private partnerships can include a variety of outsourcing and joint ventures between public and private actors (Campra et al. 2014, 32). In general, however, public-private partnerships are recognized as having three characteristics: (1) the relatively long duration of the relationship; (2) the method of funding the project, in part from the private sector, sometimes by means of complex arrangements between various players; and (3) the important role played by the economic operator, who participates at different stages in the project (design, completion, implementation, funding).

46 These private loans frequently come with interest rates of 3–7 percent rather than the 0–1 percent when taken out directly by governments. Private borrowers initially always pay higher interest rates because they, unlike governments, cannot pledge a tax base as collateral. Once the infrastructures are actually built, private investors can refinance their loans from, say, 6.5 to 4.5 percent, while the state "partner" is still contractually obliged to pay the original interest to creditors. So, in addition to the contractually agreed return of investment, private investors count on these additional windfall profits (Rügemer 2008, 44–45).

47 Public-private partnerships were initially called *private finance initiatives* (PFIs) by Tony Blair, whose government invented the term around 1997. He soon switched to the term "public-private partnerships" (Rügemer 2008, 18) in an effort to conjure the fiction of equality between partners. Yet there are many more types of predation that lurk in this form—too many for me to recount in this book. One of the most egregious are the infamous Investor State Dispute Settlement (ISDS) clauses, which allow for private water companies to claim compensation for cancelled service management contracts, or changes in future profits due to regulatory or pricing controls (Kishimoto, Lobina, and Petitjean 2015). Companies, well protected by commercial and contract law, have the upper hand, as cases are judged according to commercial law rather than public interest or service standards (Moore 2019, 9).

48 Bayliss makes the important point that companies still listed on the stock market or owned by infrastructure conglomerates have flatter group structures with "just one or two intermediaries between the regulated company and the ultimate registered parent. The finance owned companies, by contrast, have a long ladder of companies between the regulated water provider and the ultimate parent company. Most of these rungs in the ladder do little apart from receiving and paying out interest and dividends to other companies in the group" (2016, 386).

49 Note however that this capacity to borrow off the books is unequally distributed in Europe. For many municipalities, public-private partnerships are a

way to avoid stipulated debt ceilings since they don't officially get entered into the books as debt. This is not the case for countries like Greece, which has to keep even public-private partnership debt on its official books. This stricture came with the "brutally direct" pressure to privatize national assets in Greece as a result of the Eurozone crisis (Bieler 2021, 25).

50 In the case of Berlin, the original formal arrangement between the city and French multinational Veolia had taken the shape of a "silent partnership" (*stille Gesellschaft*), with the private corporation holding a financial stake in the utility without having the right to intervene into formal decision-making processes. Soon, Veolia insisted on a separate contract for the "protection of its interests" (*Interessenwahrungsvertrag*)—a contract that existed in parallel to the formal agreement and that bought them seats in the board of directors and other perks. I thank David Hartmann for a conversation at Heidi Kosche's office at the Berlin Abgeordnetenhaus in May 2016.

51 "The people," "*il popolo*," or "*das Volk*" were terms I often heard while conducting research, with their meaning ranging from "common or ordinary people" to "the sovereign" (Cody 2020, 62).

52 Many high-profile examples of urban resistance to water privatization have occurred in the Global South. See Ahlers (2010); Barraqué (2011); Barlow (2005); Beveridge and Naumann (2014); Hines (2021); Madaleno (2007); Olivera and Lewis (2004); Petrella (2001); Wu and Malaluan (2008); and Zaki and Amin (2009).

53 This is why Italians involved in the water movement would never use the term *bene comune* in the singular, but always in the plural.

54 Initially after Dublin, loans given out by the World Bank and the IMF all stipulated that water services needed to be privatized. Contracts subsequently signed all contained the basic features that contracts signed in the Global North today contain as well, including the commitment to full cost recovery. A first draft of GATT, the General Agreement on Tariffs and Trade, did not include water as a service to be commodified. That changed in 1999 when the European Union demanded the inclusion of a provision that mandated the full liberalization of water utilities in seventy-two countries, thirty of which were considered to be the poorest in the world. As already mentioned elsewhere, water corporations have since almost entirely pulled out of the African continent, with the public sector remaining the dominant source of finance for water, energy, and transport (Hall and Lobina 2010, 7). At the same time, growth is expected in India, Eastern Europe, America, and China (Moore 2019, 11), especially in a context where multinationals can push for the integration of waste, energy, and water services into multiutilities and where they can invest in wastewater management, desalination plants, consultation projects, and water-based financial products at the same time. Importantly, multiutilities usually pay more frequent returns than other utility forms (Romano and Guerrini 2019, 1).

55 In Europe, England was the only country to sell off its water infrastructures entirely. Today, the United Kingdom water market is dominated not by

mega-corporations such as Suez and Veolia, but mostly by massive private equity firms (Moore 2019, 11; Bakker 2003).

56 European water legislation can be grouped into three waves of regulation: water quality for human activities (1973–1988), pollution prevention (1988–1995), and the protection and management of water (1995–present) (Moore 2019, 14–15).

57 Each member state was required to provide a River Basin Management Plan (RBMP) by 2009, which is updated every six years. RBMPs are the translation of the WFD into local legislation (Boscheck et al. 2013). If the objectives of the WFD are not reached, the RBMP must outline how a member state aims to reach them.

58 The European Water Movement was founded in 2012 after the Alternative World Water Forum in Marseille. Adopting the Italian Water Forum's Naples Manifesto that frames water as a commons and universal right, it is organized horizontally as a critical forum to link European water movements together through the themes of ecology, remunicipalization, and antiprivatization (see Naples Water Manifesto, http://europeanwater.org/about-the-european -water-movement/naples-manifesto [last accessed January 7, 2022]). It coordinates campaigns around European water policy such as the recent Drinking Water Directive, the Water Framework Directive check-in, the Concession Directive, and the Blueprint to Safeguard Europe's Water Resources, and it has participated in the Alternative Water Forums and COP21 summits. The movement has thirty-four members across ten countries, including public water operators, trade unions, NGOs, environmental groups, and community activists (Moore 2019, 25). For the Right2Water initiative, see https://www .epsu.org/article/right2water-first-ever-european-citizens-initiative-make-it (last accessed January 20, 2022).

59 None of my interlocutors went as far as the Standing Rock water protectors, who made a somewhat similar point about the "protestor" and "activist" terminology that they find demeaning. The term *protestor*, in particular, misrepresents what people at Standing Rock said they were doing—protecting the water from capitalist incursion. Both *protestor* and *activist* were terms that my interlocutors were also sometimes not comfortable with, but they did not articulate as coherent an alternative as the Standing Rock water protectors did. See Herrera (2016).

60 This is not to say that trade unions were not crucial actors in many instances I discuss (for a detailed treatment of the coalition building between unions and civil society actors in European water movements, see Bieler [2021]). But my own research showed that water insurgencies almost without fail initially emerged "from below" on the level of households unwilling to pay soaring bills.

61 Ancient Jewish water law prioritized access according to use, with drinking water given priority, followed by irrigation and grazing. Yet the highest priority for access "was granted to those in need regardless of whether or not they belonged to the well's community of owners." Islamic water law was similar

to Jewish water law; in fact, the Arabic word for Islamic law, *sharia*, literally means "the way to water" (Salzman 2013, 50).

## Chapter 1: You Cannot Sell to Us What We Already Possess!

1   The first network of mayors in favor of managing water as a commons was formed in 2007 in the southern region of Puglia. A similar network, the Network Association of New Municipalities (Associazione Rete Nuovo Municipio), was established on the national level in 2008, when over two-hundred Italian municipalities were actively engaged in the question of public water management and in the referendum process (Bieler 2015).

2   I build on Jean Comaroff and John Comaroff's (2006) work on law and disorder in the postcolony, where they describe the rise of an "almost salvific belief" in (re)written constitutions and their capacity to conjure radical breaks with the past and visions of an equitable future. This "fetishism of constitutionality" comes "in the midst of the lawlessness that has accompanied laissez faire in so many places." While they note that this belief is particularly prevalent in postcolonial contexts, the Italian case makes clear that this sense of law and lawlessness pertains to the Global North as well (22–24). See also Brenner, Peck, and Theodore (2014).

3   The story of Napoli ABC is a complex and dramatic one that I cannot do justice to here. Suffice is to say that the utility went through several changes in the presidency after its remunicipalization and included many highly publicized spats between Napoli's mayor Luigi de Magistris and Napoli's various directors (including Ugo Mattei and Maurizio Montalto); a highly publicized court case that included compensation for one of its ex-directors; worker's struggles over wages; controversies over mode and number of inclusion of civil society groups into the participatory organ of the utility; a national media news report that falsely stated that Naples' water is undrinkable; and fears that Napoli ABC would ultimately be infiltrated by the Camorra since it was, after all, a lucrative business. Activists further feared the looming amalgamation of Naples with the larger surrounding metropolitan area; a scheme that many said would ultimately lead to the subsumption of the remunicipalized Napoli ABC under the larger, partially privatized metropolitan utility GORI. Despite these controversies, and despite activist fears that Napoli ABC might one day be privatized again, Napoli ABC remains a remarkable achievement within the larger Italian context and a pillar of hope for water activists across the country. I thank Sergio Marotta, Francesco Fusco, Renato Briganti, Ugo Mattei, and Maurizio Montalto for extended conversations on this topic.

4   This insistence that the water of Naples was "good to drink" emerged out of a national scandal that occurred when the illustrious Italian magazine *L'Espresso* made an argument about Napoli's poor water quality. *L'Espresso* based its story on the fact that members of the US military base in Naples had been warned that water off base was unfit for human consumption. The city later took the magazine to court for defamation, arguing that its water

was one of the most controlled in Italy. It is important that this article came out right after de Magistris remunicipalized the utility. He and the people of Naples' thus understood the article to be a political attack by those "who want to put their hands on our city at a decisive moment" (*Napoli Today* 2013).

5   I build on other work (Ballestero 2019; Comaroff and Comaroff 2006; Gill and Cutler 2014; Greenberg 2020) that has already commented on this judicialization of politics. This work of making the law is also, of course, a distinct form of making politics. I thank Firat Bozcali for alerting me to this distinction.

6   Carl Schmitt has long argued that the conquest of the Americas represents the original act of law creation and the solidification of the concept of sovereignty. The concept of sovereignty would later hinge on conquest's conceptual disappearance and the "ability within the West to present sovereignty as a question of 'right' rather than domination" (Reyes and Kaufman 2015, 51–53).

7   The idea of society as "constituent power" remains a contested one, since classical constitutional theory designates the capacity to constituent power to the "people" through the concept of popular sovereignty while at the same time assuming that this power is most legitimately exercised through representative democracy. The resulting paradox is often referred to as the "nonfoundational foundations of law" and may explain the exclusion of civil society actors as constituent power in traditional constitutional theory (Bailey and Mattei 2013, 969).

8   Others have commented on the jurocentrism of legal scholars, which has focused almost exclusively on the types of lawmaking coming out of formal legislatures and courts. What is obscured in the process is the fact that social movements often are the source of national and international law (Balakrishnan 2003).

9   The contract was signed with British engineers Charles Manby and Jean Albert Roberti, both of whom were associated with the General Credit and Discount Company. General Credit was founded and directed by Sir Edward Blount, an Anglo-French financier who was not only president of the Parisian bank *Société Générale*, but also president of both London's General Credit bank and London's Joint Stock bank (De Majo and Vitale 2004, 43–44).

10  The Compagnie Générale was founded in 1855 and responsible for the construction of Paris' aqueduct (De Majo and Vitale 2004, 25).

11  This fragmentation has multiple origins, including the predominance of ground-water use; the transfer of highly decentralized French administrative structures under Bourbon and Napoleonic domination, as well as the late development of the Italian nation state in 1861, which grew out of highly differentiated local traditions and diverse forms of economic organization (Lobina 2005, 108).

12  How the "remuneration of invested capital" is calculated is both a mathematical and political question and as much the result of interpretation as it is of calculation (Horacio Ortiz, personal communication; see also Ortiz 2021).

13 For a major discussion of the logics of the "Republic of Property," see Hardt and Negri (2009). For a vibrant ethnographic glimpse of the practical questioning of these liberal logics, see also Razsa and Kurnik (2012).

14 Article 42 of the Italian Constitution reads, "Property is public or private. Economic assets may belong to the State, to public bodies or to private persons. Private property is recognized and guaranteed by the law, which prescribed the ways it is acquired, enjoyed and its limitations so as to ensure its social function and make it accessible to all. In the cases provided for by the law and with provisions for compensation, private property may be expropriated for reasons of general interest. . . ."

15 Emergency law has not always been used for nefarious ends. US President Abraham Lincoln freed the slaves by decree. President Roosevelt did the same to realize the New Deal, and the new Leftist government of the Popular Front in 1930s France ruled by decree to raise taxes. Emergency law, in short, is a form of law that does not necessarily entail a particular political content.

16 There is a whole history of Italy to be told through the lens of states of emergency from above and below. I cannot do this here but refer to the work of Lumley (1990).

17 Campania currently has poverty rates exceeding 40 percent in contrast to, say the northern region of Lombardy, where poverty rates lie at 11 percent (Statista 2022).

18 I thank Firat Bozcali for this formulation.

19 I define wealth in Foster's terms to refer to wealth that far exceeds commodities "bought or sold or otherwise transacted." Wealth instead also includes things like sacred objects or family heirlooms, or even the air we breathe (Foster 2018, 292). See also Rakopoulos and Rio (2018).

20 Referenda in Italy can take only two forms: They can be abrogatory, whereby citizens can vote to abolish a formal statute (although this cannot include questions of taxation, budget, amnesty, pardon, or the ratification of international treaties). Or they can be confirmation referenda, where citizens vote to confirm a law if the constitution is changed by Parliament. In both cases, a quorum of 50 percent of voters and half a million positive votes are needed for a referendum to be successful.

21 I here build on the writing of Carrozza and Fantini (2013), Fantini (2014), Hardt and Negri (2009), Lucarelli (2013), Mattei (2013), Roggero (2010), and Petrella (2001).

22 I am indebted to Francesca Coin for pointing this out to me.

23 Italy has the highest number of bottled water consumption in Europe. The movement for the mayor's water was thus as much a political as it was an environmental one.

24 This phrase was used in a talk by Marco Bersani at a conference on water as commons (Agorà dell'acqua e dei beni comuni) in Rome in November 2015.

25 When the referendum was discussed in parliament in 2016, the responsible committee changed its content in ways that utterly undermined the original intentions, moving from obligatory remunicipalization to a law that made remunicipalization merely one option among many. The law was so ineffective that water activists opposed it. "In the end, the Forum even regarded the blocking of this law as a positive outcome" (Bieler 2021, 63).

26 Italians were called upon to vote on four questions in June of 2011, only one of which was devoted to water. The first referendum aimed at stopping the compulsory privatization of public services (including public transportation, garbage collection, nursery schools, and other public services provided by local governments). The second referendum, specifically devoted to water, aimed at abolishing a legal provision that guaranteed the "remuneration of the invested capital" as part of the final cost to the user of the water supply system. This referendum aimed to exclude the profit motive from the provisioning of water services. The third referendum was aimed at abolishing the law that reestablished an Italian nuclear program. The fourth referendum was aimed at abolishing laws providing a judicial shield to Prime Minister Berlusconi. While all were overwhelmingly approved by the voters with majorities of more than 95 percent, the question that received the most votes was the one specifically devoted to abolishing profit on water (Bailey and Mattei 2013, 988).

27 Brazilian citizens, particularly the insurgent poor of urban peripheries, participated directly in the drafting of the 1988 constitution and called themselves the Constitutional Assembly—Assembléia Constituinte (Holston 2009, 252; see also Nugent 2002, 2008).

28 The crisis of representative democracy, while evident in many parts of the world, has a long history in Italy and goes back to at least the Mani Pulite (Clean Hands) judicial investigation into political corruption that rocked the country in the 1990s and led to the demise of the so-called First Republic. Mani Pulite revealed that large parts of the political class across all political parties had been implicated in corrupt practices, with half of all members of Italy's parliament under indictment at one point. Four-hundred town and city councils were dissolved, and all major political classes suffered major losses, paving the way for parties like the right-wing Northern League (today, simply League, or Lega).

29 The emergence of future generations as subjects of law is one of the most important legal developments to emerge out of social movements who have pushed for expanded definitions of rights, obligations, and harms.

30 There are many other examples of law as play in the struggle against water privatization, one of which I recount here. On May 18, 2014, civil society groups in the Greek city of Thessaloniki organized a referendum against the privatization of their local water utility—the profitable EYATH, the Thessaloniki Water Supply and Sewage Company. The privatization of the utility, 74 percent of whose shares were still owned by the Greek state, had been

mandated by the Troika (IMF, European Commission, and European Central Bank) under the pretext of the financial crisis and the resulting austerity measures. Led by the EYATH Workers Association in 2011, a larger coordinating body called SOSte to Nero (Save Greek Water) was soon formed out of ten of the municipalities of the Thessaloniki area, Initiative 136 (a movement hoping to build a cooperative company), the Citizens' Union for Water (a second-level union of water cooperatives), and twelve nonprofit water cooperatives. The planned referendum had been declared illegal by the minister of the interior since they in Greece can only be called by the national government, not local municipalities. Yet the minister, who had publicly threatened water activists with arrests, was ignored by the soon hundreds of volunteers involved—first because they managed to get the eleven initially reticent local mayors on their side ("they were feeling our breath on their necks," as Yiorgos Archontopoulos from SOSte to Nero laughingly put it to me), and second because they played with the law: rather than have citizens cast their ballots in official voting sites such as schools and city halls, activists moved the 181 ballot boxes and stationed them outside. The ballot boxes they used had in fact been made available for a same-day election for the European parliament but had been "borrowed" by the activists for this "illegal" referendum, thus placing "legal" and "illegal" elections side by side. Rather than use official ballots that would have landed them in prison, activists used ballots but had birthdays erased from them with the help of the municipal office, thus creating population registers that were then used to authorize voters. Two hundred volunteer lawyers from the Thessaloniki Bar Association stood by these illegal ballot boxes outside of the official voting stations, thereby performatively asserting the legitimacy of the vote and making sure that all requirements of reliability were met. The local police force stood by without intervening. The votes were eventually counted at Thessaloniki City Hall by the same volunteer lawyers. Of the 218,002 citizens who voted on that day, 98 percent voted *oxi* (no) against the privatization of water (for the importance of *oxi* in Greek political life, see Bryant [2016], who argues that Greeks for specific historical reasons associate *oxi* with resistance and resilience [25]). Importantly, the referendum was held with the presence of over 30 "international observers," including Claus Kittsteiner from the Berlin Water Table. Today, Thessaloniki is a "Blue Community" that has vowed to protect water as a human right and public trust. I would like to warmly thank Kostas Nikolai from Initiative 136 for speaking to me in such detail about the referendum and for Yiorgos Archontopoulos from SOSte to Nero for doing the same and then whisking me away on a motorcycle and treating me to a Greek feast (see also Nikolaou 2018).

31  The four Italian multiutilities involved in water management are Acea (Rome), which has partnered with other local authorities in six other ATOs in central Italy, and which represents the market leader in terms of population served (15 million users); Hera, which originated in the area surrounding Bologna and today serves eleven ATOs (6.3 million users); Iren, which emerged out of a merger between Enia (Western Emilia) and Iride (Genova and nearby

areas), which also holds contracts in Sicily and Tuscany, for a total of nine ATOs (7.1 million users). Among fully privatized utilities one almost always also finds the omnipresent French multinationals Veolia and Suez, as well as the Spanish corporation Aqualia and other more minor companies (Massarutto and Ermano 2013, 25).

32  This sense of free fall was compounded in the very hot and dry summer of 2017, when Rome's private water corporation ACEA decided to shut off Rome's famous public water fountains to stave off a water scarcity crisis. The then mayor of Rome, Virginia Raggi from the Five Star Movement, initially protested but then caved to ACEA, with the case becoming highly publicized and politicized. For an article by Neapolitan missionary Alex Zanotelli on the "falling first star" of the Five Star Movement, see Zanotelli (2020).

33  For a report on the TAR decision, see a local newspaper article in *Agro 24* (2013).

34  Rather than sign the contract with GORI, the village of Roccapiemonte sought a bank loan of 900,000 euros to invest in its infrastructure. "Gori did not put a single cent into our infrastructure," as the members of the water committee proudly told me. From a fiscal point of view, the taking out of loans by the local municipality might have seemed risky, indebting the municipality heavily. But any fiscal auditors from Germany to Canada would argue that this is, in the long run, better for public institutions because ultimately cheaper than taking out more expensive loans via global investors. The fact is that governments can borrow at significantly lower rates than the private sector (Massarutto 2020, 8).

35  There have been small victories, as activists have noted, such as the fact that water shutoffs now cannot proceed without warning and without GORI contacting social services.

### Chapter 2: No More Blood from These Stones!

1  The earliest report of water meter obstruction I could find were in late January 2014, when a father of three turned away Irish Water meters about a dozen times, stating that he was "totally opposed to it because it's a completely unjust tax—this is an act of civil disobedience against an unjust law" (*thejournal.ie*, 2014).

2  Björkman (2015) describes this same process as having taken place in the 1950s and then completed in 1990s Mumbai, when the World Bank insisted that the city move its water charging system away from a variable "water tax" (with water costs approximated according to property values) to a water charges system where end-use consumption, i.e., the quantity of water consumed and measured via flowmeters, became the norm (40).

3  Ireland's independent regulator of gas and electricity services, the Commission for Energy Regulation (CER), had initially announced an average household charges limit of 240 euros until 2016, as well as a universal annual free al-

lowance of 30,000 liters, with an additional allowance for children (Dukelow 2016, 153).

4 For a short interview with Suzanne O'Flynn on the Ashbrook Heights protest, see a video uploaded to YouTube on April 23, 2014: https://www.youtube.com /watch?v=ujsHIUJeeoo (accessed January 7, 2022.) Catholic Heritage Association of Ireland, "Cork: The Rebel City," May 22, 2010, http://catholicheritage .blogspot.com/2010/05/cork-rebel-city.html.

5 Cork played an outsized role in the Irish Republican war for independence, but also in many other previous insurgencies against British rule as well.

6 Accessed on a new defunct Guardex Ireland website in 2017.

7 As Luxemburg (1951) writes, "the other aspect of the accumulation of capital concerns the relations between capitalism and the non-capitalist modes of production which start making their appearance on the international stage. Its predominant methods are colonial policy, and international loan system—a policy of spheres of interest—and war. Force, fraud, oppression, looting are openly displayed without any attempt at concealment, and it requires an effort to discover within this tangle of political violence and contests of power the stern laws of economic process" (452).

8 For Karen Doyle's stirring speech during a Cobh Community 4 Change Irish Water Protest on January 23, 2016, see "Karen Doyle, Cobh Community 4 Change Irish Water Protest 23 Jan 2016," YouTube, https://www.youtube.com /watch?v=5Ne5jnbNGKM (accessed September 10, 2022).

9 The counter insurgency specialist, David Kilcullen, frequently appears in dialogue with corporations about projected water scarcity, conflict, and water security and was a keynote speaker at the GWI Global Water Summit in 2014. While Kilcullen mostly deals with future water war scenarios and with criminal groups and war lords playing an increased role in contestations over water, he, like others in this growing field, is also involved in questions regarding the "vandalism" of water infrastructures and water theft. See, "Water Security Day Middle East: Dr. David Kilcullen Answers Your Questions," IDRICA, July 21, 2020, e.g., https://www.idrica.com/blog/water-security-day-middle-east -dr-david-kilcullen-answers-your-questions/.

10 King George I's "Riot Act" in 1714 was "an act for preventing tumults and riotous assemblies, and for the more speedy and effectual punishing of rioters. It defined a riot as "[a] violent disturbance of the peace by an assembly or body of persons; an outbreak of active lawlessness or disorder among the populace" (Clover 2016, 8).

11 I thus take issue with Clover's otherwise brilliant book, which argues that political mobilizations have moved from bread riots against the market in the eighteenth century to race riots against the state and police in the twenty-first. For my Irish interlocutors, state and market have become almost indistinguishable, with the former having been captured by the latter. The struggle against the state was thus a struggle against state capture and not

distinct from it. "Riot prime" as Clover calls it, thus continues to bear strong resemblance to the world Edward Palmer Thompson described in that the social mobilizations outlined in my book continue to focus explicitly on the question of price. Recall the most recent 2019 wave of protests in Egypt, Beirut, Chile, and Ecuador, where the demands made by the people all orbited around the demand for basic subsistence—bread, but also gasoline, and so on. In addition, I further take issue with Clover's distinction between "bread riots" of the past and "race riots" of the present—as the Irish case shows, bread riots were always race riots in the sense that the English enclosure of Irish land was explicitly articulated through a violent politics of racialization (Robinson 1983).

12  As Patrick Pearse, Irish republican political activist and one of the leaders of the 1916 Easter Rising wrote in his last political essay, "A nation may go further and determine that all sources of wealth whatsoever are the property of the nation and that all surplus wealth shall go to the national treasury to be expended on national purposes rather than be accumulated by private persons" (Pearse 1916, 2).

13  Another demonstration took place on November 1 of that year—the largest cross-country local level protest in recent Irish history. Over one hundred Right2Water protests were held around Ireland with an estimated 150,000 people participating.

14  As Robinson (1983) writes, the Irish were first "subdued" through plantations that existed parallel to the Virginia Plantation system of the sixteenth century. During this period, Scottish and English settlers were lured into Ireland with promises of access to land, while Irish "sub-humans" were driven into the hills and woods. The many rebellions that followed put major financial strains on the crown (37). It was not until the early seventeenth century that the colonization of Ireland accelerated, and by the eighteenth century turned Ireland into a dependent sector of the English economy. By the beginning of the nineteenth century, as Edward Palmer Thompson (1966) writes, the Irish were "the cheapest labor in Western Europe," a fact the British explained not out of Irish colonial history but with reference to the "primitive" and "barbaric" Irish "race." The proletarianization of Europe, in short, was intimately entangled with patterns of racialization (432).

15  In 2016 alone, fifteen million Americans had their water disconnected because of unpaid bills; a phenomenon that is growing as water affordability has reached crisis highs. Detroit, which has one of the highest poverty rates of any major US city, also has one of the highest water tariffs in the United States, with bills having gone up by as much as 400 percent in the last twenty years—unaffordable for households already struggling to keep up with rent, gas, and other payments.

16  Metering on the level of districts or neighborhoods was common in many western European and all Socialist Eastern European countries for decades. When meters began to be installed as part of the economic shock doctrine

of the 1990s, some took place without a murmur, as was the case in Berlin's eastern parts after the fall of Socialism in the early 1990s (see chapter 3). Others, in contrast, exploded in protests, such as the epic struggles against electricity metering in Georgia in the early 2000s. For a stirring documentary on the protests, see Paul Devlin, dir., *Power Trip* (New York: Act Now Productions, 2006). I thank Paul Manning for this reference.

17 As Tynan explained to me, people back then had to pay the Duke of Devonshire a fee to fish for salmon in the Blackwater River, but "we battled that" with an occupation where about two-thousand protestors fished along the banks of the Blackwater River in protest of the Duke's prerogative. To the protestors, it was unacceptable that the Duke charged the Irish for what they understood to be theirs.

18 The chant, while originally referring to the freedom of Palestine, is part of a mobile arsenal of chants that social movements repurpose to suit their own political situation and set of demands.

19 The EU Parliament's Special Rapporteur on Water, Lynn Boylan, a Sinn Féin party member now in her eighth EU parliamentary term, has been a shining example of a politics dedicated to anti-privatization on the EU level. I regret that I cannot do justice to her inspiring work in this book.

20 Note that the strategy of emphasizing the attraction of foreign capital at the expense of domestic firms has been dominant in Ireland since the 1950s (Bieler 2021, 126).

21 Material and social deprivation is an alternative measure of poverty that has been introduced in the EU and that is not necessarily income based. Instead, it is based on the material and social living conditions of households. This indicator was proposed by the Luxemburg Institute of Socio-Economic Research and subsequently adopted by the EU in 2017.

22 Irish Water operated as a subsidiary to Bord Gáis Éireann, an already existing semistate company with management expertise in the gas and energy sector and the capacity to avail Irish Water "of key expertise in raising finance" (Bresnihan 2016, 7). For this utility to be completely self-financing by 2020, it would not only be directly dependent on domestic and commercial charges but also most likely keep directly employed staff at a minimum while outsourcing the more labor-intensive functions.

23 The Irish government invested almost 5.2 billion euros in the water sector between 2000–2009. Most of this went toward filling the substantial compliance gap under the European Urban Waste Water Treatment Directive. Current operating costs of water and wastewater services are about 1.2 billion euros per year, of which around 1 billion euros was historically provided by the government through taxation, with other sources, including nondomestic water charges, contributing the rest. An estimated additional 20 billion euros investment in the water system up to 2030 is thought to be necessary (Bresnihan 2016, 117).

24 Under the 2013 Water Services Act, 970 contracts for water services were transferred from local authorities to Irish Water. Not all of these were public-private partnerships, but "they do give an indication of the range of transnational water corporations involved in providing services in Ireland. These include Veolia Ireland, which operates more than thirty plants as well as Glan Aqua, a subsidiary of the Portuguese group Mota-Engil, also operating approximately thirty water treatment plants. Other companies include Aecom whose global headquarters are in Los Angeles, as well as companies with their origins in UK water services such as Severn Trent Response, Northumbrian Water Projects, and Anglian Water International, with the latter two now being owned by global investment consortia (Dukelow 2016, 157).

25 During the late 1990s in England and Wales, an active debate about the social policy implications of water charging took place, pitting consumer rights activists (who favored low prices to protect low-income consumers and vulnerable groups) against environmental groups (who favored metering as well as higher (seasonally, temporally, or volumetrically variable) tariffs to encourage conservation (Bakker 2001, 155). This debate is grounded in a long history of antimeter sentiment among the British and Irish working classes, which have since the beginning been strongly suspicious of meters. The nineteenth-century expression "To lie like a gas meter" makes this clear (von Schnitzler 2013, 678).

26 The research on metering and its effects paints a complex picture. On the one hand, price incentives play a useful role in conservation and meters can reduce demand (Zetland 2016, 126). Volumetric prices can also incentivize households to repair leaks, replace old appliances, and reduce outdoor water use. In contrast, SIPTU (Services Industrial Professional and Technical Union) in Ireland has argued that research in the UK, Germany, and the Netherlands has shown the opposite, arguing that "metering each home makes little difference to the amount of water used by families" (SIPTU 2011). With regard to price, the research is similarly inconclusive—monthly bills can go down or up. Fifteen percent of Wessex Water consumers, e.g., reported an increase in water costs (Zetland 2016, 133). Either way, neoliberal reformers have argued for moving water services out of a "social equity" (water as a right) management paradigm in which water and costs were cross-subsidized among citizens, into an "economic equity" (pay for use) paradigm that would make it easier to assign costs *and* be more environmentally friendly. From a social policy perspective, however, problems arise if metering becomes a prelude to the unwinding of cross-subsidies across social classes and thus to an increase in water poverty. Problems also arise if metering becomes a prelude to public-private partnerships, as was clearly the case in Ireland, where water bills were also bound to go up. It is in this regard important to note that some public water utilities that do not use meters do very well, with Scottish Water being a prime example. Zeltland notes that Scottish Water is currently "supplying services at the top of the range at prices that are some of

the lowest in the UK. It might thus in fact in the long run be cheaper *and* more equitable to reduce demand via education or regulation rather than through simple technical fixes like metering. The classic (and erroneous) 'tragedy of the commons' assumption that the movement of common pool resources into private ownership will automatically improve the way resources are consumed is not born out by the research" (Zetland 2016, 125).

27  Under self-funding, approximately 50 percent of Irish Water's funding is to cover operational costs and would be derived from consumer (domestic and nondomestic) charges. The other half is raised on capital markets for infrastructural needs projected to be at least 500 million euros annually (Dukelow 2016, 159).

28  For the protests in Edenmore, see "Garda Riot Squad in Edenmore at Irish Water Protest," YouTube, https://www.youtube.com/watch?v=hVjeUMzwGF0 (last accessed September 10, 2022). For the arrest of Sharon Briggs, see Ireland Says No, "Sharon Briggs Arrested at a Water Meter Protest," YouTube, https:// www.youtube.com/watch?v=ksCMyfASsNE (last accessed September 10, 2022).

29  As Clover (2016) puts it, "There is something architectural about a riot, which is to say spatial. The barricade, that great instrument of riot, finds its origins in the chaining off of neighborhoods against incursion; the rise of the barricade is nothing but the rise of the first era of riot. . . . The new wide boulevards of the nineteenth century are, in telling after telling, designed to bring an end to barricade and riot both, industrial growth will in the end do a better job of it" (138).

30  This contrasts with the modes of behavior change of higher-income households who have the means to purchase water-saving appliances and who would have paid between 0.5 percent in the case of the seventh income decile and 0.3 percent in the case of the top income decile in water charges. Charges were changed several times under pressure from the movements, but none of these changes was progressive. Dukelow notes that "under the new regime, households in the bottom income decile pay 1.9 percent of their disposable income and households in the top income decile pay .15 percent on water services" (2016, 155).

31  As Ogle (2016) put it, "Of course, we pay for water, this is about *how* we pay for water. We currently pay for water through progressive general taxation. While water should be free at the point of use [meaning, as it flows from taps], nobody thinks water is free. Water needed to be paid for through tax" (192). See also Bieler 2021, 140.

32  I thank Anwen Tormey for clarifying aspects of the Great Irish famine for me.

33  It has been reported that Denis O'Brien purchased Siteserv, the company that won the State contract to install water meters for Irish Water, right before it was awarded the contract, and that his "political links" may have been instrumental in the purchase (O'Halloran 2014).

34 In Italy, water activists got so frustrated by mainstream media reporting on the water referendum that they occupied the seat of Italy's national broadcasting company RAI for two days (Bersani 2011, 60)

35 Modern police history begins not in Britain but in Ireland. Until the 1930s, "Ireland (and then Northern Ireland) was the official and unofficial training ground for colonial police officers. Similarly, senior-ranking officers with a background in Irish policing were dispatched the length and breadth of the Empire to provide advice and assistance to imperial police forces facing bloody challenges during the long era of decolonization" (Sinclair 2008, 173–74). The use of the Irish mode of policing as a framework for emerging police forces thus spread far and wide across the British Empire, such that there existed a "thin line separating civil and colonial styles of policing" (Sinclair 2008, 175).

36 For the online petition "Jobstown No Guilty," posted by "Friends of Jobsotwn," see https://sites.google.com/view/jobstownnotguilty/friends-of-jobstown (last accessed September 10, 2022).

37 As Peterson (2014) vividly describes for the case of Nigeria, structural adjustment led to the devaluation of the Nigerian currency, the decrease of earnings, the quadrupling of food prices within months, and the collapse of primary healthcare services because the IMF expected to recover all costs from patients who could not afford even basic food commodities (54). Soon, the 1970s Nigerian state "switched from investing in infrastructure and human capital to *violently managing* a population resistant to economic reforms. In other words, after Nigerian independence, development efforts had attempted to reduce human risk by establishing new public goods; but with structural adjustment the population itself became a risk to the state's plans to implement austerity" (56).

38 There are many examples of such arrests on Youtube. For example, "Storyful-Viral" posted the following on Dailymotion in 2015. https://www.dailymotion .com/video/x2n2c18 (last accessed September 10, 2022).

39 Boycotts have, of course, been used effectively worldwide, including in the South African post-Apartheid anti–prepaid water meter boycotts that were occurring almost simultaneously as well (Schnitzler 2013). I thank Yiorgos Archontopoulos for encouraging me to look up the Irish history of the boycott.

40 As Ogle put it, "I may be prepared to go to jail some day for not paying my water bill, but it wouldn't be much of a campaign to insist that everybody be prepared to do so. . . . Many people who oppose it pay it, not because they want to, but because they feel obliged or are afraid not to. . . . How could we build broad support if we told people like my eighty-four-year old mother who has paid every single bill that ever came in her door, that we had no interest in them?" (2016, 145–6).

41 Note that this legal case was a concerted effort by several water rights groups, including the human rights organizations France Libertés et la Coordination Eau Île-de-France.

1 All materials were accessed in May 2016.

2 Citizens can legally request information from public institutions through freedom-of-information acts, while information pertaining to private corporations is exempt from this rule. Nevertheless, German state bureaucracy is itself far from transparent and in fact highly secretive, with even major developments such as changes of ownership seldomly communicated to the public (Lanz and Eitner 2005, 20). Many others have made the argument that secrecy is a constitutive feature of both corporations and modern states more generally (Lépinay 2011; Piliavsky 2013; Agrama 2012; Nugent 2010).

3 A paradigmatic example of finance's baroque legal forms was the first public-private partnership passed by the British Parliament, the "Greater London Authority Bill" that partially privatized the London underground in 2000. This bill was the "longest and most complex law in English parliamentary history since the "Government of India Act" that regulated the dispossession of colonial India. It contained 277 paragraphs and was 28,000 pages long (Rügemer 2018, 30).

4 Weber calculated that at the time of his writing, about three-sevenths of Germany's national wealth had been brought into circulation through what he called "tributary instruments." Germany's national wealth, he wrote, "is calculated at around 180 billion DM, and the foregoing estimations [i.e., laid out in his article] make it probable that three-sevenths of it consists of interest-bearing or dividend-dispensing rights, mortgages, stocks, or obligations of all sorts. Each year about one billion (1,000 million) marks are saved anew and made available for 'investment'" ([1894] 2000, 322). For Weber, this market was indispensable to the German economy.

5 A top manager for transport in London, Tim O'Toole, referred to the public-private partnership contract governing the London underground as "diabolical" and "crazy" (Rügemer 2018, 36), while a parliamentarian from Equatorial Guinea referred to the public-private partnerships governing oil extraction in the country as a "disaster" (Appel 2019, 146).

6 The Venezuelan *mesas técnicas de aguas* (technical water tables) were first piloted by a progressive mayor in Caracas in the 1990s but then scaled up by the national government in 2001 under the mandate of president Hugo Chávez (1999–2013). These *mesas* still exist today and are neighborhood-level water committees that work with public water utilities to plan and execute local infrastructure projects and oversee service delivery. I thank Rebecca McMillan for this information.

7 The pamphlet that first called for an initial meeting on May 23, 2006 argued that water was the property of Berliners and that the task of the newly constituted group would be to stop its sell-off (*Verscherbelung*). I thank founding member Claus Kittsteiner for a scan of this early pamphlet and for several long and detailed conversations in 2015 and 2016.

8   The provisioning of water infrastructure by private English corporations was routine in Germany at the time since English technology, specifically engineering, was then considered to be vastly superior to Continental technological capacities (Mohajeri 2005, 47n57). The city of Berlin was also looking at other German cities such as Hamburg and Frankfurt, where modern sewage systems had already long been built by British engineers (Mohajeri 2005, 73).

9   Much has been written about the Nazi critique of finance capital as predatory (*raffendes*) capital that was nefariously circulated by a cosmopolitan Jewry into the German national body. The Nazis counterposed this form of capital with good, productive (*schaffendes*) German capital (see Postone 2006). This is, as many critics have noted, a woefully stunted critique of capitalism (or what in Germany is called *"eine verkürzte Kapitalismuskritik"*) that ignored capitalism's inherently exploitative features.

10  Berlin's water utility faces challenges since the city does not have major rivers for fresh water supply or for the dilution and disposal of wastewater. This means that the natural water situation in Berlin is strained and requires large-scale technological interventions and long-term planning (Lanz and Eitner 2005, 4). Berlin has historically always resorted to pumping water from deeper strata, although two thirds of all drinking water are bank or artificially filtrated and are hence strongly influenced by surface water quality. Because of the low water exchange rates in the Berlin region, water is thus effectively indirectly recycled from wastewater (Lanz and Eitner 2005, 13).

11  Eastern households were also not metered because water, like housing, was considered to be people's property (*Volkseigentum*) under Socialism. Water provisioning was heavily subsidized, and people paid for it together with their rent. Sixty thousand water meters were subsequently installed in what used to be East German households. No one I spoke to remembered any protests at the time. I thank Hermann Roloff for this information.

12  The scandal brought the Leftist party, Die Linke, to power in a red-red coalition with the SPD. As a direct consequence, a party that had opposed privatization came to lead the Senate for Economy, which was responsible for the regulation and public share of the water company. Although Die Linke did not initially call for a reversal of the privatization, a more aggressive approach to the private partners was taken (see Behnis 2020).

13  The insurance company Allianz originally also held 5 percent of the shares but sold them to Véolia and RWE in 2002 (Lanz and Eitner 2005, 5).

14  The year 2005 saw the so-called locust debate in Germany—a debate sparked by Social Democratic politician Sigmar Gabriel when he spoke of US investment firms as "locusts" that preyed on the productive German economy and were going to destroy it. This language, critics were quick to note, was haunted by the Nazi association of finance capital with a predatory cosmopolitan Jewry, frequently also referred to as "parasites," "lice," and so on (see Schindler 2018; Raffles 2007; Postone 2006). Needless to say, this language and its implied

stunted critique of capitalism haunts the rise of the European right-wing movements today.

15 The city was ruled by the Social Democrats and the Christian Democrats (SPD/CDU). Opposition was the PDS party (now called the Party of the Left [Die Linke]) and the Greens (Bündnis 90/Die Grünen).

16 The wave of early retirements was also linked to the fact that Berlin had two utilities—everything, including employees, existed doubly because of Berlin's divided history.

17 The city was ruled by the rot-schwarz (SPD/CDU) coalition. Opposition was the PDS party (now called the Party of the Left [Die Linke]) and the Greens (Bündnis 90/Die Grünen).

18 I thank Ulrike von Wiesenau for this delightful detail. For a thorough analysis of Schermer's political work and trajectory, see Von Wiesenau (2012).

19 In contrast to Berlin, where drinking water and sewage cost 5.09 euros/m³, these services cost 3.06 euros/m³ in Munich, 3.17 euros/m³ in Cologne, and 3.62 euros/m³ in Hamburg (Kosche 2014, 14).

20 This ruling in 2004 was interesting because the court ruled that the BWB was subject to laws undergirding the calculation of fees (*Gebührenrecht*) rather than to laws governing pricing. I take up the distinction between fees and price in chapter 4.

21 The Wassertisch chose this route because popular initiatives at the time were prohibited from intervening into ongoing budgetary issues pertaining to the city. This is why the Wassertisch focused on the contract itself rather than on the remunicipalization of the utility. This limitation on popular initiatives was eventually overturned by Berlin's Constitutional Court.

22 They were eventually successful in 2007, but only after several court cases.

23 It seemed that infrastructural investments had significantly declined, as is often the case with public-private partnerships (Peck and Whiteside 2016). As the director of Grenoble's remunicipalized water utility explains, "The [private] contract dictates a deadline within which the provider must be profitable. The maintenance of a pipe is thus not their priority because there is no return on investment. It's a rhythm that does not correlate with the life-cycle of the shared water heritage, which extends over sixty to eighty years" (Binctin 2018). And yet, unlike Southern Italy where infrastructural decline was much more blatantly visible, members of the Wassertisch like Mathias Behnis noted, "It wasn't like brown water was coming out of the taps." This means that they had to use other means to "prove that structural maintenance had declined." Critics did so by closely reading the BWB's end-of-year reports and doing the numbers. The reports revealed that the utility had contractually committed to an annual average investment of 256 million euros (= DM 500 million) over the first ten years. This was a significant drop from the investments that had taken place before partial privatization and was further decreased to

200 million euros after 2007. The BWB investments that did take place were focused on extending connections to the sewer system and on upgrading sewage treatment plants. Meanwhile, the underground infrastructure—drinking water pipes and sewers in particular—suffered from underinvestment, with many environmentally harmful effects such as contaminated wastewater leakages into groundwater. In 2000, the first full year under private management, the number of sewer rehabilitation measures reportedly went down by 90 percent from 2,200 (in 1999) to 220 (10 percent), with few provisions made for a "continuous rehabilitation of the system" (Lanz and Eitner 2005, 12–13).

Still, the damages incurred to the infrastructure were difficult to prove. Like some of the activists I met in Southern Italy, the Wassertisch began to create a list of burst pipes in the city, monitoring what they perceived to be a significant deterioration of the infrastructure under partial privatization. The Wassertisch not only kept track of burst pipes but also of the downsizing that was occurring at the BWB. They argued that a reduction in employees would result in a compressed work day for workers who could simply not keep up with maintenance. In addition, the large-scale early retirement of BWB workers meant a loss of valuable know-how about subterranean piping systems and infrastructural vulnerabilities; a knowledge that is often acquired over years. The Wassertisch cited the well-documented failures of Thames Water in London, which had been acquired by RWE a year after Berlin's partial privatization, where the corporation sought to remedy London's steady infrastructural decline by decreasing the water pressure ("Imagine! People on the third and fourth floors of apartment buildings were suddenly not receiving water anymore!").

24 Thanks to Firat Bozcali for this observation on these dual payments across Ireland and Germany.

25 For example, the majority of Berlin's drinking water wells were at that time located in the Russian sector, and 34.6 percent of the water was "exported" to the Western sector. However, the Western water utility was not willing to pay the price requested by the East Berlin authorities, which is why pipes were at times disconnected. Soon, West Berlin began to massively expand its own independent water works in order to not be too dependent on the East (Schug et al. 2014, 176).

26 There is a fascinating history that has been told about the assimilation of the East German water utility VEB WAB with its Western counterpart (Schug et al. 2014). I cannot do that history justice here but thank Timothy Moss and Christa Hecht for fascinating conversations on the topic (see also Moss 2020).

27 This includes popular initiatives (*Volksinitiativen*), referenda (*Volksbegehren*), plebiscites (*Volksentscheide*), and constitutional complaints (*Verfassungsbeschwerde*), including the right to introduce changes to Berlin's constitution (*Befugnis der Verfassungsänderung*).

28 This opinion by the Berlin House of Representatives (Drucksache 16/2723, 29.10.2009) can be downloaded from the House of Representative's online archive, at https://www.parlament-berlin.de/ados/16/IIIPlen/vorgang/d16-2723.pdf.

29  The term "bürgerliches Recht" is part of "Zivilrecht" (also called "Privatrecht") in the German context. It is best translated as "private law" in the US American context. I thank Anya Bernstein for this clarification.

30  The Wassertisch was inspired by a similar logo originally created in Hamburg.

31  In addition to these "fictive costs," activists pointed out that either way, necessary infrastructural investments were not made and that Berliners should only be charged for actual repairs, not fictive future investments (Kosche 2014, 6).

32  Hannah Appel writes extensively about these fiscal stability clauses through which corporations attempt to guarantee the stability of returns. Often, these clauses represent some of the most "egregious contractual methods companies use to profit from inequality" (2019, 167–8).

33  Michael Efler was one of the founders of Berlin's Energietisch (Berlin Energy Table), which was named after the Wassertisch. Here, a coalition of fifty-six local civil society groups sought to remunicipalize Berlin's privatized energy distribution grid (Berlin Energie) and transform it into a Berlin-owned local energy supplier (Berliner Stadtwerke). The quorum for the referendum was narrowly missed. Since then, the city has seen a plethora of referenda take off and significantly impact the political culture of the city, notably, and most recently an attempt to expropriate one of Europe's leading publicly listed property companies.

34  See Kishimoto, Lobina, and Petitjean (2015); Kishimoto, Steinfort, and Petitjean (2020); McDonald and Swyngedouw (2019); and McDonald (2016).

35  See also the Berliner Wassercharta, written by the Berlin Wasserrat (Water Assembly), many of whose founding members consist of members of the Wassertisch. It proposes a number of political, economic, ecological, and legal principles for a public and democratically managed water utility. For a look at the charter, see https://berliner-wassertisch.net/content/docs/charta.php (last accessed September 10, 2022).

### Chapter 4: Just Price

1  Parthenope is also the original name of the city of Naples when it was a Greek colony around the ninth to eighth century BC. When Parthenope burned down, it was renamed "Neapolis" (New City) in the sixth-century BC by the Greeks. I thank Salvatore Giusto for alerting me to this fact.

2  On November 9, 2018, GORI again signed a long-term industrial agreement with the region of Campania and the Campanian Water Authority (Ente Idrico Campano), establishing the terms and conditions based on which the company will complete its takeover of the facilities and operation of the integrated water services within the respective water district.

3  ACEA SpA (originally an acronym for Azienda Comunale Elettricità e Acque; Electricity and Water Municipal Utility) is a multiutility operative in the management and development of networks and services in the water, energy,

and environmental sectors. It is a leading actor in the Italian water sector and serves around nine million inhabitants in four regions. It also operates in Latin American countries such as Honduras, the Dominican Republic, Colombia, and Peru. ACEA is one of four major Italian water corporations (*le quattro sorelle dell'acqua*; the four sisters of water) as a recent Italian news report sarcastically referred to them (Giovannini 2017, 9).

4 Anthropologist Michael Taussig has perhaps most famously written about the devil as the figure that often mediates conflicts "between precapitalist and capitalist modes of objectifying the human condition" (1980, xvi).

5 Although Napoli ABC did raise its prices by 40 percent in 2019 (Mormone 2019), it also staggers its water pricing, allowing for reduced water rates for tens of thousands of poor families in the city.

6 Andrea Ballestero offers a detailed example of the public price setting in Costa Rica, where the country's Public Service Regulation Authority is committed to water pricing as an ethical exercise grounded in public transparency (2019).

7 All quotations taken from Allianz Global Water website, https://updates .allianzgi.com/en-gb/investment-ideas/sdg-investing/our-strategies/allianz -global-water (last accessed January 20, 2022).

8 The 7 percent was initially envisioned to be only provisional; with the MTN prescribing that this remuneration mechanism would be regularly updated depending on market conditions. But this never happened. On the contrary, and especially after the 2008 financial crisis when it became clear that investments into water utilities would generate secure returns for investors, the return rates embedded within the pricing mechanisms were always 7 percent or even higher than originally capped (Massarutto 2015, 213).

9 Tariffs hardly allowed the recovery of operational costs before the Galli law in 1994, since investments were financed by the public budget. As a result, Italian residential water tariffs were extremely low and hardly noticeable in the family budget. In addition, billing and revenue collection efficiency was often poor, especially in the south, where people often did not pay anything. Sanitation, sewage collection, and treatment charges rely on a uniform charge, proportional to volume, which was set at the national level by budget law. At the launch of the reform, the sanitation charge was 170 and 500 ITL/ $m^3$ (corresponding to 0.35 euros/$m^3$ in total) (Massarutto 2015, 211).

10 This estimate was made by the "pioneering" regulator of the water sector in England and Wales, Ofwat (Massarutto 2020, 7).

11 Note that proliferation is of course integral to profits: The Global Water Intelligence tariff survey from 2019, e.g., includes a whole section on the separate storm-water rates that utilities are increasingly charging because of climate change; see https://globalwaterintel-info.com/p/36G3–5QE/gwi-2019-water -tariff-infographic-nb?fbclid=IwAR2NQS2dRBhSyUklyXCB8xo3mUiorhzHm qPlGJBwyAq58qftcy2TiYgWu4Y (last accessed January 7, 2022).

12  This is authorized by two provisions in the MTI, which caps prices at 9 percent instead of 6.5 percent for "virtuous firms" that promised investments in 2014–2017, and that introduced a further tariff component (FNI) for financing new investments promised by virtuous firms or undercapitalized utilities. The ex-post paradigm is further weakened by the "time lag" mechanism that recognizes a spread of 0.1 percent on financial costs charged in tariffs, to compensate for the two-year delay on investment remuneration. Price, in short, is generated out of promises that are hard to verify. It is hardly surprising that utilities were immediately incentivized to increase their promises on future investments after the adoption of MTI (Romano, Guerrini, and Campedelli 2015, 52).

13  German observers noted similar critiques of water price composition. In Berlin before the referendum, for example, a large part of the water price consisted not of real but of calculatory (fictive) costs.

14  Enzo Alliegro beautifully documents the complex struggles against oil extraction in the Southern Italian region of Basilicata, where people similarly speak of "authorized theft" or *furto autorizzato* (Alliegro 2012, 163).

15  Local TV and online news source *RTA Live*, https://rtalive.it/2016/07/nocera -inferiore-cercasi-fontanine-disperatamente/35875/ (last accessed January 7, 2022).

16  As Jane Schneider has noted, state-mafia entanglements have long been acknowledged by Italians, who refer to these relations as *intrecci* (an interweaving of state with organized crime networks). Most importantly, she argues that these entanglements are not the result of an ineffective or absent state, but more of a matter of mutual accommodation, especially under conditions of rapid capitalist developments (Schneider 2016, 8).

17  As the authors describe, the Italian system of public procurement is vulnerable to infiltration by organized crime, particularly in Calabria, Campania, and Sicily. There, organized crime enters the public sector by creating businesses that can influence the adjudication of public contracts through bribery and intimidation.

18  As Li and Semedi put it: "A critical term sometimes used in Indonesia to describe rent seeking is mafia, a word [that] in this context does not signal the activity of a criminal family or gang, but rather that of tollbooths that uses choke points in bureaucratic structures to extract value for personal gain." Hence there is a school mafia that extracts tolls from parents through multiple fees that must be paid for children to sit their exams, a land mafia that extracts tolls whenever a signature is needed for land transaction and so on. It's about "capturing a share of the wealth" (2021, 41).

19  Amedeo Laboccetta was a close ally of Sarro, who in turn was closely allied with Nicola Cosentino, the Campanian politician accused by a Camorra informer of having facilitated the illegal disposal of toxic waste in exchange for the sum of 50,000 euros. In 2009, magistrates of Naples' antimafia commission sent a

request for Cosentino's arrest to the chamber of deputies, but the chamber's commission refused. "It's always the same people," a lawyer wearily said to me.

20  This slogan was the heartbreaking epilogue to the already existing slogan, in dialect, which said, *C'at accis a salut* (You have killed our health).

21  It is noteworthy to say that these practices of autoreduction can be found in the gas and electricity sector, too, although they are not graced with the "legality" that the autoreduction of water bills is in the aftermath of the referendum. The price for gas and electricity has soared in Italy—almost 50 percent since 2004—giving rise to what one journalist called "Robin Hood electricians" who "fix" meters for customers who cannot pay. Working like the "struggle electricians" documented by Antina von Schnitzler (2013; see also Anand 2017, 105–6), these energy heroes insist that their technically illegal acts are in fact ethical because they are not helping their clients forego payment altogether but instead making sure that impoverished households are charged sums they can actually pay. As one Neapolitan electrician explained, people can either hook themselves up to the electricity grid for free and escape payment altogether or opt for a "partial" solution that goes unnoticed by authorities because bills are still sent and paid. The difference is that the electrician "fixes" the meter in a way that some household electrical consumption is not counted. The bill is thus reduced by 30–40 percent—a "fix" he performs for the "little people," as he put it, "the *gente del popolino*—with four to five children, the husband in prison, or for pensioners who receive maybe only 300 euros a month." For the video *Energy Thieves* (*Ladri di Energia*), see https://www.la7.it/piazzapulita/video/ladri-di-energia-25-11-2016-198890 ?fbclid=IwAR0StLQeOI578zHJ4TWM7QU-ATtP3p3DlT9J9ztQF4PilSFrbW-0ATx _OJ8 (last accessed January 7, 2022). I thank Salvatore Giusto for alerting me to this story.

22  De Angelis (2017) describes radical price setting practiced by other grassroots agricultural initiatives in Italy, such as by the Genuino Clandestino (genuine clandestine) network in and around Bologna. The network is dedicated to participatory food sovereignty practices, and prices are decided at regular assemblies among consumers and producers. In some cases, boxes and scales are done away with altogether, with people taking from the warehouse simply what they need after having paid an amount proportionate to their household income at the beginning of the year (294–98).

23  In response, Publiacqua sent all mayors a letter, threatening to block all money for investments if the new tariff structure was not accepted (Sasso and Sironi 2013).

24  For the full report, see the Italian Forum for Water Movements' website: https://www.acquabenecomune.org/notizie/53-raccolta-firme-referendum /notizie/1987-tar-toscana-vittoria-del-forum (last accessed January 7, 2022).

25  As Nikhil Anand (2017) puts it, the state and its biopolitical projects are not simply "extended from the center as much is it pulled, tugged, and demanded, often quite materially, from the margins" (161).

26 The phenomenon of the fiscal strike has a long history in Italy (Guano 2010).

27 By 2017, GORI had again amassed 100 million euros in debt even as its users continued to report regular breakdowns of infrastructure and constantly struggled with unannounced water shortages. By 2019, major Italian financial news outlets reported that the region of Campania had just seen the most important financial restructuring that the Campanian water and wastewater sector had ever seen; 80 million euros worth of long-term loans provided to GORI by numerous banks and Acea itself (*Il Gazzettino Vesuviano* 2017).

28 A post on Facebook by the Rete Civica (accessed on October 27, 2020) notes that an eighty-year old woman in Nola just had her water cut off by an "unknown man" who was not immediately identifiable as a GORI employee and who entered the gate of her residence without identifying himself or knocking—and this in the middle of the COVID-19 pandemic. Her only fault, the post noted, was that she had sent an official complaint against GORI. Another case was a family with two small children in Massa di Somma that had similarly launched a complaint against the utility after receiving a bill of 2000 euros.

29 This sense of criminalization has a long history in a country that did just that. A long genealogy of anthropologists in Italy insisted that racialized, lower-class Southern Italians were "savage races" with a tendency for fury, vengeance, and carnal love, thus making them "born criminals" (Schneider and Schneider 2008, 353).

30 This slogan or variants of it has been reiterated many times by political movements across Europe (Razsa and Kurnik 2012, 239).

31 Since 2015, Campania has been governed by the EIC and consists of one single regional ATO that is subdivided into five water districts. Only one, the Sarnese Vesuviano district, is in a public-private partnership with GORI, which could be liquidated if the Sarnese-Vesuviano district's governing council, consisting of thirty mayors, vote in favor of liquidation. At present, the district is split in two factions: those who are in favor of a return to the public management of integrated water services (*Comuni per l'acqua pubblica*) and those that are not (the pro-GORI group), which calls itself Protection for All (Tutela per tutti), with the latter group holding a slight majority (Il Mediano 2020)

32 In Castellammare, e.g., the mayor was forced into the network because activists presented the local town council with a motion insisting that "the will of the people be respected" and the water referendum be implemented. The majority of the council voted in favor of the motion—not surprising since many of its members at the time belonged to the Five Star Movement.

## Epilogue

1 For a summary by Anne Le Strat, see "Paris: Local Authorities Regain Control of Water Management," TNI, August 10, 2010, https://www.tni.org/en/article /paris-local-authorities-regain-control-of-water-management.

2  This is enshrined in the law (Code Général des Collectivités Territoriales) and is thus in line with both the Water Framework Directive as well as the principle "Water pays for Water." I am grateful to Thierry Uso for sharing this information, and for his profound generosity and time.

3  People in Paris were worried about the scaling up of utility management to metropolitan levels, which could entail the city of Paris being agglomerated with its surrounding areas. The worry was that Eau de Paris would be managed under a metropolitan utility that would include surrounding utilities managed by Suez and Veolia. The problems that might emerge from metropolitan-level utility management were recently demonstrated in the Northern Italian city of Turin, where the attempt on the part of the city of Turin to remunicipalize its water utility was thwarted by the smaller, mostly center-right municipalities that surround the city but that together form the "Turin Metropolitan City." For the full text, written by the Italian Forum for Water Movements, see Forum Italiano dei Movimenti per l'Acqua, "Turin: A New Stop to the Long March towards Water Remunicipalization," European Water Movement, http://europeanwater.org/actions/country-city-focus/970 -turin-a-new-stop-to-the-long-march-towards-water-remunicipalization (last accessed January 7, 2022).

4  Many of my interlocutors who were involved in the remunicipalization of previously privatized utilities talked about how complex it was to disambiguate the corporate culture from what they perceived to be a more transparent, public culture of service provisioning. In Paris, for example, my interlocutors stressed the differences between public accounting and private accounting systems, and how difficult it had been to move from the one back to the other. This is only one of the many themes I was not able to follow up on in this book but hope that others might take up. There is an urgent need for ethnographic studies on the move from corporate back to public municipal management.

5  In Orbán's Hungary, initial remunicipalizations were accompanied by the reiteration of the populist surface critiques of finance capitalism that were first articulated at the beginning of the twentieth century with the rise of National Socialism and Fascism—a "widespread rage" against the finance sector as rent-seeking, parasitic, and, above all, rooted in an "international Jewry" that undermines the social health of the nation (Postone 2006). Here, one "bad" form of rent-seeking capitalism is played off against a "good" and "productive" form of capitalism; a contrast that disregards the mutual constitution of both expropriation and labor exploitation as two sides of the same regime of accumulation (Mahmud 2020; Clover 2016, 131–32).

6  For the Transnational Institute's global database on remunicipalized public services, see publicfutures.org.

7  Rennes, now also a member of France Eau Publique (FEP), a network of public water operators in France, has contracted with around two thousand local farms who have pledged to shift to pesticide free farming. This pledge helps protect Rennes's water resources, lessens the cost of water treatment, and

today provides around eleven thousand organic school meals on a daily basis. This initiative is identical to the system pioneered by Eau de Paris.

8 More specifically, central governments have sometimes paid directly for the water service so that there is virtually no role for charges (Ireland). Governments also distribute some part of central tax revenue to support local authority spending on water and other services (Canada), provide cheap loan finance for local authorities to use for capital investment (US), or collect water charges centrally and redistribute them to authorities that need to invest (France). In Europe, the EU itself plays a major role in public financing of water systems in poorer states through the cohesion and solidarity funds, and through low interest loans from its public sector development instrument, the European Investment Bank (Hall and Lobina 2012, 5).

9 These "basic principles" (*Grundsätze*) can be found on their website (translation by author). See GiB, "Grundsätze," December 29, 2010, https://www .gemeingut.org/uber-uns/grundsaetze-2/.

10 Agamben (2013) asks these questions through his narration of the history of the Fraticelli (Little Brethren) Franciscans, who were part of a growing group of religious movements that practiced forms of life where no one claimed ownership of any possession at all (93). Heretics to the church because they proposed a new type of order—the common life—the Fraticelli held everything they owned in common. They renounced everything except de facto use itself, since use was necessary to survival and human life. Because the Fraticelli attempted to live outside of regimes of appropriation, ownership, and property, their form of life was thought of as an animal form of life; analogous to the lives of little children (who do not own but only use the property of the father) as well as madmen "who all lack the disposition to possess" (112). The pope, in response to religious movements such as those of the Fraticelli, established a juridical separation between the church and its property and the "minor friar's" use of books and other moveable property etc. (124–25). It was thus a Papal Bull, written by Gregorius IX, that first distinguished between ownership and use, retaining the former for the Pope and the Church while conceding the latter to the friars. It is from this sharp distinction between ownership and use, made by a pope in the eleventh century, that the first theory of ownership emerged (134). It was at this historical moment, with the Church creating laws of ownership in response to Franciscan heretics, that "being proprietary" became a "genuinely distinct sociological type" (134).

# REFERENCES

Agamben, Giorgio. 2005. *State of Exception*. Translated by Kevin Attell. Chicago: University of Chicago Press.

Agamben, Giorgio. 2013. *The Highest Poverty: Monastic Rules and Form-of-Life*. Translated by Adam Kotsko. Stanford, CA: Stanford University Press.

Agrama, Hussein Ali. 2012. *Questioning Secularism: Islam, Sovereignty, and the Rule of Law in Modern Egypt*. Chicago: University of Chicago Press.

*Agro 24*. 2013. "Roccapiemonte: Il TAR boccia la Gori; Acqua nelle mani del comune." *Agro 24* (blog). Accessed January 6, 2022. https://www.agro24.it/2013/04/roccapiemonte-il-tar-boccia-la-gori-acqua-nelle-mani-del-comune/.

*Agro 24*. 2015. "Gori: Il Tar Campania annulla le ordinanze dei sindaci." *Agro 24* (blog). Accessed January 6, 2022. https://www.agro24.it/2015/04/gori-il-tar-campania-annulla-le-ordinanze-dei-sindaci/.

*Agro 24*. 2020. "Roccapiemonte: No all'acqua privata, prosegue la battaglia." *Agro 24* (blog). Accessed January 6, 2022. https://www.agro24.it/2020/07/roccapiemonte-no-allacqua-privata-prosegue-la-battaglia/.

Ahlers, Rhodante. 2010. "Fixing and Nixing: The Politics of Water Privatization." *Review of Radical Political Economics* 42, no. 2: 213–30.

Allianz Global Investors. 2021. "Water Infrastructure: Why Investment Is So Urgently Needed." Accessed April 10, 2022. https://us.allianzgi.com/en-us/sustainability/sustainable-ideas/water-infrastructure.

Alliegro, Enzo Vinicio. 2012. *Il totem nero: Petrolio, sviluppo e conflitti in Basilicata*. Rome: CISU.

Alliegro, Enzo Vinicio. 2020. *Out of Place, Out of Control: Antropologia dell'ambiente in crisi*. Rome: CISU.

Anand, Nikhil. 2017. *Hydraulic City: Water and the Infrastructures of Citizenship in Mumbai*. Durham, NC: Duke University Press.

Anand, Nikhil. 2011. "Pressure: The Politechnics of Water Supply in Mumbai." *Cultural Anthropology* 26, no. 4: 542–64.

Angier, Natalie. 2008. "The Wonders of Blood." *New York Times*, October 21, 2008. https://www.nytimes.com/2008/10/21/science/21angi.html.

Appel, Hannah. 2019. *The Licit Life of Capitalism: US Oil in Equatorial Guinea*. Durham, NC: Duke University Press.

Arendt, Hannah. 1976. *The Origins of Totalitarianism*. New York: Harcourt Brace Jovanovich.

Arendt, Hannah. 1998. *The Human Condition*. 2nd ed. Chicago: University of Chicago Press.

Aretxaga, Begoña. 2000. "Playing Terrorist: Ghastly Plots and the Ghostly State." *Journal of Spanish Cultural Studies* 1: 43–58.

Aretxaga, Begoña. 2003. "Maddening States." *Annual Review of Anthropology* 32, no. 1: 393–410.

Armiero, Marco, and Giacomo D'Alisa. 2013. "Voices, Clues, Numbers: Roaming among Waste in Campania." *Capitalism Nature Socialism* 24, no. 4: 7–16.

Arrighi, Giovanni. 1994. *The Long Twentieth Century*. London: Verso.

Baccaro, Andreina, and Antonio Musella. 2013. *Il Paese dei veleni: Biocidio; Viaggio nell'Italia contaminata*. Rome: Round Robin Editrice.

Badiou, Alain. 2012. *The Rebirth of History: Times of Riots and Uprisings*. London: Verso.

Bailey, Saki, and Ugo Mattei. 2013. "Social Movements as Constituent Power: The Italian Struggle for the Commons." *Indiana Journal of Global Legal Studies* 20, no. 2: 965–1013.

Bakhtin, Mikhail. 1984. *Rabelais and His World*. Translated by Hélène Iswolsky. Bloomington: Indiana University Press.

Bakke, Gretchen. 2016. *The Grid: The Fraying Wires between Americans and Our Energy Future*. London: Bloomsbury.

Bakker, Karen. 2001. "Paying for Water: Water Pricing and Equity in England and Wales." *Transactions of the Institute of British Geographers* 26, no. 2: 143–64.

Bakker, Karen. 2004. *An Uncooperative Commodity: Privatizing Water in England and Wales*. Oxford: Oxford University Press.

Bakker, Karen. 2007. "The 'Commons' versus the 'Commodity': Alter-globalization, Anti-privatization, and the Human Right to Water in the Global South." *Antipode* 39, no. 3: 430–55.

Bakker, Karen. 2010. *Privatizing Water: Governance Failure and the World's Urban Water Crisis*. Ithaca, NY: Cornell University Press.

Bakker, Karen. 2013. "Neoliberal versus Postneoliberal Water: Geographies of Privatization and Resistance." *Annals of the Association of American Geographers* 103, no. 2: 253–60.

Balakrishnan, Rajagopal. 2003. *International Law from Below: Development, Social Movements, and Third World Resistance.* Cambridge: Cambridge University Press.

Ballestero, Andrea. 2015. "The Ethics of a Formula: Calculating a Financial-Humanitarian Price for Water." *American Ethnologist* 42, no. 2: 262–78.

Ballestero, Andrea. 2019. *A Future History of Water.* Durham, NC: Duke University Press.

Ballestero, Andrea, Andrea Muehlebach, and Gloria Pérez-Rivera. Forthcoming. "What Is a Financial Frontier?" *Journal of Cultural Economy.*

Barlow, Maude. 2005. *Blue Gold: The Fight to Stop The Corporate Theft of the World's Water.* New York: New Press.

Barlow, Maude. 2019. *Whose Water Is It Anyway? Taking Water Protection into Public Hands.* Toronto: ECW Press.

Barnes, Jessica. 2013. "Who Is a Water User? The Politics of Gender in Egypt's Water User Associations." In *Contemporary Water Governance in the Global South: Scarcity, Marketization, and Participation,* edited by Leila Harris, Jacqueline Goldin, and Christopher Sneddon, 185–98. London: Routledge.

Barnes, Jessica. 2014. *Cultivating the Nile: The Everyday Politics of Water in Egypt.* Durham, NC: Duke University Press.

Barraqué, Bernard. 2011. *Urban Water Conflicts.* Boca Raton, FL: CRC Press.

Bayliss, Kate. 2014. "The Financialization of Water." *Review of Radical Political Economics* 46, no. 3: 292–307.

Bayliss, Kate. 2017. "Material Cultures of Water Financialization in England and Wales." *New Political Economy* 22, no. 4: 383–97.

Bear, Laura. 2015. *Navigating Austerity: Currents of Debt along a South Asian River.* Stanford, CA: Stanford University Press.

Bear, Laura. 2017. "'Alternatives' to Austerity: A Critique of Financialized Infrastructure in India and Beyond." *Anthropology Today* 33, no. 5: 3–7.

Bear, Laura. 2018. "Global Water Wars and the Public Good." Public Books, February 5, 2018. https://www.publicbooks.org/global-water-wars-and-the-public-good/.

Bear, Laura. 2020. "Speculations on Infrastructure: From Colonial Public Works to a Postcolonial Global Asset Class on the Indian Railways, 1840–2017." *Economy and Society* 49, no. 1: 1–26.

Bear, Laura, Ritu Birla, and Stine Simonsen Puri. 2015. "Speculation: Futures and Capitalism in India." *Comparative Studies of South Asia, Africa and the Middle East* 35, no. 3: 387–91.

Beggs, Mike, Dick Bryan, and Michael Rafferty. 2014. "Shoplifters of the World Unite! Law and Culture in Financialized Times." *Cultural Studies* 28, nos. 5–6: 976–96.

Behnis, Mathias. 2009. "Kein Grund zum Feiern." *Junge Welt,* October 29, 2009, 10. https://www.jungewelt.de/artikel/133808.kein-grund-zum-feiern.html.

Behnis, Mathias. 2020. *Die Rekommunalisierung der Berliner Wasserbetriebe: Einmal Privatisierung und Zurück.* Berlin: Berliner Wissenschafts Verlag.

Bersani, Marco. 2011. *Come abbiamo vinto il referendum: Dalla battaglia per l'acqua pubblica alla democrazia dei beni comuni.* Rome: Tempi Moderni.

Besky, Sarah. 2016. "The Future of Price: Communicative Infrastructures and the Financialization of Indian Tea." *Cultural Anthropology* 31, no. 1: 4–29.

Besky, Sarah. 2021. "Teawords: Science, Brokerage, and Experiments with Quality in Industrial Tea Production." *American Anthropologist* 123, no. 1: 96–107.

Beveridge, Ross. 2012. "Consultants, Depoliticization and Arena-Shifting in the Policy Process: Privatizing Water in Berlin." *Policy Sciences* 45, no. 1: 47–68.

Beveridge, Ross, and Matthias Naumann. 2014. "Global Norms, Local Contestation: Privatisation and de/Politicisation in Berlin." *Policy and Politics; London* 42, no. 2: 275–91.

Beveridge, Ross, Frank Hüesker, and Matthias Naumann. 2014. "From Post-politics to a Politics of Possibility? Unraveling the Privatization of the Berlin Water Company." *Geoforum* 5: 66–74.

Bieler, Andreas. 2015. "'Sic Vos Non Vobis' (For You, But Not Yours): The Struggle for Public Water in Italy." *Monthly Review*, October 1, 2015. https://monthlyreview.org /2015/10/01/sic-vos-non-vobis-for-you-but-not-yours/.

Bieler, Andreas. 2021. *Fighting for Water: Resisting Privatization in Europe.* London: Bloomsbury Publishing.

Binctin, Barnabe. 2018. "How Did Grenoble Start a French Water Revolution? It Made Its Water Management Public." *openDemocracy* May 7, 2018. https://www.opendemocracy .net/en/tc-grenoble-water-municipalisation/.

Birla, Ritu. 2009. *Stages of Capital: Law, Culture, and Market Governance in Late Colonial India.* Durham, NC: Duke University Press.

Björkman, Lisa. 2015. *Pipe Politics, Contested Waters: Embedded Infrastructures of Millennial Mumbai.* Durham, NC: Duke University Press.

Blackstone, William. 2016. *Commentaries on the Laws of England, Book II: Of the Rights of Things.* Oxford: Oxford University Press.

Blauel, Celia. 2020. "Paris Celebrates a Decade of Public Water Success." *The Future Is Public.* Accessed January 6, 2022. https://www.tni.org/en/futureispublic.

Block, Fred. 2001. "Introduction." In *The Great Transformation: The Political and Economic Origins of Our Time*, 2nd ed. Boston: Beacon Press.

Blyth, Mark. 2013. *Austerity: The History of a Dangerous Idea.* Oxford: Oxford University Press.

Boewe, Jörn. 2009. "Sizilianisierung der Gewinne." *Berliner Wasser—Alles Klar?* (blog). Accessed January 6, 2022. https://berliner-wasser.blogspot.com/2009/03 /sizilianisierung-der-gewinne.html.

Boscheck, Ralf, Judith C. Clifton, Daniel Díaz-Fuentes, Mark Oelmann, Christoph Czichy, Monica Alessi, Sébastien Treyer, Janet Wright, and Martin Cave. 2013. "The Regulation of Water Services in the EU." *Intereconomics* 48, no. 3: 136–58.

Boyer, Dominic. 2019. *Energopolitics: Wind and Power in the Anthropocene.* Durham, NC: Duke University Press.

Bradshaw, Jonathan, and Meg Huby. 2013. "Water Poverty in England and Wales." *Journal of Poverty and Social Justice* 21, no. 2: 137–48.

Brenner, Neil, Jamie Peck, and Nik Theodore. 2014. "New Constitutionalism and Variegated Neo-liberalization." In *New Constitutionalism and World Order*, edited by Stephen Gill and A. Claire Cutler, 126–42. Cambridge: Cambridge University Press.

Bresnihan, Patrick. 2016. "The Bio-financialization of Irish Water: New Advances in the Neoliberalization of Vital Services." *Utilities Policy* 40 (June): 115–24.

Brockington, Dan. 2011. "Ecosystem Services and Fictitious Commodities." *Environmental Conservation* 38, no. 4: 367–69.

Brophy, Daragh. 2015. "The Story of 'No.' 15 Moments That Have Defined the Irish Water Protest Movement." *thejournal.ie*, August 29, 2015.

Brown, Maia. 2019. "Stopping Veolia: A Report from Seattle." *e-flux Architecture*, June. https://www.e-flux.com/architecture/liquid-utility/259654/stopping-veolia-a-report-from-seattle/.

Brown, Wendy. 2015. *Undoing the Demos: Neoliberalism's Stealth Revolution*. New York: Zone Books.

Browne, Craig, and Simon Susen. 2014. "Austerity and Its Antithesis: Practical Negations of Capitalist Legitimacy." *South Atlantic Quarterly* 113, no. 2: 217–30.

Bryant, Rebecca. 2016. "On Critical Times: Return, Repetition, and the Uncanny Present." *History and Anthropology* 27, no. 1: 19–31.

Butler, Judith. 2015. *Notes Toward a Performative Theory of Assembly*. Cambridge, MA: Harvard University Press.

Byrd, Jodi A., Alyosha Goldstein, Jodi Melamed, and Chandan Reddy. 2018. "Predatory Value: Economies of Dispossession and Disturbed Relationalities." *Social Text* 36, no. 2: 1–18.

Calderone, Antonino, and Pino Arlacchi. 1993. *Men of Dishonor: Inside the Sicilian Mafia; An Account of Antonino Calderone*. New York: Morrow.

Campra, Maura, Gianluca Oricchio, Eugenio Mario Braja, and Paolo Esposito. 2014. *Sovereign Risk and Public-Private Partnership during the Euro Crisis*. London: Palgrave Macmillan.

Caneppele, Stefano, Francesco Calderoni, and Sara Martocchia. 2009. "Not Only Banks: Criminological Models on the Infiltration of Public Contracts by Italian Organized Crime." *Journal of Money Laundering Control* 12, no. 2: 151–72.

Capone, Nicola. 2013. "The Assemblies of the City of Naples: A Long Battle to Defend the Landscape and Environment." *Capitalism Nature Socialism* 24, no. 4: 46–54.

Carroll, Michael P. 1999. *Irish Pilgrimage: Holy Wells and Popular Catholic Devotion*. Baltimore, MD: Johns Hopkins University Press.

Carrozza, Chiara, and Emanuele Fantini. 2013. *Si scrive acqua . . . Attori, pratiche e discorsi nel movimento italiano per l'acqua comune*. Prima edizione. Turin, Italy: Accademia University Press.

Carrozza, Chiara, and Emanuele Fantini. 2016. "The Italian Water Movement and the Politics of the Commons." *Water Alternatives* 9, no. 1: 99–119.

Cattelino, Jessica. 2015a. "The Cultural Politics of Water in the Everglades and Beyond." Transcript of the Lewis Henry Morgan Lecture. *HAU: Journal of Ethnographic Theory* 5, no. 3: 235–50.

Cattelino, Jessica. 2015b. "Valuing Nature." Fieldsights—Theorizing the Contemporary, *Society for Cultural Anthropology*, March 30, 2015. https://culanth.org/fieldsights/valuing-nature.

Césaire, Aimé. 2000. *Discourse on Colonialism*. New York: Monthly Review Press.

Chakrabarty, Dipesh. 2000. *Provincializing Europe. Postcolonial Thought and Historical Difference*. Princeton, NJ. Princeton University Press.

Chiasson, Chrissy. 2019. "'I Am the River; the River Is Me'—Legal Personhood for Waters." International Joint Commission. Accessed January 6, 2022. https://ijc .org/en/i-am-river-river-me-legal-personhood-waters.

Christophers, Brett, and Ben Fine. 2020. "The Value of Financialization and the Financialization of Value." In *The Routledge International Handbook of Financialization*, edited by Philip Mader, Daniel Mertens, and Natascha van der Zwan, 19–30. London: Routledge.

Christopherson, Susan, Ron Martin, and Jane Pollard. 2013. "Financialisation: Roots and Repercussions." *Cambridge Journal of Regions, Economy and Society* 6, no. 3: 351–57.

Chu, Julie Y. 2014. "When Infrastructures Attack: The Workings of Disrepair in China." *American Ethnologist* 41, no. 2: 351–67.

Clover, Joshua. 2016. *Riot. Strike. Riot: The New Era of Uprisings*. London: Verso.

Cody, Francis. 2011. "Publics and Politics." *Annual Review of Anthropology* 40, no. 1: 37–52.

Cody, Francis. 2016. "The Obligation to Act: Gender and Reciprocity in Political Mobilization." *HAU: Journal of Ethnographic Theory* 6, no. 3: 179–99.

Cody, Francis. 2020. "Metamorphoses of Popular Sovereignty: Cimena, Short Circuits, and Digitization in Tamil India." *Anthropological Quarterly* 93, no. 2: 57–88.

Colamonaco, Giuseppe. 2015. "TAR campania: Respinte sette ordinanze contro i distacchi." *RTALive* (blog). Accessed January 6, 2022. https://rtalive.it/2015/04/tar -campania-respinte-ordinanze-contro-i-distacchi/20723/.

Coleman, Gabriella. 2009. "Code Is Speech: Legal Tinkering, Expertise, and Protest among Free and Open Software Developers." *Cultural Anthropology* 24, no. 3: 420–54.

Collier, Stephen J. 2011. *Post-Soviet Social: Neoliberalism, Social Modernity, Biopolitics*. Princeton, NJ: Princeton University Press.

Collier, Stephen J., and Andrew Lakoff. 2015. "Vital Systems Security: Reflexive Biopolitics and the Government of Emergency." *Theory, Culture and Society* 32, no. 2: 19–51.

Collins, Jane L. 2017. *The Politics of Value: Three Movements to Change How We Think about the Economy*. Chicago: University of Chicago Press.

Comaroff, Jean, and John L. Comaroff, eds. 2006. *Law and Disorder in the Postcolony*. Chicago: University of Chicago Press.

Commissione Rodotà. 2010. XVI Legislatura, Disegno di Legge e Relazioni. Delega al Governo per la modificadel codice civile in materia di beni pubblici. *Senato della Repubblica*, no. 2031 (February 24). https://www.senato.it/service/PDF/PDFServer /DF/217244.pdf.

Cooper, Melinda. 2008. *Life as Surplus: Biotechnology and Capitalism in the Neoliberal Era*. In Vivo: A Mclellan Book. Seattle: University of Washington Press.

Cooper, Melinda, and Angela Mitropoulos. 2009. "The Household Frontier." *Ephemera: Theory and Politics in Organization* 9, no. 4: 363–68.

*Corriere della Sera*. 2016. "Acqua, ancora aumenti delle tariffe Proteste in 20 Comuni dell'ex Ato3." Accessed January 6, 2022. http://corrieredelmezzogiorno.corriere .it/napoli/economia/16_settembre_29/acqua-ancora-aumenti-tariffe-proteste-20 -comuni-dell-ex-ato3-425c2074-8618-11e6-832a-cce4cd3e89ac.shtml.

Cozzolino, Adriano. 2019. "Reconfiguring the State: Executive Powers, Emergency Legislation, and Neoliberalization in Italy." *Globalizations* 16, no. 3: 336–52. https:// doi.org/10.1080/14747731.2018.1502495.

Croce, Raffaele Della, and Juan Yermo. 2013. "Institutional Investors and Infrastructure Financing." Accessed January 6, 2022. http://sefifrance.fr/images/documents/oc deinstitutionalinvestorsandinfrastructurefinancing.pdf.

D'Alisa, Giacomo, and Marco Armiero. 2013. "What Happened to the Trash? Political Miracles and Real Statistics in an Emergency Regime." *Capitalism Nature Socialism* 24, no. 4: 29–45.

De Angelis, Massimo. 2017. *Omnia Sunt Communia: On the Commons and the Transformation to Postcapitalism.* London: Zed.

De Biase, Marco. 2015. "Fires of Pianura: The Antidump Struggle in the Western Outskirt of Naples." *Capitalism Nature Socialism* 26, no. 1: 39–58.

De la Cadena, Marisol. 2015. "*Uncommoning Nature.*" *e-flux*, no. 65. https://www.e-flux .com/journal/65/336365/uncommoning-nature/.

Della Croce, Raffaele, and Juan Yermo. 2013. "Institutional Investors and Infrastructure Financing." OECD Working Papers on Finance, Insurance and Private Pensions, no. 36. Accessed January 6, 2022. http://sefifrance.fr/images/documents/ocdein stitutionalinvestorsandinfrastructurefinancing.pdf.

De Majo, Silvio, and Augusto Vitale. 2004. *L'acquedotto di Napoli.* Naples, Italy: Azienda Risorse Idriche Napoli.

Di Costanzo, Gianpaolo, and Stefania Ferraro. 2013. "The Landfill in the Countryside: Waste Management and Government of the Population in Campania." *Capitalism Nature Socialism* 24, no. 4: 17–28.

Doris, Yvonne, Cliona Ni Eidhin, Nigel Hayes, Brendan Wall, Darragh Page, Derval Devaney, Aoife Loughnane, David Flynn, and Gerard O'Leary. 2013. *Drinking Water Report.* Environmental Protection Agency. Accessed September 11, 2022. https:// www.epa.ie/publications/compliance-enforcement/drinking-water/Drinking -Water-Report-Web.pdf.

Dukelow, Fiona. 2016. "Irish Water Services Reform: Past, Present and Future." In *The Irish Welfare State in the Twenty-First Century*, 141–65. London: Palgrave Macmillan.

Duncan, Pamela. 2015. "Irish Water to Inherit €100m in Unpaid Commercial Charges." *Irish Times*, March 23, 2015. https://www.irishtimes.com/news/consumer/irish -water-to-inherit-100m-in-unpaid-commercial-charges-1.2149222.

Eagleton, Oliver. 2017. "Criminalizing Anti-austerity in Ireland." *Jacobin*, April 21, 2017. https://jacobinmag.com/2017/04/jobstown-not-guilty-ireland-water-privatization -austerity/.

Eliade, Mircea. 1958. *Patterns in Comparative Religion.* Translated by R. Sheed. London: Sheed and Ward.

Elyachar, Julia. 2005. *Markets of Dispossession: NGOs, Economic Development, and the State in Cairo.* Durham, NC: Duke University Press.

Elyachar, Julia. 2012. "The Passions of Credit and the Dangers of Debt." Fieldsights—Theorizing the Contemporary. *Society for Cultural Anthropology*, May 15, 2012. https://culanth.org/fieldsights/the-passions-of-credit-and-the-dangers -of-debt.

Estes, Nick. 2019. *Our History Is the Future: Standing Rock versus the Dakota Pipeline, and the Long Tradition of Indigenous Resistance.* London, NY: Verso Books.

EuroNomade. 2018. "Il governo degli equivoci, la giustizia proprietaria, e il popolo sovrano." June 3, 2018. http://www.euronomade.info/?p=10753.

European Environment Agency. 2015. *The European Environment. State and Outlook 2015. Synthesis Report.* European Environment Agency, Luxembourg.

Fahrun, Joachim. 2010. "Verkauf der Wasserbetriebe war ein Irrtum." *Morgen Post,* November 2, 2010. https://www.morgenpost.de/berlin/article104801025/Verkauf -der-Wasserbetriebe-war-ein-Irrtum.html.

Fantini, Emanuele. 2014. "Catholics in the Making of the Italian Water Movement: A Moral Economy." *Partecipazione e Conflitto: The Open Journal of Sociopolitical Studies* 7, no. 1: 35–57.

Farha, Leilani, Juan Pablo Bohoslavsky, Koumbou Boly Barry, Léo Heller, Olivier de Schutter, and Magdalena Sepúlveda Carmona. 2020. "Covid-19 has exposed the catastrophic impact of privatising vital services." *Guardian,* October 19, 2020. https://www.theguardian.com/society/2020/oct/19/covid-19-exposed-catastrophic -impact-privatising-vital-services.

Farthing, Linda, and Nicole Fabricant. 2018. "Open Veins Revisited: Charting the Social, Economic, and Political Contours of the New Extractivism in Latin America." *Latin American Perspectives* 45, no. 5: 4–17.

Fattori, Tommaso. 2011. "Fluid Democracy: The Italian Water Revolution." Tansform! Europe, October 27, 2011. https://www.transform-network.net/publications /yearbook/overview/article/journal-092011/fluid-democracy-the-italian-water -revolution.

Fattori, Tommaso. 2013. "From the Water Commons Movement to the Commonification of the Public Realm." *South Atlantic Quarterly* 112, no. 2: 377–87.

Federici, Silvia. 2004. *Caliban and the Witch.* New York: Autonomedia.

Federici, Silvia. 2015. "Re-enchanting the World: Technology, the Body, and the Construction of the Commons." In *Anomie of the Earth: Philosophy, Politics, and Autonomy in Europe and the Americas,* edited by Federico Luisetti, John Pickles, and Wilson Kaiser, 202–214. Durham, NC: Duke University Press.

Fennell, Catherine. 2016. "Are We All Flint?" *Limn,* no. 7: *Public Infrastructures/ Infrastructural Publics.* Accessed January 6, 2022. https://limn.it/articles/are -we-all-flint/.

Finanza Repubblica. 2020. "Codacons: Bollette italiane tra le più care d'Europa." 2020. *La Repubblica,* July 21, 2020. https://finanza.repubblica.it/News/2020/07/21 /codacons_bollette_italiane_tra_le_piu_care_deuropa-101/

Fitzpatrick, Brian. 2015. "From Detroit to Dublin, a Fight for the Right to Water." *Nation,* January 29, 2015. https://www.thenation.com/article/archive/detroit -dublin-fight-right-water/.

Food and Water Watch. 2021. "Massive Water Merger Would Create Monopoly." Food and Water Watch, April 12, 2021. https://www.foodandwaterwatch.org/2021/04/12 /massive-water-merger-would-create-dangerous-corporate-monopoly/.

Forum Italiano dei Movimenti per l'Acqua. 2012. "Vademecum per la Campagna di 'Obbedienza Civile.'" 2012. Accessed September 12, 2022.https://csaintifada.org /wp/wp-content/uploads/2012/02/VADEMECUM-obbedienza-civile-Empoli2.pdf.

Forum Italiano dei Movimenti per l'Acqua. 2014a. "Arezzo, Mille Famiglie Aderiscono Alla Campagna Di Obbedienza Civile." January 12, 2021. https://www

.acquabenecomune.org/toscana-iniziative/1318-arezzo-mille-famiglie-aderiscono -alla-campagna-di-obbedienza-civile.

Forum Italiano dei Movimenti per l'Acqua. 2014b. "I nuovi processi di privatizzazione e finanziarizzazione dei beni comuni: Dal decreto 'Sblocca Italia' alla legge di stabilità passando per la 'Spending Review.'" Accessed September 10, 2022. http://www .unioneinquilini.it/public/doc/Documento_nuovi_processi__privatizzazione.pdf.

Foster, Robert J. 2018. "Entropy, Alchemy and Negative Pigs: Obviating the Matter of Wealth." *History and Anthropology* 29, no. 3: 3, 292–306.

Foster, John B., and Fred Magdoff. 2009. *The Great Financial Crisis: Causes and Consequences*. New York: NYU Press.

Fraser, Nancy. 2016. "Expropriation and Exploitation in Racialized Capitalism: A Reply to Michael Dawson." *Critical Historical Studies* 3, no. 1: 163–78.

Franquesa, Jaume. 2018. *Power Struggles: Dignity, Value, and the Renewable Energy Frontier in Spain*. Bloomington: Indiana University Press.

Fruschki, Andreas and Alina Donets. 2018. "Water Your Assets for Growth." Accessed January 12, 2023. https://nordic.allianzgi.com/-/media/allianzgi/eu/luxembourg/ documents/water-your-assets-for-growth.pdf.

Fusco, Francesco. 2014. "Castellammare di Stabia: Acqua della Madonna, fonti ancora chiuse." *Stabiesi.Net*, July 14 2014. https://stabiesi.net/2014/07/castellammare-di -stabia-acqua-della-madonna-fonti-ancora-chiuse/.

Gago, Verónica. 2015. "Financialization of Popular Life and the Extractive Operations of Capital: A Perspective from Argentina." *South Atlantic Quarterly* 114, no. 1: 11–28.

Gandy, Matthew. 2008. "Landscapes of Disaster: Water, Modernity, and Urban Fragmentation in Mumbai." *Environment and Planning A: Economy and Space* 40, no. 1: 108–30.

Gandy, Matthew. 2014. *The Fabric of Space: Water, Modernity, and the Urban Imagination*. Cambridge, MA: MIT Press.

Gara, Francesca. 2015. "Gori: In arrivo le 'Case dell'Acqua' in quindici comuni del napoletano." *LoStrillone.TV*, March 8, 2015. https://lostrillone.tv/gori-in-arrivo-le -case-dellacqua-in-quindici-comuni-del-napoletano/3957.html.

Gemma, Alessio. 2016. "Inchiesta Gori, consulenze nel mirino: Morosità record per il caro bollette." *La Repubblica Edizione*, June 4, 2016. https://napoli.repubblica .it/cronaca/2016/06/04/news/inchiesta_gori_consulenze_nel_mirino_morosita _record_per_il_caro_bollette-141261596/.

Gill, Stephen, and A. Claire Cutler, eds. 2014. *New Constitutionalism and World Order*. Cambridge: Cambridge University Press.

Gillespie, Kelly. 2022. "Orders of Protection: Feminist Politics and Authoritarianism in South Africa." *Cultural Anthropology* 37, no. 4: 599–624.

Gillespie, Kelly, and Leigh-Ann Naidoo. 2019. "Between the Cold War and the Fire: The Student Movement, Antiassimilation, and the Question of the Future in South Africa." *South Atlantic Quarterly* 188, no. 1: 226–39.

Giovannini, Roberto. 2017. "Le quattro sorelle dell'acqua: Ecco i padroni dei rubinetti italiani." *La Stampa*, July 7, 2017. https://www.lastampa.it/tuttogreen/2017/07/07/news /le-quattro-sorelle-dell-acqua-ecco-i-padroni-dei-rubinetti-italiani-1.34448241.

Giusto, Salvatore. 2018. "La Terra dei Fuochi: Cultural Labeling, Ecological Crimes, and Social (Re)action in Mediacratic Italy." *International Journal of Semiotics and Visual Rhetoric* 2, no. 1: 15–28.

Giusto, Salvatore. 2019. "'One of Us': The Neomelodic Music Industry as a Camorra-mediated Space of Subaltern Publicity in Contemporary Naples." *Global Crime* 20, no. 1: 134–55.

Giusto, Salvatore. 2020. "Through the Looking-Glass: Televised Politics in Contemporary Populist Italy." *PoLAR: Political and Legal Anthropology Review* 43, no. 1: 87–102.

Gómez-Barris, Macarena. 2017. *The Extractive Zone: Social Ecologies and Decolonial Perspectives*. Durham, NC: Duke University Press.

Graeber, David. 2001. *Toward an Anthropological Theory of Value: The False Coin of Our Own Dreams*. New York: Palgrave.

Graeber, David. 2004. *Fragments of an Anarchist Anthropology*. Chicago: Prickly Paradigm Press.

Graeber, David. 2011. *Debt: The First 5000 Years*. New York: Melville House Publishing.

Gramsci, Antonio. 2005. *The Southern Question*. Montreal: Guernica Editions.

Greenberg, Jessica. 2014. *After the Revolution: Youth, Democracy, and the Politics of Disappointment in Serbia*. Stanford, CA: Stanford University Press.

Greenberg, Jessica. 2020. "Law, Politics, and Efficacy at the European Court of Human Rights." *American Ethnologist* 47, no. 4: 417–31.

Guano, Georgia. 2010. "Taxpayers, Thieves, and the State: Fiscal Citizenship in Contemporary Italy." *Ethnos* 75, no. 4: 471–95.

Guerrini, Andrea, and Giulia Romano. 2014. "Water Management in Italy: Governance, Performance, and Sustainability." *Springer Briefs in Water Science and Technology*. Heidelberg: Springer International Publishing.

Guerrini, Andrea, and Giulia Romano. 2013. "The Process of Tariff Setting in an Unstable Legal Framework: An Italian Case Study." *Utilities Policy* 24 (March): 78–85.

Gupta, Akhil. 2018. "The Future in Ruins: Thoughts on the Temporality of Infrastructure." In *The Promise of Infrastructure*, edited by Nikhil Anand, Akhil Gupta, and Hannah Appel, 62–79. Durham, NC: Duke University Press.

Guyer, Jane I. 2009. "Composites, Fictions, and Risk: Toward an Ethnography of Price." In *Market and Society*, edited by Chris Hann and Keith Hart, 203–20. Cambridge: Cambridge University Press.

Hall, David and Emanuele Lobina. 2010. "The Past, Present and Future of Finance for Investment in Water Systems." PSIRU: Public Services International Research Unit. Accessed September 11, 2022. http://www.psiru.org/reports/past-present-and-future-finance-investment-water-systems.html.

Hall, David, and Emanuele Lobina. 2012. *Financing Water and Sanitation: Public Realities*. Public Services International for the 6th World Water Forum. March 2012. http://world-psi.org/sites/default/files/documents/research/psiru_financing_water_sanitation.pdf.

Halpern, Orit. 2019. "Golden Futures," *limn*, no. 10: *Chokepoints*. Accessed December 5, 2022. https://limn.it/articles/golden-futures/.

Hardt, Michael. 2010. "The Common in Communism." *Rethinking Marxism* 22, no. 3: 346–56.

Hardt, Michael, and Antonio Negri. 2000. *Empire*. Cambridge, MA: Harvard University Press.

Hardt, Michael, and Antonio Negri. 2009. *Commonwealth*. Cambridge, MA: Belknap Press.

Hart, Keith, and Horacio Ortiz. 2014. "The Anthropology of Money and Finance: Between Ethnography and World History." *Annual Review of Anthropology* 43, no. 1: 465–82.

Harvey, David. 2004. "The 'New' Imperialism: Accumulation by Dispossession." *Socialist Register* 40 (2004): 63–87.

Harvey, David. 2013. *Rebel Cities: From the Right to the City to the Urban Revolution.* London: Verso.

Healy, Paul. 2015. "Rogue Group of 'Fairies' Will Come and Make Your Water Meter 'Disappear.'" *Independent*, June 2, 2015. https://www.independent.ie/irish-news/water/irish-water-crisis/rogue-group-of-fairies-will-come-and-make-your-water-meter-disappear-31271846.html

Hearne, Rory. 2015. "The Irish Water War." *Interface* 7, no. 1: 309–21.

Helmreich, Stefan. 2008. "Species of Biocapital." *Science as Culture* 17, no. 4: 463–78.

Helmreich, Stefan. 2011. "Nature/Culture/Seawater." *American Anthropologist* 113, no. 1: 132–44.

Herrera, Allison. 2016. "Standing Rock Activists: Don't Call us Protestors; We're Water Protectors." *World*, October 31, 2016. https://theworld.org/stories/2016–10–31/standing-rock-activists-dont-call-us-protesters-were-water-protectors.

Herzberg, Carsten. 2015. *Legitimation durch Beteiligung: Stadt- und Wasserwerke in Deutschland und Frankreich.* Hamburg: VSA.

Herzberg, Carsten, and Thomas Blanchet. 2016. "Von der Bürgerkommune zu Bürgerstadtwerken." SpringerProfessional, January 6, 2016. https://www.springerprofessional.de/von-der-buergerkommune-zu-buergerstadtwerken/10803348.

Herzfeld, Michael. 2002. "The Absent Presence: Discourses of Crypto-Colonialism." *South Atlantic Quarterly* 101, no. 4: 899–26.

Heslop, Luke. 2020. "A Journey through 'Infraspace': The Financial Architecture of Infrastructure." *Economy and Society* 49, no. 3: 364–81.

Hines, Sarah. 2021. *Water for All: Community, Property, and Revolution in Modern Bolivia.* Berkeley: University of California Press.

Ho, Karen. 2009. *Liquidated: An Ethnography of Wall Street.* Durham, NC: Duke University Press.

Ho, Karen. 2018. "Markets, Myths, and Misrecognitions: Economic Populism in the Age of Financialization and Hyperinequality." *Economic Anthropology* 5, no. 1: 148–50.

Ho, Karen. 2020. "Why the Stock Market Is Rising amidst a Pandemic and Record, Racialized Inequality." American Ethnological Society, October 12, 2020. https://americanethnologist.org/features/pandemic-diaries/introduction-intersecting-crises/why-the-stock-market-is-rising-amidst-a-pandemic-and-record-racialized-inequality.

Holston, James. 2009. *Insurgent Citizenship: Disjunctions of Democracy and Modernity in Brazil.* Princeton, NJ: Princeton University Press.

Hopman, Luca, Satoko Kishimoto, Bertie Russell, and Louisa Valentin. 2021. *Democratic and Collective Ownership of Public Goods and Services: Exploring Public-Community Collaborations.* Amsterdam: Transnational Institute (TNI). https://www.tni.org/en/publication/democratic-and-collective-ownership-of-public-goods-and-services.

Horváth, Tamás M. 2016. "From Municipalisation to Centralism: Changes to Local Public Service Delivery in Hungary." In *Public and Social Services in Europe: From Public and Municipal to Private Sector Provision*, edited by Hellmut Wollman, Ivan Koprić, and Gérard Marcou, 185–99. London: Palgrave Macmillan.

Humphreys, Elena, Andrea van der Kerk, and Catarina Fonsecca. 2018. "Finance for Water Infrastructure Development and Its Practical Challenges for Small Towns." *Water Policy* 20 (S1): 100–111.

*Il Gazzettino Vesuviano.* 2017. "Gori accumula debiti, sventare aumenti in bolletta: L'allarme del M5s." November 12, 2017. https://www.ilgazzettinovesuviano.com /2017/11/12/gori-accumula-debiti-sventare-aumenti-bolletta-lallarme-del-m5s/.

Illich, Ivan. 1985. *H$_2$O and the Waters of Forgetfulness: Ideas in Progress.* London: Boyars.

*Independent.* 2014.

*Independent,* November 6, 2014. "Leo Varadkar Slams 'Sinister Fringe' to Water Protests." November 6, 2014. https://www.independent.ie/irish-news/water/leo-varadkar -slams-sinister-fringe-to-water-protests-30723122.html.

Jaffee, Daniel, and Robert Case. 2018. "Draining Us Dry: Scarcity Discourses in Contention over Bottled Water Extraction." Portland State University Sociology Faculty Publications and Presentations. https://pdxscholar.library.pdx.edu/soc_fac/79/.

James, Ian, and Geoff Hing. 2021. "Investors Are Buying Up Rural Arizona Farmland to Sell the Water to Urban Homebuilders." *Arizona Republic,* November 25, 2021. https://www.azcentral.com/story/news/local/arizona-environment/2021/11/25 /investors-buying-up-arizona-farmland-valuable-water-rights/8655703002/.

Jones, Graham M. 2014. "Secrecy." *Annual Review of Anthropology* 43, no. 1: 53–69.

Juuti, Petri S., Tapio S. Katko, and University of Tampere. 2005. *Water, Time and European Cities—History Matters for the Futures.* Accessed January 6, 2022. https://trepo .tuni.fi/handle/10024/65706.

Kaika, Maria. 2003. "The Water Framework Directive: A New Directive for a Changing Social, Political and Economic European Framework." *European Planning Studies* 11, no. 3 (April): 299–316.

Kalb, Don. 2020. "Introduction: Transitions to What? On the Social Relations of Financialization in Anthropology and History." In *Financialization: Relational Approaches,* edited by Chris Hann and Don Kalb, 1–42. Oxford: Berghahn Books.

Kaplan, Martha. 2007. "Local Politics and a Global Commodity: Fijian Water in Fiji and New York." *Cultural Anthropology* 22, no. 4: 685–706.

Kaplan, Martha. 2012. "Lonely Drinking Fountains and Comforting Coolers." *Cultural Anthropology* 26, no. 4: 514–41.

Kar, Sohini, and Caroline Schuster. 2021. "Subprime Empire: On the In-Betweenness of Finance." *Current Anthropology* 62, no. 4: 389–411.

Khalili, Laleh. 2021. *Sinews of War and Trade: Shipping and Capitalism in the Arabian Peninsula.* London: Verso.

Kishimoto, Satoko, Emanuele Lobina, and Olivier Petitjean. 2015. *Our Public Water Future: The Global Experience with Remunicipalisation.* Amsterdam: Transnational Institute. https://www.tni.org/files/download/ourpublicwaterfuture-1.pdf.

Kishimoto, Satoko, Lavinia Steinfort, and Olivier Petitjean. 2019. *The Future Is Public: Democratic Ownership of Public Services.* Transnational Institute Report. https:// www.tni.org/en/futureispublic.

Kishimoto, Satoko, Olivier Petitjean, and Lavinia Steinfort. 2017. *Reclaiming Public Services.* Transnational Institute Report. https://www.tni.org/en/publication /reclaiming-public-services.

Knight, Daniel. 2021. *Vertiginous Life: An Anthropology of Time and the Unforeseen.* New York: Berhahn Books.

Kockelman, Paul. 2016. *The Chicken and the Quetzal.* Durham, NC: Duke University Press.

Kockelman, Paul. 2020. *Kinds of Value: An Experiment in Modal Anthropology.* Chicago: Prickly Paradigm Press.

Kosche, Heidi. 2014. "Endabrechnung Wasserprivatisierung." Flyer. (MdA Der Fraktion Bündnis 90/Die Grünen Im Abgeordnetenhaus von Berlin)."

Laaninen, Tarja. 2018. "Revision of the Drinking Water Directive." European Parliament, *At A Glance,* October 11, 2018. https://www.europarl.europa.eu/RegData /etudes/ATAG/2018/628279/EPRS_ATA(2018)628279_EN.pdf.

LaDuke, Winona, and Deborah Cowen. 2020. "Beyond Wiindigo Infrastructure." *South Atlantic Quarterly* 119, no. 2: 243–68.

Landriani, Loris, Gabriella D'Amore, Stefano Pozzoli, Federico Alvino, and Luigi Lepore. 2019. "Decorporatization of a Municipal Water Utility: A Case Study from Italy." *Utilities Policy* 57 (April): 43–47.

Langley, Paul. 2012. "The Fear Index and Frankenstein Finance." Fieldsights— Theorizing the Contemporary. *Society for Cultural Anthropology,* May 15, 2012. https://culanth.org/fieldsights/the-fear-index-and-frankenstein-finance.

Langley, Paul. 2018. "Frontier Financialization: Urban Infrastructure in the United Kingdom." *Economic Anthropology* 5, no. 2: 172–84.

Langley, Paul. 2020a. "Assets and Assetization in Financialized Capitalism." *Review of International Political Economy* 28, no. 2: 328–93.

Langley, Paul. 2020b. *The Financialization of Life: The Routledge International Handbook of Financialization.* New York: Routledge.

Langley, Paul. 2020c. "The Folds of Social Finance: Making Markets, Remaking the Social." *Environment and Planning A: Economy and Space* 52, no. 1: 130–47.

Lanz, Klaus, and K. Eitner. 2005. "WaterTime Case Study—Berlin, Germany, WaterTime Deliverable D12." Research project on "Decision making in water systems in European cities" (WATERTIME), European Commission, 5th Framework Programme, 2002–2005. Accessed January 6, 2022. http://www.watertime.net/docs/WP2/D12_Berlin.doc.

Lanz, Klaus, and Stephan Scheuer. 2001. *EEB Handbook on EU Water Policy under the Water Framework Directive.* https://www.rivernet.org/general/docs/handbook.pdf.

Lappé, Anna. 2014. "Detroit's Fight for Public Water Is Also the Nation's."*Aljazeera America,* June 30, 2014. http://america.aljazeera.com/opinions/2014/6/detroit -public-watershutoffsunitednationsprivatization.html.

Lazar, Sian. 2007. *El Alto, Rebel City: Self and Citizenship in Andean Bolivia.* Durham, NC: Duke University Press.

Lazzarato, Maurizio. 2012. *The Making of the Indebted Man: An Essay on the Neoliberal Condition.* Translated by Joshua David Jordan. Cambridge, MA: MIT Press.

Leahy, Pat. 2016. "Denis O'Brien's Media Power Must Be Addressed, Report Says." *Irish Times,* October 23, 2016. https://www.irishtimes.com/news/politics/denis-o -brien-s-media-power-must-be-addressed-report-says-1.2840470.

Lederer, Klaus. 2010. "Verkauftes Wasser: die Geschichte einer Teilprivatisierung und ihre Folgen für Berlin." Fraktion die Linke im Abgeordnetenhaus Berlin. https:// www.linksfraktion.berlin/fileadmin/download/2010/verkauftes_wasser.pdf.

Legambiente. 2020. "H$_2$O la chimica che inquina l'acqua." Ufficio Scientifico di Legambiente. https://www.legambiente.it/wp-content/uploads/2020/06/rapporto _H2o_la-chimica-che-inquina_2020.pdf.

Leins, Stefan. 2018. *Stories of Capitalism: Inside the Role of Financial Analysts*. Chicago: University of Chicago Press.

Leins, Stefan. 2020. "Responsible Investment: ESG and the Post-crisis Ethical Order." *Economy and Society* 49, no. 1: 1–21.

Lépinay, Vincent Antonin. 2011. *Codes of Finance: Engineering Derivatives in a Global Bank*. Princeton, NJ: Princeton University Press.

Lepselter, Susan. 2016. *The Resonance of Unseen Things*. Ann Arbor: University of Michigan Press.

Le Strat, Anne. 2010. "Paris: Local Authorities Regain Control of Water Management." Transnational Institute. August 24, 2021. https://www.tni.org/en/article/paris-local -authorities-regain-control-of-water-management.

Lewis, Norman. (1978) 2005. *Naples '44: A World War II Diary of Occupied Italy*. Reprint. New York: Da Capo Press.

Leyshon, Andrew, and Nigel Thrift. 2007. "The Capitalization of Almost Everything: The Future of Finance and Capitalism." *Theory, Culture and Society* 24, nos. 7–8: 97–115. https://doi.org/10.1177/0263276407084699.

Li, Tania Murray. 2007. *The Will to Improve: Governmentality, Politics, and the Practice of Politics*. Durham, NC: Duke University Press.

Li, Tania Murray. 2014. "What Is Land? Assembling a Resource for Global Inverstment." *Transactions of the Institute of British Geographers*. April 10, 2014. https:// www.academia.edu/21142777/What_is_land_Assembling_a_resource_for_global _investment.

Li, Tania Murray, and Pujo Semedi. 2021. *Plantation Life: Corporate Occupation in Indonesia's Oil Palm Zone*. Durham, NC: Duke University Press.

Limbert, Mandana E. 2001. "The Senses of Water in an Omani Town." *Social Text* 19, no. 3: 35–55.

Lipari, Lucio. 2015. "A cimitile inaugurata la 'Casa dell'Acqua' gori." *Il Mezzogiorno*. Accessed January 6, 2022. http://www.ilmezzogiorno.info/2015/10/03/a-cimitile -inaugurata-la-casa-dellacqua-gori/.

Lobina, Emanuele. 2005. "Italy." In *Water, Time and European Cities*, edited by Petri Juuti and Tapio Katko, 106–22. Tampere, Finland: Tampere University Press.

Lobina, Emanuele. 2014. "Troubled Waters: Misleading Industry PR and the Case for Public Water." Corporate Accountability International. Accessed September 11, 2022. http://www.psiru.org/sites/default/files/2014-11-W-TroubledWaters.pdf.

Lobina, Emanuele, Satoko Kishimoto, and Olivier Petitjean. 2014. "Here to Stay: Water Remunicipalisation as a Global Trend." Public Services International Research Unit (PSIRU) website. Accessed September 12, 2022. https://www.tni.org/files/ download/heretostay-en.pdf.

Locke, John. 1823. *Two Treatises of Government*. Vol. 5. London: Thomas Tegg.

Lucarelli, Alberto. 2013. *La democrazia dei beni comuni: Nuove frontiere del diritto pubblico*. Bari, Italy: Editori Laterza.

Lucarelli, Alberto. 2018. "Il progetto Rodotà diventa legge di iniziativa popolare." *Il Manifesto*. Accessed September 10, 2022. https://ilmanifesto.it/il-progetto-rodota -diventa-legge-di-iniziativa-popolare/.

Lumley, Robert. 1990. *States of Emergency: Cultures of Revolt in Italy from 1968 to 1978*. London: Verso.

Luxemburg, Rosa. 1913. *Die Akkumulation des Kapitals: Ein Beitrag zur ökonomischen Erklärung des Imperialismus*. Berlin: Buchhandlung Vorwärts Paul Singer.

Luxemburg, Rosa. 1951. *The Accumulation of Capital: Rare Masterpieces of Philosophy and Science*. Edited by Dr. W. Sark. London: Routledge and Kegan Paul.

Macpherson, C. B. 2011. *The Political Theory of Possessive Individualism: Hobbes to Locke*. New York: Oxford University Press.

Madaleno, I. M. 2007. "The Privatisation of Water and Its Impacts on Settlement and Traditional Cultural Practices in Northern Chile." *Scottish Geographical Journal* 123 (September 1, 2007): 193–208. https://doi.org/10.1080/14702540701855394.

Mahmud, Lilith. 2020. "Fascism, a Haunting: Spectral Politics and Antifascist Resistance in Twenty-First-Century Italy." In *Beyond Populism*, edited by Jeff Maskovsky. Morgantown: West Virginia University Press.

Manjapra, Kris. 2019. "Necrospeculation: Postemancipation Finance and Black Redress." *Social Text* 37, no. 2: 29–65.

Manning, Peter K. 2012. "Trust and Accountability in Ireland: The Case of An Garda Síochána." *Policing and Society* 22, no. 3: 346–61.

Maraini, Dacia. 2020. "L'acqua sprecata della rete nostra idrica." *Corriere della Sera*, November 23, 2020. https://www.corriere.it/opinioni/20_novembre_23/acqua -sprecata-nostra-rete-idrica-00b475d8-2d79-11eb-b83d-41802abb4d33.shtml.

Marois, Thomas. 2021. *Public Banks: Decarbonisation, Definancialisation, and Democratisation*. SOAS University of London and UCL Institute for Innovation and Public Purpose.

Marotta, Sergio. 2012. "Le tariffe del servizio idrico integrato dopo il referendum" *Munus: Rivista Giuridica Dei Servizi Pubblici*, no. 3: 657–66.

Marotta, Sergio. 2014. "On the Critical Relationship between Citizenship and Governance: The Case of Water Management in Italy." *Urbanities* 4, no. 2: 12.

Marotta, Sergio. 2015. "Legge sull'acqua in Campania, vi spiego perché è un passo indietro." *Corriere della Sera*. Accessed January 6, 2022, http://corrieredelmezzogiorno .corriere.it/napoli/economia/15_novembre_18/legge-sull-acqua-campania-vi -spiego-perche-passo-indietro-c73c099c-8e27-11e5-98d3-3cfe8f434bbc.shtml.

Martin, Randy. 2002. *Financialization of Daily Life*. Philadelphia: Temple University Press.

Marx, Karl, and Friedrich Engels. 1967. *The Communist Manifesto*. Edited and with an introduction by A. J. P. Taylor. Pelican Books. Harmondsworth, UK: Penguin.

Massarutto, Antonio. 2015. "Water Pricing in Italy: Beyond Full-Cost Recovery." In *Water Pricing Experiences and Innovations*, edited by Ariel Dinar, Víctor Pochat, and José Albiac-Murillo, 201–30. Global Issues in Water Policy. Berlin: Springer.

Massarutto, Antonio. 2020. "Servant of Too Many Masters: Residential Water Pricing and the Challenge of Sustainability." *Utilities Policy* 63 (April). https://doi.org/10 .1016/j.jup.2020.101018.

Massarutto, Antonio. 2011. "Urban Water Reform in Italy: A Live Bomb behind Outward Unanimity." In *Urban Water Conflicts: UNESCO-IHP*, edited by Bernard Barraque, 247–68. Boca Raton, FL: CRC Press.

Massarutto, Antonio, and Paolo Ermano. 2013. "Drowned in an Inch of Water: How Poor Regulation Has Weakened the Italian Water Reform." *Utilities Policy* 24 (March): 20–31.

Mattei, Ugo. 2013. "Protecting the Commons: Water, Culture, and Nature; The Commons Movement in the Italian Struggle against Neoliberal Governance." *South Atlantic Quarterly* 112, no. 2: 366–76.

Mattei, Ugo, and Laura Nader. 2008. *Plunder: When the Rule of Law Is Illegal.* Malden, MA: Blackwell Publishing.

Mattert, Jana, Laura Valentukeviciute und Carl Waßmuth. 2017. Gemeinwohl als Zukunftsaufgabe: Öffentliche Infrastrukturen zwischen Daseinsvorsorge und Finanzmärkten. Berlin: Heinrich-Böll-Stiftung, with Gemeingut in BürgerInnenhand (GiB) e.V.

Mattioli, Fabio. 2020. *Dark Finance: Illiquidity and Authoritarianism at the Margins of Europe.* Stanford, CA: Stanford University Press.

Mbembe, Achille. 2019. *Necropolitics.* Durham, NC: Duke University Press.

Mbembe, Achille, and Janet Roitman. 1995. "Figures of the Subject in Times of Crisis." *Public Culture* 7, no. 2: 323–52.

McCarthy, James. 2019. "Authoritarianism, Populism, and the Environment: Comparative Experiences, Insights, and Perspectives." *Annals of the American Association of Geographers* 109, no. 2: 301–13.

McDonald, David A., ed. 2016. *Making Public in a Privatized World: The Struggle for Essential Services.* London: Zed Books.

McDonald, David A. 2018. "Remunicipalization: The Future of Water Services?" *Geoforum* 91 (May): 47–56.

McDonald, David A., and Erik Swyngedouw. 2019. "The New Water Wars: Struggles for Remunicipalisation." *Water Alternatives* 12, no. 2: 322–33.

McDonald, David A., Thomas Marois, and Susan Spronk. 2021. "Public Banks + Public Water = SDG6?" *Water Alternatives* 14, no. 1: 117–34.

McDonald, David A., and Susan Spronk. 2021. "Covid-19 Has Decimated Water Systems Globally, but Privatization Is Not the Answer." *Conversation*, March 17, 2021. https://theconversation.com/covid-19-has-decimated-water-systems-globally-but -privatization-is-not-the-answer-155689.

McGee, Harry. 2015. "Water Protests First to Go Viral on Irish Social Media." *Irish Times*, March 2, 2015. https://www.irishtimes.com/news/politics/water-protests -first-to-go-viral-on-irish-social-media-1.2122292.

McManus, Ruth. 2011. "Suburban and Urban Housing in the Twentieth Century." Special issue, *Proceedings of the Royal Irish Academy: Archaeology, Culture, History, Literature,* 111C: 253–86.

McNiffe, Liam. 1997. *A History of the Garda Siochana: A Social History of the Force 1922–52, with an Overview of the Years 1952–97.* Dublin: Wolfhound.

Merry, Sally Engle. 1996. "Legal Vernacularization and Ka Ho'okolokolonui Kanaka Maoli: The People's International Tribunal, Hawai'i 1993." *Political and Legal Anthropology Review* 19, no. 1: 67–82. http://www.jstor.org/stable/24498064.

Mezzadra, Sandro. 2015. "Resonances of the Common" In *The Anomie of the Earth: Philosophy, Politics, and Autonomy in Europe and the Americas,* edited by Federico Luisetti, John Pickles, and Wilson Kaiser, 215–26. Durham, NC: Duke University Press.

Micciarelli, Giuseppe. 2021. "Path for New and Urban Commons: Legal and Political Acts for the Recognition of Urban Civic and Collective Use Starting from Naples." European Union, Urbact, Civic eState.

Mimosa, Oriol, and Leila M. Harris. 2012. "Human Right to Water: Contemporary Challenges and Contours of a Global Debate." *Antipode* 44, no. 3: 932–49. https://doi.org/10.1111/j.1467-8330.2011.00929.x.

Mitchell, Timothy. 2020. "Infrastructures Work on Time." *e-flux Architecture,* January. https://www.e-flux.com/architecture/new-silk-roads/312596/infrastructures-works-on-time/.

Miyazaki, Hirokazu. 2012. "The End of Finance?" Fieldsights—Theorizing the Contemporary. *Society for Cultural Anthropology,* May 15, 2012. https://culanth.org/fieldsights/the-end-of-finance.

Mohajeri, Shahrooz. 2005. *100 Jahre Berliner Wasserversorgung und Abwasserentsorgung 1840–1940.* Stuttgart, Germany: Franz Steiner Verlag.

Mohajeri, Shahrooz. 2006. "Die Privatisierung der Berliner Wasserbetriebe damals und heute: Eine kritische Betrachtung." In *Hydropolis: Wasser und die Stadt der Moderne,* edited by Susanne Frank and Matthew Gandy, 169–87. Frankfurt: Campus Verlag.

Molé Liston, Noelle. 2020. *The Truth Society: Science, Disinformation, and Politics in Berlusconi's Italy.* Ithaca, NY: Cornell University Press.

Montalto, Maurizio. 2018. *La rapina perfetta: L'attacco delle multinazionali alle fonti d'acqua italiane.* Roma: StradeBianchedi Stampa Alternativa.

Moore, Madelaine. 2019. "Wellsprings of Resistance: Struggles over Water in Europe." RLS Brüssel, March 5, 2019. https://www.rosalux.eu/en/article/1366.wellsprings-of-resistance.html.

Mormone, Luigi Maria. 2019. "Abc, stangata sulle bollette: Tariffe dell'acqua aumentate del 40 percent." *2a News* (blog). Accessed January 6, 2022. https://www.2anews.it/abc-stangata-sulle-bollette-tariffe-dellacqua-aumentate-del-40/.

Morris, Rosalind C. 2016. "Ursprüngliche Akkumulation: The Secret of an Originary Mistranslation." *boundary 2* 43, no. 3: 29–77.

Moss, Timothy. 2020. *Remaking Berlin: A History of the City through Infrastructure, 1920–2020.* Cambridge, MA: MIT Press.

Moten, Fred. 2013. "The Subprime and the Beautiful." *African Identities* 11, no. 2: 237–45.

Muehlebach, Andrea. 2017. "The Irish Water Insurgency: No More Blood from These Stones." *Roar Magazine,* February 6, 2017. https://roarmag.org/essays/ireland-anti-austerity-water-protests/.

Muehlebach, Andrea. 2018a. "Commonwealth: On Democracy and Dispossession in Italy." *History and Anthropology* 29, no. 3: 342–58.

Muehlebach, Andrea. 2018b. "Sister Water." Accessed January 6, 2022. https://www.blackwoodgallery.ca//publications/sduk/commuting/sister-water.

Muehlmann, Shaylih. 2012. "Rhizomes and Other Uncountables: The Malaise of Enumeration in Mexico's Colorado River Delta." *American Ethnologist* 39, no. 2: 339–53.

Muehlmann, Shaylih. 2013. *Where the River Ends: Contested Indigeneity in the Mexican Colorado Delta.* Durham, NC: Duke University Press.

Muniesa, Fabian. 2012. "Coping with the Discount Rate." Fieldsights—Theorizing the Contemporary. *Society for Cultural Anthropology*, May 15, 2012. https://culanth.org /fieldsights/coping-with-the-discount-rate.

Muniesa, Fabian, Liliana Doganova, Horacio Ortiz, Álvaro Pina-Stranger, Florence Paterson, Alaric Bourgoin, Véra Ehrenstein, Pierre-André Juven, David Pontille, and Basak Saraç-Lesavre. 2017. *Capitalization: A Cultural Guide*. Paris: Presses des Mines via Open Edition Books.

Murphy, Michelle. 2017. *The Economization of Life*. Durham, NC: Duke University Press.

Murphy, Noreen. 2019. "Overview of the Anti–Water Privatisation Campaign in Ireland." European Water Movement. Accessed January 6, 2022. http://europeanwater.org /actions/country-city-focus/899-anti-water-privatisation-campaign-in-ireland.

Naguib, Nefissa. 2009. *Women, Water, and Memory: Recasting Lives in Palestine*. Leiden, Netherlands: Brill.

Napolitano, Valentina. 2015. *Migrant Hearts and the Atlantic Return: Transnationalism and the Roman Catholic Church*. New York: Fordham University Press.

*Napoli Today*. 2013. "'Bevi Napoli e Poi Muori,' Il Comune Fa Causa All'Espresso." November 15, 2013. https://www.napolitoday.it/cronaca/bevi-napoli-e-poi-muori -espresso-causa-comune.html.

Narotzky, Susana, and Niko Besnier. 2014. "Crisis, Value, and Hope: Rethinking the Economy: An Introduction to Supplement 9." *Current Anthropology* 55, no. S9: S4–16.

Neimanis, Astrida. 2017. *Bodies of Water: Posthuman Feminist Phenomenology*. London: Bloomsbury Academic.

Neimanis, Astrida. 2019. "The Weather Underwater: Blackness, White Feminism, and the Breathless Sea." *Australian Feminist Studies* 34, no. 102: 490–508.

Nichols, Robert. 2017. "Theft Is Property! The Recursive Logic of Dispossession." *Political Theory*. 46, no. 1: 3–28.

Nikolaou, Kostas. 2018. "The Referendum on the Water of Thessaloniki." European Water Movement. Accessed January 6, 2022. http://europeanwater.org/actions /country-city-focus/456-the-referendum-on-the-water-of-thessaloniki.

Noys, Benjamin. 2015. "The Savage Ontology of Insurrection: Negativity, Life, Anarchy." In *The Anomie of the Earth: Philosophy, Politics, and Autonomy in Europe and the Americas*, eds. Federico Luisetti, John Pickles, and Wilson Kaiser, 174–91. Durham, NC: Duke University Press.

Nugent, David. 2002. "Alternative Democracies: The Evolution of the Public Sphere in 20th Century Peru." *PoLAR: Political and Legal Anthropology Review* 25, no. 1: 151–63.

Nugent, David. 2008. "Democracy Otherwise: Struggles over Popular Rule in the Northern Peruvian Andes." In *Democracy: Anthropological Approaches*, edited by Julia Paley, 21–62. Santa Fe, NM: School of American Research.

Nugent, David. 2010. "States, Secrecy, Subversives: APRA and Political Fantasy in Mid-20th-Century Peru." *American Ethnologist* 37, no. 4: 681–702.

O'Brien, Suzanne J. Crawford. 2008. "Well, Water, Rock: Holy Wells, Mass Rocks and Reconciling Identity in the Republic of Ireland." *Material Religion* 4, no. 3: 326–48.

Ogle, Brendan. 2016. *From Bended Knee to a New Republic: How the Fight for Water Is Changing Ireland*. Dublin, Ireland: Liffey Press.

O'Halloran, Marie. 2014. "O'Brien's Political Links in Meter Contract Influential, TD Claims." *Irish Times*, October 10, 2014. https://www.irishtimes.com/news/politics /oireachtas/o-brien-s-political-links-in-meter-contract-influential-td-claims-1 .1958326.

Olivera, Oscar, and Tom Lewis. 2004. *Cochabamba!: Water War in Bolivia*. Boston: South End Press.

O'Rourke, David. 2015. "Myths about Irish Water to Pay or Not to Pay." *Carrickmacross Citizens Group* (blog). Accessed January 6, 2022, https://carrickmacrosscitizensgroup .wordpress.com/2015/02/08/myths-about-irish-water-to-pay-or-not-to-pay/.

Ortiz, Horacio. 2012. "Anthropology—of the Financial Crisis." In *A Handbook of Economic Anthropology*, 2nd ed., edited by James G. Carrier, chap. 35. Cheltenham, UK: Edward Elgar Press.

Ortiz, Horacio. 2021. "Political Imaginaries of the Weighted Average Cost of Capital: A Conceptual Analysis." *Valuation Studies* 8, no. 2: 5–36.

O'Shanahan, Catherine. 2015. "Austerity 'Had Huge Impact' on Suicide." *Irish Examiner*, June 17, 2015. https://www.irishexaminer.com/ireland/austerity-had-huge -impact-on-suicide-337377.html.

Palladino, Andrea. 2016. "Acqua, referendum tradito: Gli 'obbedienti civili' di Arezzo si tagliano la bolletta; E l'azienda toglie le forniture." *Il Fatto Quotidiano*, April 13, 2016. http://www.ilfattoquotidiano.it/2016/04/13/acqua-referendum-tradito-gli -obbedienti-civili-di-arezzo-si-tagliano-la-bolletta-e-lazienda-toglie-le-forniture /2622598/.

Palomera, Jaime. 2015. "Investing without Wealth: The Financialization of Social Reproduction #Crisis." *Allegra* (blog). Accessed January 6, 2022. https:// allegralaboratory.net/investing-without-wealth-the-financialization-of-social -reproduction-crisis/.

Papadopoulos, Dimitris. 2017. "The Two Endings of the Precarious Movement." In *Mapping Precariousness, Labour Insecurity and Uncertain Livelihoods*, edited by Emiliana Armano, Arianna Bove, and Annalisa Murgia, 137–48. Oxfordshire, UK: Routledge.

Passadakis, Alexis. 2006. "The Berlin Water Works: From Commercialization and Partial Privatization to Public Democratic Water Enterprises." Study on Behalf of the European Deputy Sahra Wagenknecht. *Berlin and Brussels: Vereinigte Europäische Linke/Nordische Grüne Linke, Europäisches Parliament* 10: 1–49.

Pasternak, Shiri, and Tia Dafnos. 2018. "How Does a Settler State Secure the Circuitry of Capital?" *Environment and Planning D: Society and Space* 36, no. 4: 739–57.

Pearse, Padraic. 1916. *The Sovereign People*. Dublin: Whelan and Son.

Peck, Jamie, and Heather Whiteside. 2016. "Financializing Detroit." *Economic Geography* 92, no. 3: 235–68.

Peterson, Kristin. 2014. *Speculative Markets: Drug Circuits and Derivative Life in Nigeria*. Durham, NC: Duke University Press.

Petrella, Riccardo. 2001. *The Water Manifesto: Arguments for a World Water Contract*. London: Verso.

Phemister, Andrew. 2019. "'The Surging Tide of Pauper Democracy': Irish Boycotting and Anglo-American Liberalism." *Radical History Review* 134 (May): 29–57.

Piliavsky, Anastasia. 2013. "Where Is the Public Sphere? Political Communications and the Morality of Disclosure in Rural Rajasthan." *Cambridge Journal of Anthropology* 31, no. 2: 104–22.

Pipyrou, Stavroula. 2016. "Adrift in Time: Lived and Silenced Pasts in Calabria, South Italy." *History and Anthropology* 27, no. 1: 45–59.

Pistor, Katharina. 2019. *The Code of Capital: How the Law Creates Wealth and Inequality.* Princeton, NJ: Princeton University Press.

Polanyi, Karl. 2001. *The Great Transformation: The Political and Economic Origins of Our Time.* 2nd ed. Boston, MA: Beacon Press.

Polonyi, Anna. 2020. "How Paris's Public Water Supply Is Beating Covid." Open Democracy. November 12, 2020. https://www.opendemocracy.net/en/oureconomy/how-pariss-public-water-supply-beating-covid/.

Portelli, Stefano. 2017. "Stato e mafia sul litorale: Ostia come capro espiatorio." January 27, 2017. https://www.academia.edu/37472152/Stato_e_mafia_sul_litorale_Ostia_come_capro_espiatorio.

Postone, Moishe. 2006. "History and Helplessness: Mass Mobilization and Contemporary Forms of Anticapitalism." *Public Culture* 18, no. 1: 93–110.

Povinelli, Elizabeth. 2016. *Geontologies.* Durham, NC: Duke University Press.

Public Services International. 2015. "French Constitutional Council Bans Water Cut-Offs." June 2, 2015. http://world-psi.org/en/french-constitutional-council-bans-water-cut-offs.

Radin, Margaret Jane. 2012. *Boilerplate: The Fine Print, Vanishing Rights, and the Rule of Law.* Princeton, NJ: Princeton University Press.

Raffles, Hugh. 2007. "Jews, Lice, and History." *Public Culture* 19, no. 3: 521–66.

Rakopoulos, Theodoros. 2020. "Notes on the 500 Euro: On Mafias and Instituted Precarity." In *Who's Cashing In? Contemporary Perspectives on New Monies and Global Cashlessness,* edited by Atreyee Sen, Johan Lindquist, and Marie Kolling, 131–42.

Rakopoulos, Theodoros, and Knut Rio. 2018. "Introduction to an Anthropology of Wealth." *History and Anthropology* 29, no. 3: 275–91.

Ray, Celeste. 2011. "The Sacred and the Body Politic at Ireland's Holy Wells." *International Social Science Journal* 62, nos. 205–6: 271–85.

Razsa, Maple. 2015. *Bastards of Utopia: Living Radical Politics after Socialism.* Global Research Studies. Bloomington: Indiana University Press.

Razsa, Maple, and Andrej Kurnik. 2012. "The Occupy Movement in Žižek's Hometown: Direct Democracy and a Politics of Becoming." *American Ethnologist* 39, no. 2: 238–58.

Redirossi, A. and M. Ferazzoli. 2016. Frosinone: I cittadini bruciano le bollette Acea sotto la Prefettura; Anche fatture da 14mila Euro. *L'inchiesta,* May 26, 2016. https://www.linchiestaquotidiano.it/news/2016/05/28/frosinone-i-cittadini-bruciano-le-bollette-acea-sotto-la-pr/14236.

Reyes, Alvaro, and Mara Kaufman. 2015. "Sovereignty, Indigeneity, Territory: Zapatista Autonomy and the New Practices of Decolonization." In *The Anomie of the Earth: Philosophy, Politics, and Autonomy in Europe and the Americas,* edited by Federico Luisetti, John Pickles, and Wilson Kaiser, 44–68. Durham, NC: Duke University Press.

Robbins, Richard. 2020. "Financialization, Plutocracy and the Debtor's Economy: Consequences and Limits." In *Financialization: Relational Approaches*, edited by Chris Hann and Don Kalb, 43–63. New York: Berghahn Books.

Roberts, Adrienne. 2008. "Privatizing Social Reproduction: The Primitive Accumulation of Water in an Era of Neoliberalism." *Antipode* 40, no. 4: 535–60.

Robertson, Morgan M. 2006. "The Nature That Capital Can See: Science, State, and Market in the Commodification of Ecosystem Services." *Environment and Planning D: Society and Space* 24, no. 3: 367–87.

Robinson, Cedric J. (1983) 2000. *Black Marxism: The Making of the Black Radical Tradition*. Chapel Hill: University of North Carolina Press.

Romano, Giulia, and Andrea Guerrini. 2014. "The Effects of Ownership, Board Size and Board Composition on the Performance of Italian Water Utilities." *Utilities Policy* 31 (2014): 18–28.

Romano, Giulia, and Andrea Guerrini. 2019. "Paying Returns to Shareholders of Water Utilities: Evidence from Italy." *Sustainability* 11, no. 7: 2033.

Romano, Giulia, Andrea Guerrini, and Bettina Campedelli. 2015. "The New Italian Water Tariff Method: A Launching Point for Novel Infrastructures or a Backwards Step?" *Utilities Policy* 34 (June): 45–53.

*RTA Live*. 2016. "Nocera Inferiore: cercasi fontanine disperatamente." July 21, 2016. https://rtalive.it/2016/07/nocera-inferiore-cercasi-fontanine-disperatamente/35875/.

Rügemer, Werner. 2008. *Heuschrecken im öffentlichen Raum: Public Private Partnership— Anatomie eines globalen Finanzinstruments*. Bielefeld: Transcript Verlag.

Rügemer, Werner. 2018. *Die Kapitalisten des 21. Jahrhunderts: Gemeinverständlicher Abriss zum Aufstieg der neuen Finanzakteure*. Köln: Papyrossa Verlags, 2018.

Roggero, Gigi. 2010. "Five Thesis on the Common." *Rethinking Marxism: A Journal of Economics, Culture and Society* 22, no. 3: 357–73.

Ryan, Órla. 2015. "Two Thirds of the Money Diverted to Irish Water Came from Your Motor Tax." *thejournal.ie*, February 5, 2012. https://www.thejournal.ie/how-much-will-it-cost-to-set-up-irish-water-1921250-Feb2015/.

Sahlins, Marshall. 1974. "The Original Affluent Society." *Ecologist* 4, no. 5: 181.

*SalernoNotizie*. 2020. "Roccapiemonte: Aperto conto corrente per difendere l'acqua pubblica." *Salernonotizie.it* (blog). Accessed January 6, 2022. https://www.salernonotizie.it/2020/08/26/roccapiemonte-aperto-conto-corrente-per-difendere-lacqua-pubblica/.

Salzman, James. 2013. *Drinking Water: A History*. New York: Overlook Duckworth.

Sannino, Conchita. 2014. "Acqua pubblica, blitz alla Gori: Amedeo Labocetta presidente." *La Repubblica*, September 12, 2014. https://napoli.repubblica.it/cronaca/2014/02/01/news/acqua_blitz_alla_gori_labocetta_presidente-77421929/.

Sasso, Michele, and Francesca Sironi. 2013. "Acqua, il referendum tradito." *L'Espresso*, June 12, 2016. http://espresso.repubblica.it/attualita/cronaca/2013/06/12/news/acqua-il-referendum-tradito-1.55462.

Satsuka, Shiho. 2019. "Rhapsody in the Forest: Wild Mushrooms and the Multispecies Multitude." In *How Nature Works: Rethinking Labor on a Troubled Planet*, edited by Sarah Besky and Alex Blanchette, 191–209. Albuquerque: University of New Mexico Press.

Schermer, Gerlinde. 2011. *Hintergrundinformationen zum Volksentscheid am 13. Februar 2011*. Accessed December 19, 2020. https://berliner-wassertisch.net/assets/pdf/VE/Gerlinde%20Schermer%20-%20Hintergrundinfos.pdf.

Schindler, Frederik. 2018. "Die Linke und die Heuschrecken." *Jüdische Allgemeine*, May 31, 2022. https://www.juedische-allgemeine.de/politik/die-linke-und-die-heuschrecken/.

Schneider, Jane. 1998. *Italy's "Southern Question": Orientalism in One Country*. Oxfordshire, UK: Routledge.

Schneider, Jane. 2016. "Mafia Emergence: What Kind of State?" *Italian American Review* 6, no. 1: 7–30.

Schneider, Jane, and Peter Schneider. 2008. "The Anthropology of Crime and Criminalization." *Annual Review of Anthropology* 37, no. 1: 351–73.

Schudoma, Sabine. 2012. *Zwanzig Jahre Berliner Verfassungsgerichtsbarkeit: Ansprachen anlässlich des Festaktes*. Frankfurt: Carl Heymanns Verlag.

Schwenkel, Christina. 2015. "Spectacular Infrastructure and Its Breakdown in Socialist Vietnam." *American Ethnologist* 42, no. 3: 520–34.

Sewell, William. 2008. "The Temporalities of Capitalism." *Socio-Economic Review* 6, no. 3: 517–37.

Shiva, Vandana. 2016. *Water Wars: Privatization, Pollution and Profit*. New Delhi, India: India Research Press.

Shoshan, Nitzan. 2016. *The Management of Hate: Nation, Affect, and the Governance of Right-Wing Extremism in Germany*. Princeton, NJ: Princeton University Press.

Simpson, Audra. 2020. "The Sovereignty of Critique." *South Atlantic Quarterly* 119, no. 4: 685–99.

Simpson, Leanne Betasamosake. 2017. *As We Have Always Done: Indigenous Freedom through Radical Resistance*. Minneapolis: University of Minnesota Press.

Simpson, Leanne Betasamosake. 2021. *A Short History of the Blockade: Giant Beavers, Diplomacy, and Regeneration in Nishnaabewin*. Edmonton, Canada: University of Alberta Press.

Sinclair, Georgina. 2008. "The 'Irish' Policeman and the Empire: Influencing the Policing of the British Empire—Commonwealth." *Irish Historical Studies* 36, no. 142: 173–87.

Sirvent, Robert. 2018. "BAR Book Forum: Fred Moten's 'Consent Not to Be a Single Being.'" Black Agenda Report. July 25, 2018. https://www.blackagendareport.com/bar-book-forum-fred-motens-consent-not-be-single-being.

Skerrett, Kevin. 2018. "Canada's Public Pension Funds: The 'New Masters of the (Neoliberal) Universe.'" In *The Contradictions of Pension Fund Capitalism*, edited by Kevin Skerrett, Johanna Weststar, Simon Archer and Chris Roberts, 121–52. Ithaca, NY: Cornell University Press.

Smith, Adam. 1937. *The Wealth of Nations [1776]*. Chicago: University of Chicago Press.

Smith, Gavin. 2020. "Afterword: Financialization Beyond Crisis." In *Financialization: Relational Approaches*, edited by Chris Hann and Don Kalb, 321–32. New York: Berghahn Books.

Song, Jesook. 2009. *South Koreans in the Debt Crisis: The Creation of a Neoliberal Welfare Society*. Durham, NC: Duke University Press.

Song, Jesook. 2014. *Living on Your Own: Single Women, Rental Housing, and Post-revolutionary Affect in Contemporary South Korea*. Albany: State University of New York Press.

Sopranzetti, Claudio. 2017. *Owners of the Map: Motorcycle Taxi Drivers, Mobility, and Politics in Bangkok*. Berkeley: University of California Press.

Squillace, Germana. 2015. "L'acqua della Madonna, tesoro liquido di Castellammare di Stabia." *Vesuvio Live*, December 19, 2015. https://www.vesuviolive.it/cultura -napoletana/124644-lacqua-della-madonna-castellammare-stabia-perche-si-chiama -cosi/.

Statista. 2022. "Italy: Risk of Poverty Rate by Region." Statista. Accessed September 12, 2022, https://www.statista.com/statistics/647996/at-risk-of-poverty-rate -italy-by-region/.

Stout, Noelle. 2019. *Dispossessed: How Predatory Bureaucracy Foreclosed on the American Middle Class*. Berkeley: University of California Press.

Strang, Veronica. 2004. *The Meaning of Water*. Oxford, UK: Berg.

Strang, Veronica. 2005. "Common Senses: Water, Sensory Experience and the Generation of Meaning." *Journal of Material Culture* 10, no. 1: 92–120.

Strang, Veronica. 2015. *Water, Nature and Culture*. London: Reaktion Books.

Strang, Veronica. 2016. "Infrastructural Relations: Water, Political Power, and the Rise of a New 'Despotic Regime'." *Water Alternatives* 9, no. 2: 292–318.

Subramanian, Ajantha. 2009. *Shorelines: Space and Rights in South India*. Stanford, CA: Stanford University Press.

Sullivan, Sian. 2013. "Banking Nature? The Spectacular Financialisation of Environmental Conservation." *Antipode* 45, no. 1: 198–217.

Sunder Rajan, Kaushik. 2006. *Biocapital*. Durham, NC: Duke University Press.

Susser, Ida. 2017. "Commoning in New York City, Barcelona, and Paris," *Focaal* 79 (2017): 6–22.

Susser, Ida, and Molly Doane. 2014. "Introduction." *Anthropology Now* 6, no. 3: 1–7.

Swyngedouw, Erik. 2005. "Dispossessing H$_2$O: The Contested Terrain of Water Privatization." *Capitalism Nature Socialism* 16, no. 1: 81–98.

Swyngedouw, Erik. 2018. *Promises of the Political: Insurgent Cities in a Post-political Environment*. Cambridge, MA: MIT Press.

Swyngedouw, Erik. 2019. "The New Water Wars: Struggles for Remunicipalisation." *Water Alternatives* 12, no. 2: 322–33.

Tansel, Cemal Burak. 2018. "Authoritarian Neoliberalism and Democratic Backsliding in Turkey: Beyond the Narratives of Progress." *South European Society and Politics* 23, no. 2: 197–217.

Tappe, Anneken. 2020. "Investors Can Now Trade Water Futures." *CNN Business*, December 7, 2020. https://www.cnn.com/2020/12/07/investing/water-futures -trading/index.html.

Taussig, Michael T. 1980. *The Devil and Commodity Fetishism in South America*. Chapel Hill: University of North Carolina Press.

*thejournal.ie*. 2014. "Dublin Man Stops Irish Water Workers Installing Meter at Home 12 Different Times." January 29, 2014. https://www.thejournal.ie,/water-meter -dublin-man-1286824-Jan2014/.

Thompson, Edward Palmer. 1966. *The Making of the English Working Class.* New York: Vintage, Vintage Edition.

Thompson, Edward Palmer 1971. "The Moral Economy of the English Crowd in the Eighteenth Century." *Past and Present* 50, no. 71: 76–136.

Thompson, Edward Palmer. 1975. *Whigs and Hunters: The Origin of the Black Act.* New York: Pantheon Books.

Trocchia, Nello. 2017. "'Ecco chi sono i giganti che inquinano l'ambiente': Le accuse choc della procura nazionale antimafia." *Tiscali Notizie.* Accessed January 6, 2022. https://notizie.tiscali.it/cronaca/articoli/giganti-inquinano.ambiente-procura-antimafia/.

Trommer, Silke. 2019. "Watering Down Austerity: Scalar Politics and Disruptive Resistance in Ireland." *New Political Economy* 24, no. 2: 218–34.

Tsing, Anna Lowenhaupt. 2003. "Natural Resources and Capitalist Frontiers." *Economic and Political Weekly* 38, no. 48: 5100–06.

Vande Panne, Valerie. 2018. "Detroiters Fear Losing Their Water May Mean Losing Their Kids." *In These Times*, September 11, 2018. https://inthesetimes.com/article/detroit-water-shutoffs-child-services-debt.

Veblen, Thorstein. 1923. *Absentee Ownership and Business Enterprise in Recent Times: The Case of America.* New York: B. W. Huebsch.

Verfassungsgerichtshof des Landes Berlin. 2009. Im *Namen des Volkes: Urteil* (Ruling), Publikation. L. No. VERfGH 63/08 (2009). Accessed September 12, 2022. https://berliner-wassertisch.net/assets/Historie/Erste%20Stufe/urteil_verfgh_63_08.pdf.

Vogl, Joseph. 2017. *The Ascendancy of Finance.* Hoboken, NJ: Wiley.

Von Schnitzler, Antina. 2016. *Democracy's Infrastructure: Techno-Politics and Protest after Apartheid.* Princeton, NJ: Princeton University Press.

Von Schnitzler, Antina. 2013. "Traveling Technologies. Infrastructure, Ethical Regimes, and the Materiality of Politics in South Africa." *Cultural Anthropology* 28, no. 4: 670–93.

Walsh, Dermot. 2018. "Adapting the Police Authority Concept to a Centralised National Police Service: Appearance over Substance in the Republic of Ireland?" *Modern Law Review* 81, no. 4: 622–45.

Warne, Kennedy. 2019. "This River in New Zealand Is a Legal Person: How Will It Use Its Voice?" *National Geographic.* Accessed January 6, 2022. https://www.nationalgeographic.com/culture/2019/04/maori-river-in-new-zealand-is-a-legal-person/.

Schug, Alexander, Bernd Kessinger, Katja Roeckner, and Petrasch Frank. 2014. *Berliner Wasser: Die Geschichte einer Lebensnotwendigkeit.* Berlin: Vergangenheitsverlag.

Von Wiesenau, Ulrike. 2012. "Höchster Wasserpreis in Deutschland." *Neue Rheinische Zeitung.* Accessed September 10, 2022. http://www.nrhz.de/flyer/beitrag.php?id=17512.

Von Wiesenau, Ulrike. 2011 "Beutegemeinschaft auf Kosten der Wasserkunden." *Neue Rheinische Zeitung.* Accessed January 6, 2022. http://www.nrhz.de/flyer/beitrag.php?id=17322.

Watts, Michael J. 2016. "The Mafia of a Sicilian Village, 1860–1960; a Study of Violent Peasant Entrepreneurs, by Anton Blok." *Journal of Peasant Studies* 43, no. 1: 67–91.

Weber, Max. 2000 (1894). "Stock and Commodity Exchanges [Die Börse]." *Theory and Society* 29, no. 3: 305–38.

Weiner, Annette B. 1992. *Inalienable Possessions: The Paradox of Keeping While Giving.* Berkeley: University of California Press.

Weiss, Hadas. 2018. "Popfinance: From the Economic Man to the Schwabian Housewife." *HAU: Journal of Ethnographic Theory* 8, no. 3: 455–66.

Weiss, Hadas. 2022. "From Desire to Endurance: Hanging on in a Spanish Village." *Cultural Anthropology* 37, no. 1: 45–68.

Weston, Kath. 2017. *Animate Planet: Making Visceral Sense of Living in a High-Tech Ecologically Damaged World.* Durham, NC: Duke University Press.

Whiteside, Heather. 2018. "Public Works: Better, Faster, Cheaper Infrastructure" *Studies in Political Economy* 99, no. 1: 2–19.

Whiteside, Heather. 2019. "Advanced Perspectives on Financialised Urban Infrastructures." *Urban Studies* 56, no. 7: 1477–84.

Wu, Xun, and Nepomuceno A. Malaluan. 2008. "A Tale of Two Concessionaires: A Natural Experiment of Water Privatisation in Metro Manila." *Urban Studies* 45, no. 1: 207–29.

Yang, Jo-Shing. 2020. "The New 'Water Barons': Wall Street Mega-Banks Are Buying Up the World's Water." *Global Research*, July 14, 2020. https://www.globalresearch.ca/the-new-water-barons-wall-street-mega-banks-are-buying-up-the-worlds-water/5383274.

Zaki, Saeed, and ATM Nurul Amin. 2009. "Does Basic Services Privatisation Benefit the Urban Poor? Some Evidence from Water Supply Privatisation in Thailand." *Urban Studies* 46, no. 11: 2301–27.

Zaloom, Caitlin. 2017. "Finance." Fieldsights—Theorizing the Contemporary. *Society for Cultural Anthropology*, August 7, 2017. https://culanth.org/fieldsights/the-household-finance.

Zaloom, Caitlin. 2019. *Indebted: How Families Make College Work at Any Cost.* Princeton, NJ: Princeton University Press.

Zanotelli, Alex. 2020. "Tradimento a 5 stelle." *Peacelink*, September 17, 2020. https://www.peacelink.it/zanotelli/a/47986.html.

Zetland, David. 2016. "Water Metering in England and Wales." *Water Alternatives* 9, no. 1: 120–38.

Zimmer, Zac. 2015. "The Enclosure of the Nomos." In *The Anomie of the Earth: Philosophy, Politics, and Autonomy in Europe and the Americas*, edited by Federico Luisetti, John Pickles, and Wilson Kaiser, 137–56. Durham, NC: Duke University Press.

Zinn, Dorothy Louise. 2001. *La raccomandazione: Clientelismo vecchio e nuovo.* Rome: Donzelli Editore.

# INDEX

*Page locators in italics refer to figures*

Communist Party (Italy), 48, 61, 149
Compagnie de Suez, 22
Compagnie Générale des Eaux pour les Étrangers, 40, 190n10
consent, 96–100, 97
"constituent powers," 38, 190n7
Constitutional Council (France), 99–100
Constitutional Court (Berlin), 116, 119, 123–27, 152
Constitutional Court (Italy), 157
constitutional law, 55, 175–76
consumer rights advocates, 120, 162–64, 169, 198n25
contract, Berlin water provision: as "contract of trust" (Vertrag des Vertrauens), 116; demands for disclosure of, 120, 122–24, 203n21; disclosure of forced by people's law, 2, 34, 104–5, 108, 127–30; "efficiency enhancement clause," 117; guaranteed returns, 118–21, 128; judicial review of, 116–18; Paragraph 23.7 ("circumvention paragraph"), 106, 118–20, 131; risk surcharge (R+2 percent), 116–17, 119; state as guarantor, 117–21; trial, 121–28. See also Berlin; referendum against water privatization (Berlin, 2011)
contracts: circumvention of public law by, 115; consent not given, 96–99, 97; financial frontiers as zones of struggle over, 105–6; and future projected revenue, 111, 131, 205n32; length of, 11, 18, 59, 101, 110–11, 115, 118, 131, 184n30; liberal capitalist fantasy of contractual equality, 27, 98–99, 106, 107, 123–24; pacta sunt servanda, 118; politicization of, 99–100; predatory practices rendered legal by, 106, 108, private as "higher ranking," 124; "proprietary information," 106, 107, 120, 127. See also contract, Berlin water provision; social contract
Coonan, Noel, 69
Cooper, Melinda, 106, 181n12
Coordinadora de defensa del agua y la vida (Committee for the Defence of Water and Life), 29–30
Cork, Ireland, 2, 67–68, 195n5
corporate culture, 80, 133, 210n4
Costa Rica, 144, 206n6
Court of Cassation (Rome), 51
COVID-19 pandemic, vii, viii, xi, 64, 101, 102, 209n28
Cozzolino, Adriano, 10, 45

Crampton, Thomas Russell, 109–10
"crazy bills" (bollette pazze), 1–2, 7, 49, 60, 136–40; "Civil Obedience Campaign," 139, 156–65, 157; "consumer victims," reimbursement for, 59; intergenerational effects of, 162; protests against, 137–38; and regulatory authority, 144; retroactive (partite pregresse), 137, 140, 162–64. See also Campania, Italy; Civil Obedience Campaign (Italy); water bills
criminalization of social protest, 34, 91–94, 209n29
Criminal Justice and Public Order Act (Ireland, 1994), 91
Curtis, Maeve, 72

Dean, Sharon, 83
debt: automatic deductions, 98; Berlin's, 108, 113–14, 133–34; as cult of blame, 27; cyclical debt forgiveness, 163; durable rent structure, 17–18; futurity of, 11, 15; as goal of financialization, 4, 9; increased by contractually guaranteed profits, 14–15, 118, 119; intergenerational bondage to, 15, 70; Schuld, as term for debt and guilt, 113; and sovereignty, 185–86n44; as violence, 72, 77, 95
debt financing, 4, 9, 13–15; conditions for created by laws, 42; socialization of bank debt, 77, 86
Debtor's Act (Ireland, 1872), 98
decree, rule by, 44–46, 191n15
Delanoë, Bertrand, 169
de Magistris, Luigi, 35, 37, 39, 46, 65, 156, 189n3, 190n4
democracy: authoritarian, 33, 37–38, 54; direct, 57–58, 123, 132; embodied memory of, 66; "of appropriation," 64–65; participatory, 38, 50–51; public water fountains as infrastructure of, 61–62; representative, 57–58, 190n7, 192n28; "slow," 54; Socialist Easterners' insights into, 117–18
"democracy experts," 32
Detroit, 29, 72–73, 86, 196n15
Devonshire, Duke of, 76, 197n17
direct democracy, 57–58, 123, 132
dispossession, 3, 38, 66; accumulation by, 69–70, 107, 179n1; frontiers of, 16, 21; law as instrument of, 63–64; recursivity of, 20–21; of shareholders, rhetoric of, 124

financialization: debt as goal of, 4, 9; as
    intimate social formation, 7; of life,
    12–18; move from "social equity" to
    "economic equity," 74–75, 143, 198n26;
    recursivity of, 20–21, 23; of value, 3;
    water futures, 181–82n13
Fine Gael (Ireland), 91, 101
fiscal strikes (*sciopero fiscale*), 162–63,
    209n26
fishing rights, 75, 76, 197n17
"A Five Star Betrayal" (Zanotelli), 65–66
Five Star Movement (Italy), 58–69, 65–66,
    162, 194n32, 209n32
Fizzarotti, Emanuele, 40–41
Flanagan, Luke Ming, 78
Flint water scandal, 29, 73
Florence (Tuscany, Italy), 49
Fox, Charles, 109–10
France: *Compagnie de Suez*, 22; Consti-
    tutional Council, 99–100; Grenoble,
    168, 203n23; remunicipalizations, 34,
    168–71; water basin authorities, 6. *See
    also* Paris, France; Suez (corporation)
*France Eau Publique* (FEP), 210n7
Francis of Assisi, Saint, 48
Fraticelli (Little Brethren) Franciscans,
    211n10
freedom, 74–75
Freisler, Roland, 124–25
"frontier priests" (*preti di frontiera*), 48
frontiers: battle over common goods, 30; of
    dispossession, 16, 21; as global process,
    3; multiple local-to-global scales, 154;
    of political imagining, 33; as zones
    of law creation, 38. *See also* financial
    frontiers
Fugmann-Heesing, Annette, 114
full cost recovery, 2, 31, 47, 76, 139, 142, 144,
    149, 187n54, 206n9
future generations, 11, 15, 53, 56, 162,
    192n29; future projected revenue ex-
    propriated from, 111, 131, 133, 205n32;
    interests of, 11, 41, 53

Galli law (Italy, 1994), 41–42, 46, 49, 55
GAP (Gruppi d'Azione Partigiana), 165
GAP (*Gruppo Antidistacco Popolare*, "Super
    Marios"), 88, 165–66, 166, 208n21
Garda Síochána (Guardians of the Peace,
    Ireland), 68, 69, 95–96
GATT (General Agreement on Tariffs and
    Trade), 187n54

*Gemeingut* (common good), 28–29
*Gemeingut in BürgerInnenhand* (Common
    Goods in Citizens' Hands), 26, 176
gendered nature of insurgencies, 21, 32–33,
    71, 83, 85
General Credit and Discount Company, 23,
    40, 190n9
*Genuino Clandestino* (genuine clandestine)
    network, 208n22
George I, 71, 195n10
German Alliance for Public Water Works,
    148, 180n5
German National Audit Office, 113
Germany: citizens' initiatives, 120; federal
    law, 122–23, 124, 125; Nazi, 112, 172,
    202–3n14, 202n9; partial privatization
    of water, 120; unification, 113, 121.
    *See also* Berlin
*Gestione Ottimale Risorse Idriche* (Optimal
    Water Resources Management, GORI
    SpA), 1–2, 35–36, 59–61, 136–40, 194n34,
    205n2; cases lost by, 99; class action
    lawsuit against, 164; debt of forgiven
    by government, 163; mayors "bought"
    by, 46, 59, 62, 148, 153; No Gori Civic
    Network (*Rete Civica No Gori*), 138, 145,
    162–65, 209n28; obscure price-setting
    practices, 137–38, 140, 144–45; seen as
    predatory, 140, 149–50; shares owned
    by Sarnese Vesuviano SRL, 60, 64, 137;
    "We will not pay GORI's debts" slogan,
    164, 209n30
Gibney, David, 73, 80, 90
Global North, 184n31, 189n2; structural
    adjustment equivalencies in, 13–14,
    25–26, 108–9; struggles in Global South
    returning to, 30, 47, 50, 72, 187n54
Global South: insurgencies in, 5, 10, 71–72,
    183n24; "insurgent citizenship," 10;
    secrecy, critiques of, 108; structural
    adjustment policies imposed on, 13–14,
    71–72; struggles in returning to Global
    North, 30, 47, 50, 72, 187n54
Global Water Intelligence (GWI), vii–viii,
    12, 14, 206n11; counterinsurgency
    activities, 70–71, 195n9; global water
    tariff survey, 102; Ireland watched by,
    70–71, 102
Global Water Summit (London, 2019), 12–13
"God of the City" (Heym), 134
Gola, Giuseppe, 60, 64
Grauso, Giuseppe, 59, 63, 164

Greece, 81, 187n49, 192–93n30
Greek myth, 136
Green Party (Berlin), 127
Green Party (Ireland), 81
Gregorius IX, 211n10
Grenoble, France, 168, 203n23
Grillo, Beppe, 162
groundwater, 41–42, 190n11
guaranteed returns, 14–15, 118–19, 128, 145
guarantor, state as, 117–21, 131–32, 143, 145
Guardex, 68, 93
Guardia di Finanza (Italian financial police), 150

Hardt, Michael, 53, 54, 184n35
Härlin, Dorothea, 30, 76, 107–8, 133
Hartmann, David, 132
Harvey, David, 20, 52–53
Hecht, Christa, 148, 180n5
Heinrich, Rainer, 130
Heym, Georg, 134
Hobbes, Thomas, 36
Hogan, Phil, 79
holy wells, 76. *See also* mineral waters
household, 10; as captive income stream, 14; at center of Suez corporation, 22; gendered division of labor, 32–33, 71; needs not taken into consideration, 144; as site of wealth extraction, 18, 32
human right, water as, 7, 11, 16, 32, 140
Hungary, 172, 210n5

"illegality of the law," 11, 38–39, 51, 152–53; and intensification of emergency rule, 56–57
imperialism, 21–23, 87
inalienable possessions, 6–7
India, 23, 71, 126–27, 150, 183n24
indigenous movements, 8, 11, 75–76, 188n59
infrastructures, 6–8; as already part of global regime, 22–23; antiquated, 80; as asset class, 11, 181n13; built environment, 73; and durable rent structure, 18; financialized, across space and time, 20–21, 23; future returns calculated into, 133; life as, 8; local knowledge about, 63; neglect of, 150; and pricing, 146; public water fountains and democracy, 61–62; reduced investments in, 120–21, 203–4n23; security apparatus merged with, 70; social, 131–34; vital, 8, 11, 81, 134; of working-class neighborhoods, 83–84

insurgency, as term, 10
"insurgent questions," 84
International Monetary Fund (IMF), 77, 88, 200n37
investment: "adequate remuneration of invested capital," 43, 52, 54–55, 58, 115, 142–44, 157–60, 190n12, 192n26; future returns calculated into infrastructures, 133; guaranteed returns, 14–15, 118–19, 128, 145; planned, 142, 145
Irace, Alberto, 149
Ireland, 10; antiausterity mass mobilization, 68, 82, 86; anticolonial struggle against British enclosure, 23, 75, 86–87, 196n14; antiquated water infrastructure, 80; austerity, 33, 67–68; Ballyhea, 78; boycotts, 92, 98, 200n39; Commission for Energy Regulation (CER), 194–95n3; Constitution, 101; corporate tax benefits, 77, 96; deprivation rate, 77–78; "domestic rates grant," 74; and financial crisis of 2007–2008, 76–78; holy wells, 76; housing and homelessness battles, 101; investment in water sector, 197n23; Irish, racialization of, 72, 92, 196n11; National Recovery Plan of 2011–2014, 79; nineteenth century protests, 92; police, 68, 69, 70, 90–96; Social Welfare and Pensions Bill, 91–92; state support of Irish Water, 68; unions, 68, 73, 80, 81–82; Water Services Bill (2013), 79, 198n24; water use per person per annum, 81; women as backbone of water movement, 32–33. *See also* Irish Water; water meters, Ireland; water movement, Ireland
*Iren,* 159, 193–94n31
"Irish Exemption" (WFD), 76
Irish Land League, 92
*Irish Times,* 68
Irish Water, 2, 67–68, 197n22; changes to, 78–79; corporate culture, 80; debt capacity of, 14; Eurostat test, 79, 95; funding sources, 199n27; legibility of to future global investors, 76, 79, 100, 102; police presence at work sites, 68–69, 69, 94; refusal to register with, 85; as state water company, 79. *See also* water movement, Ireland
Italian Civil Code, 43, 175–76
Italian Constitution, 51, 55–56, 191n14
Italian Constitutional Court, 57–58

water: anthropomorphization of, 103–4, 105; as asset class, 8, 11, 31–32, 181n13; body composed of, 49; as commodity, 9, 12, 50, 91, 138–39, 181n13, 182n15; as commons, 6, 38, 47, 52–53, 75–76, 160; conservation of, 3, 198–99n26, 198n25; debt owed to, 15; early examples of provisioning, 19–20; as fictitious commodity, 182n15; as fixed-demand service, 17–18; as free, 74; as human right, 7, 11, 16, 32, 41, 140; as "immovable wealth," 47; kinship language for, 11, 48–49, 165; "murdering" of, 156, 208n20; poetics of, 15, 74, 112, 134; as public good, 32, 41, 46; sacrality of, 27, 47–48, 76, 139; value of as immeasurable, 4, 9–10

water bills, 7; autoreduction of, 158, 163, 208n21; proportion of income spent on water, 86–87, 143, 147, 199n30. *See also* "crazy bills" *(bollette pazze)*

water bonus *(bonus idrico)*, 60, 64

*Water Charta* (Berlin *Wasserrrat*), 205n35

water committees, Italy, 33, 46, 137, 158–59

water crisis, as manufactured, 25, 30, 185n39

water cultures, 6, 47

"water fairies," 85, 88–90, 165

Water Framework Directive (European Union, 2000), 31, 76, 210n2

water insurgencies: Black, in US, 72–73; emerging, 171–74; as frontiers, 5; GAP (*Gruppo Antidistaccho Popolare*, 88, 165–66, *166*, 208n21; as gendered, 21, 32–33, 71, 83, 85; German, 23–24; India, 71–72; laughter as weapon, 89; social sources of, 32; "water fairies," 85, 88–90

water leakages, 63, 141–42, 151, 204n23

water meters, Ireland, 2, 7, 10, 33, 67; district level, 74, 87–88; "double payment," 75, 90; ecological arguments, 81; older cast-iron vs. newer plastic, 87–89

water meters, Italy, 150

water movement, Ireland, 67–68, 194n1; 1915–1916, 87; anticolonial registers in water meter protests, 23; "From the river to the sea: Irish water will be free!" chant, 2, 76, 197n18; hunger strikes, 93; Irish accused of not wanting to pay, 75, 76, 87, 90–91; "Our Water is Not for Sale" initiative, 81–82;

Right2Water initiative, 32, 72, 80, 85–86; "Says No" movement, 78–79, 81; slow marches, 78; "water fairies," 85, 88–90; as working-class led mobilization, 73; yellow reflective vests of police and protestors, 95. *See also* Irish Water

water movement, Italy, 47; Civil Obedience Campaign, 139, *157*, 158–64; National Assembly of Water Movements, 51; and preexisting mobilizations, 50–51; social forum on water (2003), 49; *sorella acqua* (sister water), 11, 48–49, 165; specter of unaffordability countered by, 66; successes of, 65; "Super Marios," 88, 165–66, *166*

water movements: political imagining by, 5–6, 29, 33, 171; struggle against hegemony of finance, 3; terrains of, 29–34

"Water pays for Water" principle, 170, 210n2

water poverty, 86, 196n15, 198n26

Water Services (No.2) Act (Ireland, 2013), 98, 198n24

Water Services Act of 2014 (Ireland), 98

water shutoffs, 32, 163; and Civil Obedience Campaign, 160; court cases, 99–100; Detroit, 73, 196n15; France, 99–100; Italy, 35, 60; ordinances against, 63–64; retaliatory, 209n28

water tables *(mesas de agua)*, 108, 201n6

water tasters *(goûteurs d'eau)*, 167–68

*The Wealth of Nations* (Smith), 19

Weber, Max, 106, 110, 133, 201n4

"We're done with Secret Contracts! We Berliners Want Our Water Back" campaign, 108, 122–23

White Rose resistance group, 124–25

Williams, DeMeeko, 73

Wolf, Harald, 118

Wolfhagen, Germany, 174

Wollner, Hermann, 120, 122–23

working class: antimeter sentiment, 198n25; and built environment, 73; fishing rights, 75, 76, 197n17; neighborhood infrastructure, 83–84

working-class estates, 2, 67; features of, 83–84

World Bank, 30, 71, 181n12, 194n2

World Social Forum (Porto Alegre, 2001), 30

Zanotelli, Padre, 50, 65–66, 155

www.ingramcontent.com/pod-product-compliance
Lightning Source LLC
LaVergne TN
LVHW091453050925
820306LV00025B/365